Turkey Tails and Tales from Across the USA

Volume 4

By Tom "Doc" Weddle

© 2023 Tom Weddle
All rights reserved.

No part of this publication may be reproduced, stored in a retrieval system, or transmitted, in any form or by any means, electronic, mechanical, photocopying, recording or otherwise, without the written permission of the author.

ISBN: 978-1-7354419-6-2

Printed in the United States of America

Volume 4 is dedicated to the many friends and family who have already passed away. The tragedy of living a long life is in seeing loved ones die before we do. Every single one of them has helped to make me who I am, and I will never forget that!

Two of the best, and too many others already gone; all loved!

Contents

Ephemera 7

Chapter 1
2007 15

Chapter 2
2008 39

Chapter 3
2009 64

Chapter 4
2010 84

Chapter 5
2011 101

Chapter 6
2012 123

Chapter 7
2013 144

Chapter 8
2014 158

Chapter 9
2015 185

Chapter 10
2016 204

Chapter 11
2017... 221

Chapter 12
2018... 248

Epilogue 268

Signed copies of this book and other volumes in the series can be purchased directly from me. Hardcovers are $39 and paperbacks are $29. I'll take care of postage. I can accept funds via PayPal sent to my email address of tdocweddle@comcast.net, or checks/money orders can be mailed to:

Tom Weddle
PO Box 7281
Bloomington, IN 47407

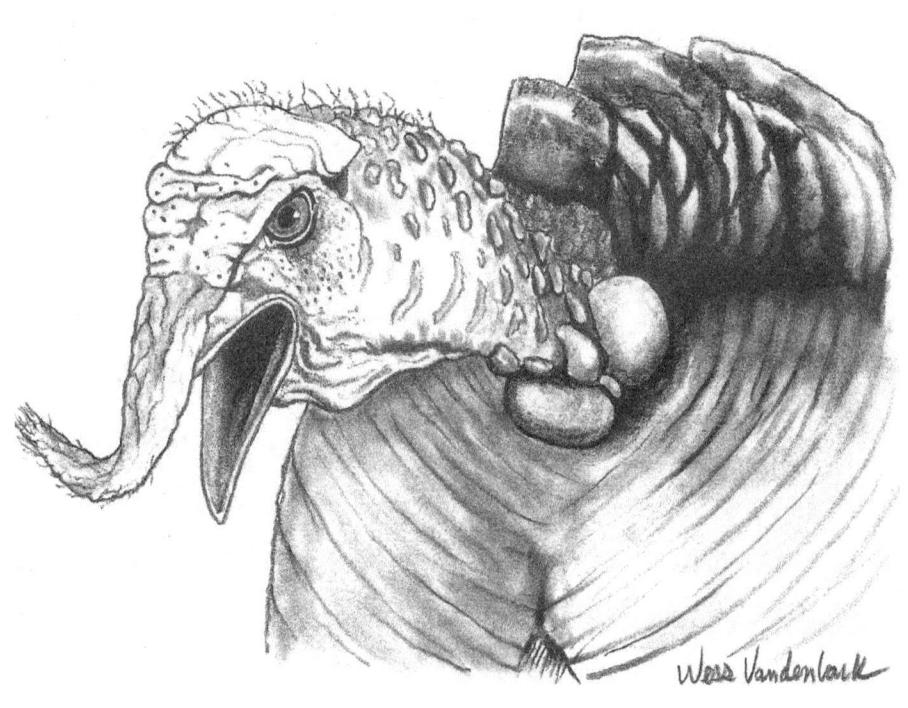

Ephemera

In my first three books I detailed a portion of my life which I consider to be very well-spent…those 24 years following an initial introduction to the wild turkey. During that timeframe I'd grown from a neophyte who had never even seen a turkey in his first 23 years on this planet, to someone having attained a number of rather lofty achievements in the sport of hunting them. Perhaps the most illustrious of these was conquering a U.S. Super Slam, which is the act of killing a wild turkey in all 49 states which support a spring season for these wondrous birds. I've always considered myself to be an over-achiever in whatever tasks are deemed important by me personally, and to be certain, that's a characteristic of which I take great pride. The aforementioned "Super Slam" was a perfect case in point. I was extremely proud in doing that, and even still today, I consider it to be one of my greatest accomplishments in life.

But, as has also been a notable trait of myself, I am not one to sit back and gloat on things already done. Moving forward is the only way I know to go. Striving ever-onward towards something far off and yet attainable is how my brain operates at its best, and by setting my goals high, I'm afforded the motivation and sense of direction needed to get there. Thus, as soon as that final bird of the U.S. Super Slam had been brought to bag, I came up with some brand new ambitions. Then, I began chipping away at turning them into reality.

I finished up that initial U.S. Super Slam in 2006, and soon thereafter, the wheels were set in motion for conquering a second one. So far as I knew at the time, nobody else had ever achieved such an outlandish thing, and with only 24 states remaining where I had killed but a single tom, I figured that I could work my way through that list in a few more seasons and become the first-ever holder of two U.S. Super Slams.

I was also keenly aware that there were just seven states on my life list where I hadn't killed turkeys on public land. Since I consider myself to be a public land hunter above anything else, I felt like it was very important to rectify this particular aberration. Heck; the reality of the matter is that I prefer to hunt on ground open to the masses, and I've long made it a mission of sorts to do that almost exclusively in my travels around the country. Becoming the first person to claim such a Public Land Super Slam seemed like an ambition befitting my priorities and values.

Now, before this treatise perhaps heads off in a direction unintended, I'd like to first clarify that I do not view turkey hunting as any sort of a competitive sport; not in any way, shape, or form! I also abhor braggarts of all kinds. But, there is no denying that my inner soul has a competitive edge to it, and conquering these two quests was something which I thought worthy of note. However, only from a very *personal* perspective! I wasn't out to gain bragging rights over anyone else, or to project myself as being better than other hunters, and I most certainly wasn't going forth in order to gain any sort of attention or fame. No; my motivations were much more innocent of ill intent. I just wanted to prove to *myself* that I was worthy of being mentioned in the same company as a league of fine outdoorsmen who had come before me, and for whom I in turn beheld the utmost respect. This list of people did include some nationally well-known turkey hunters, but of even more import were the names of a couple people whom I considered to be absolute heroes in my eyes.

The first of those was my original turkey hunting mentor, Bill Madden. I've mentioned him in all of my books. Bill was a great man of fine moral character, as well as being an extremely knowledgeable wildlife biologist with the Indiana Department of Natural Resources. He was also the first turkey hunter that I'd ever met, and his stories of both conquests and defeats in the turkey woods were directly responsible for inspiring me to take up this sport. From my very first days of hunting turkeys, I always measured how I felt like I had performed in the battles against my worthy adversaries with how I thought Bill would view those same actions. Whether (or not) I conducted myself honorably and intelligently was ultimately all that mattered, because I knew that this was how Bill Madden hunted.

The other person on that short list of heroes was my Dad, and while he never hunted turkeys a day in his life, that's only because these magnificent creatures weren't a part of the landscape when he was growing up around Franklin.

Turkeys had been extirpated from Indiana way back around the turn of the 20th century, and the birds hadn't been reintroduced until 1970. Like Bill, Dad was a lifelong DNR employee, with his most notable professional position being the longtime property manager for Lake Monroe, which is Indiana's largest man-made reservoir. My father was a gifted hunter with a special passion for waterfowl, squirrels, and ruffed grouse, so I'm quite certain that he would've been a tremendous turkey hunter, too.

These two men were the greatest role models in my life. If I could look back on any of my own accomplishments in the woods and waters and feel like they might have given me the slightest nod of approval or felt a modicum of respect towards me as a fellow outdoorsman, then that is all I might ever hope for, or strive towards. That was true the day I set my first muskrat trap with my Dad looking over my shoulder, it was true the moment Bill shook my hand after I'd brought in a mink taken from a "blind" set he had overseen me build, and it was true the very first time I stepped foot into the inky black depths of an early spring morning in hopes of discovering what made turkey hunting so mysterious and appealing. That still holds true even today, when memories of their lessons and inspirations are all that I have left from their physical presence.

Here's another thing that I'd like to get straight right from the start: I am most certainly not the greatest turkey hunter to have ever walked this planet! No if's, and's, or but's needed to addend that statement. However, through shear will and determination, and a brain that is at least moderately functional on occasion, I've become fairly adept at figuring out a creature which generally befuddles many of the folks who hunt them. In other words; through pure perseverance, patience, repetition, and relentless pursuit, I've become pretty good at what I do in the turkey woods.

Oh, I've heard my name bantered around as being some sort of a GOAT, or "legend" in this sport, but I can't even begin to tell you how hearing that descriptor always cracks me up. Trust me when I say that I would refute such an ill-gained moniker vociferously on any day of the week! I make silly mistakes and get schooled by my feathered adversaries on a daily basis, and I do so in ways that the most inept of turkey hunters would find bewildering or amusing. Always have, and I'm sure, always will!

In short, I'm just a regular guy who likes to turkey hunt....a *lot*! I'm nothing more, and nothing special. In fact, I think of myself as terribly flawed on many, many levels. Perhaps the most obvious of these is a complete inability to control this burning desire to hunt turkeys all around the country at every opportunity. That rabid, singular focus which holds such an ironclad grasp on my psyche has been the bane of all duties and responsibilities in my life requiring far more importance, and the only defense I can offer of said charge is that I readily admit to consciously and with malice aforethought intentionally setting up my entire existence in a manner which actually creates those opportunities. In other words: I've purposefully designed my life so that turkey hunting is *the* sole priority for which I live! Does that make me legendary? HARDLY! I would much more likely characterize myself as simply insane and dysfunctional on a grand scale.

So, having tried to nip in the bud any preconceived notions that Doc Weddle is anything other than a bumbling honyawk in the turkey woods, I think it's simply time to jump right back into the telling of some tales. There's no need or value in wasting more space on worthless drivel. After all, these books are merely the recollections of said fanatical turkey hunter, as retold only for the purpose of sharing them with my fellow cohorts, companions, and commiserators. Writing these stories down is, if nothing more, simply a way in which to preserve for all of eternity those wonderful days of my life spent afield in the company of the greatest of all gamebirds. I'd like to say that I'm recording these tales as a preemptive before my memories begin to fade away as part of the aging process, but that wouldn't be totally true…I've *always* had a very poor memory! Well, that's not totally true, either. My claim is that the memory acquisition software in my brain is just fine, but the data retrieval system has a glitch.

This generally weak ability to remember stuff is undoubtedly part of the reason why I've diligently kept and maintained a hunting journal containing notes and data from nearly every day that I've ever spent pursuing turkeys. One of these diaries is always in my vest, as they are what I consider to be a vital piece of hunting gear. I try to jot down the details of a hunt soon after it happens and the memories are still fresh. That way, when I read them later on, it allows my mind to seamlessly slip right back into the thoughts and emotions which I was feeling at the time. It doesn't matter how many hours, days, weeks, or years have passed since the hunt. Keeping a written record has also proven to be invaluable in facilitating the writing of these books.

As I've done previously, I'm going to arrange this volume in chronological order. The difference this time is that I've decided to eliminate the chapters in between hunting stories, where I had previously expounded upon themes which I just felt like discussing. While each of my other books highlighted five or six hunting seasons sandwiched around those divergent chapters, I need this one to cover more ground. I'm not getting these things out to press fast enough, and time might be of the essence. You see; as I write this, I am still recovering from surgery to remove part of a kidney, along with its hated and heinous parasitic tumor. At this point I don't know what the ultimate outcome will be, but my take on the ordeal is that I need to get rolling and finish up some things which I've always wanted to accomplish in life, or others that I've been putting off for far too long. The quality of the writing in this particular edition quite simply isn't going to be up to the standards that I've always set for myself, but there's just too much ground to cover. This book will thus be more or less a condensed version of my hunting journals, with select tales further expounded upon. I apologize in advance for falling short of your expectations.

Another notable difference will be in the number of photos plastered across these pages. As digital cameras became more and more prevalent during my hunting career, I found myself taking many more pictures every year. I love looking back on old photos, so I've included a *bunch* in this book in hopes that you'll enjoy some of them, too. This book is going to be really picture-heavy, but hey, it's my life's story, and photos have always been a big part of that.

Volume 3 took us up through the completion of my first U.S. Super Slam in 2006. This one will see me attain a second Slam finished up in 2011, and it will also bear witness to tidying up those last seven states (CT, KY, MI, NH, VA, TX, and VT) needed for the public land version mentioned earlier. Only after those two goals had been met did I ever even dream about or set forth on a course towards a whole new level of insanity...trying for yet a third Super Slam, which was achieved in 2018. That year will be the last chapter of this book. Tales of my fourth and fifth Slams won't make it onto paper until Volume 5. See: I told you that I was insane!

Once again, I've kept the cover art for all of my books identical, using only a different color scheme to differentiate each one from its brethren. And, just as in the three volumes which precede it, I'm going to keep the first and last illustrations the same, as well. Their intended inclusion from the very beginning has been to first lead the reader into the stories ahead with a strident tom gobbling in their face, and then to show them the way out while at the same time offering promises for more tales to come in future books via a strutter fading away into the timber. I am *so greatly* indebted to Wess Vandenbark for these fantastic works of art which he created for me, and I am grateful beyond measure for his kindness in allowing their continued usage. Wess's immense talents and skillset are truly inspirational for someone like me who can't even begin to draw an adequate stick figure, and I stand in awe of having his work showcased in these books.

Once again and for always onward, my Mom's artwork can be seen in the turkey tracks at the beginning of this chapter and the feather renditions at every title page thereafter. I am humbled not only by Joanne Weddle's abilities to render vision to paper, but in her eternal willingness to stand behind me through thick and thin. Thanks seem inadequate, but thanks, Mom!

So, too; another shout-out goes to Kevin Rhoades for his expertise at book design and color usage on the covers. Kevin has done a tremendous job on these last two volumes, and I can't thank him enough.

As for editing, I'm afraid that it is I who sits solely to blame for any and all snafus, misspellings, clunky phraseology, etc. I'm well-aware of the wisdom in hiring a professional editor in order to achieve professional results, but of course, I've ignored the intelligent way to do things. Instead, I've self-edited this manuscript just under a bazillion times, and for good or bad, this book is the result of that ill-thought-out decision. As Kevin has often reminded me whenever I make annoying changes post-submission, "there is no such thing as a perfect book." At some point the author has just got to let go and sign off on living with the imperfections. That's a very hard thing to do personally, for I am fully aware of just how far these treatises drift away from anything even closely resembling the aforementioned "perfection." I can only hope that my readers won't judge me too harshly for the way in which these books have turned out, because, as I've stated numerous times in my writing, "I'm doing the best that I can with the brain I've been given."

OK; enough of this perfunctory stuff. Let's dive right back into turkey hunting tales. I've got quite a few stories left to tell…

Makin' Plans

Photo by Stephen Spurlock

Chapter 1

2007

I first hunted Hawaii back in 2005, becoming instantly enchanted by all that I'd found there. Making a return visit was of paramount importance to me, and I could hardly wait to go back! During the summer following my initial trip to the islands I'd become romantically involved with Jen Roberts, who would subsequently become a big part of my life for the next decade (our first qualifying date being a frog-gigging expedition where she'd been persuaded to wade in mud and muck up to her neck for hours on end), but classes at Indiana University prevented her from accompanying me back to Hawaii in 2007. Too bad for Miss Jenny; I went alone. Nobody said being my girlfriend was gonna be easy!

I spent nine glorious days on the Big Island in 2007, and found it to be every bit as awe-inspiring as it had been when traveling with Frank and Nancy Emert two years earlier. Hawaii is an incredible wonderland; an absolute dream destination on so very many levels. And yet, it's a land of stark contrasts, and even, danger. The scenery is certainly too beautiful to describe, and the local denizens are wonderfully warm and friendly, but don't let that fool you. The terrain up high on the slopes of Mauna Kea (where most of the public land options exist) is absolutely *the* most brutal, punishing, and debilitating footing that I've ever encountered! Additionally, the birds which inhabit that wicked ground have always given me fits and made me work hard for every victory gained. Perhaps it's these contrasts themselves which have so enamored me of the place, but for whatever the reason, I absolutely love my time spent island-bound.

A few more details need follow on that hellish Hawaiian terrain. The slopes of Mauna Kea are made up of the most vicious, sharp, ankle-rolling, knee-twisting, skin-abrading lava rock imaginable. A lot of that "ground" is also covered in deep, thickly matted grass that effectively hides where your next step will land, so traversing across it on foot is an absolute nightmare; truly and truthfully a horrendous experience! I tell anyone going there that it's of utmost importance to remain focused on *every single step* taken for the entire duration of the hunt. That's the only way to lessen the risk of breaking a leg or taking a serious injury-producing tumble...both of which can easily happen in the blink of an eye. I'm totally serious here, and cannot stress these points strongly enough! And yet; no matter how stridently I might overemphasize the warnings, I don't believe the human brain can adequately fathom how bad it can be until you've been there/done that.

When you add in the constantly changing weather patterns up there at the 7,000 – 9,000 foot elevations where most of the non-resident hunting takes place, those contrasts of which I spoke earlier begin to make even more sense. Things can quite literally go from freezing cold and snowing, to 90 degrees and baking-hot in a matter of minutes...and it does so quite regularly and all day long! Consistently high winds are one of the only things that you can count on. All of these varied, contrasting, and oftentimes vicious climatic conditions are not exactly what one would think of when initially planning a trip to "paradise," but that is the reality of the situation.

And yet, there are certainly turkeys to be found among those craggy cliffs, even if they do tend to be incredibly henned-up and reluctant to come to a call during that first week of March, when the island's turkey season kicks off. At least that's been my own experience during all four times when I've hunted there. I've had to fight hard for every victory gained on that fascinating chunk of Pacific cinder, and more often than not, the toms taken have been a result of tactical maneuvers instead of calling prowess. Oh; you'll hear lots of gobbling, but most of it will be down in the lower elevations and on the private land holdings of the surrounding Parker Ranch. Up on the public ground the toms don't gobble nearly as much. Even the hens are usually quiet, demure, and shy, despite their Rio Grande heredity.

These differences between up-high and down-low are yet another in the long line of stark contrasts alluded to earlier, and the difference in the quality of the hunting at those respective elevations is equally as much a case in point. I've known people who hunted on the private lands and were absolutely dumbstruck by how many turkeys they encountered and how easily they came to a call. You'll just have to trust me on this next claim: hunting on the Parker Ranch ain't *nothing* like what's found up-slope!

In the nine days spent hunting on Hawaii in 2007, I heard exactly one turkey gobble from his evening roost. Then, almost every single bird which gobbled in the early morning hours did so only a few times before shutting up for the entire day. Out of all my calling attempts using either a pot and peg or diaphragms, I was answered exactly twice, and although I did kill two toms, I crippled and lost the only bird which actually came in like they're supposed to. Never in my life had I encountered turkeys *that* henned up, and afterward, as noted in my journal, I described the entire experience as being "tough, tough, and tough!" Still, I had a blast kicking around on the island solo, and I knew even before the trip had come to an end that I would be coming back. I truly do love Hawaii and *all* of her contrasting charms!

Florida offers far fewer contrasts than does Hawaii, other than the differences found on public land versus private ground. The turkey hunting on each of those is like night and day from one another, with private opportunities coming *far* more easily than what's found on the crowded ground open to everyone and their brother.

A Hawaiian tourist lookout

And a Hawaiian turkey hunter's lookout

Zane Caudill and I had once again lined up four clients on some prime private holdings in Polk County, and by the third day of the season they had all killed a bird. Contrast that with my own success rate during the following few days, when I'd struck out thoroughly and completely while competing for space with seemingly all of the masses of humanity in the back woods of Green Swamp WMA. I do love Florida public land hunting, but that ground gets heavily pressured and it's seldom an easy task to kill a tom there. I suppose the most redeeming aspect of competing on these large tracts of public land is that any victory gained makes you feel like you've truly *earned* it. Succeeding in spite of the difficulties encountered tends to give a feller a boost of confidence that he can kill turkeys anywhere else in America.

Over the winter I had been conversing on several internet turkey hunting talk forums about guiding a young man with ALS (Lou Gehrig's disease) to help him finish up his Grand Slam. My work with the Wheelin' Sportsmen group during the last couple of years had put me in a great position to help out with that request, so members of these forums had worked hard to gather up all the funds necessary to fly Eric Corey and his parents from their home in northern Indiana and rent them a motel room in Lakeland. We even raised enough money to acquire a handicapped-accessible van and cover all of their food and sundry travel expenses.

On the day of our hunt, I pulled up to the Hampton Inn early in the morning and met Eric and his parents Doug and Carol for the first time. From the second we shook hands, Eric (age 20) touched my soul. It was obvious right from the start that he was a true hunter through and through, and we immediately formed a bond which would stretch far beyond that of a guide and his client. We were fellow hunters, but more importantly, we instantly became solid friends.

Eric came from good stock, too. His mom and dad are some of the kindest and most gentle folks whom I've ever known, and their love and support of their son serves as an inspiration which I will carry forth until my dying day. They are wonderful people, and now, some 16 years later, I consider them to be friends whom I could always count on at the mere hint or a phone call. I hope they know that it goes both ways.

On the first morning of our hunt, Carol was feeling a little run-down, so she stayed in the hotel to catch up on some rest while Doug, Eric, and I, along with videographer Mike Walters hit the woods. The preceding day I had set up a pair of blinds side-by-side in a great area of the Hampton Unit of Green Swamp WMA (a section which is only hunted a couple of times per year by handicapped participants), and at dawn we heard a number of distant toms gobbling hard. But, as happens on most turkey hunts, the toms went silent after flydown and plumb evaded us thereafter. By 11 a.m. it was hot as blazes in those blinds and Eric needed a rest, so we headed back into town. After stopping in for a delicious lunch at the Quail House Restaurant, a nap was called for in the air conditioned rooms of the hotel.

However, by 2 o'clock Eric was wide awake and ready to return to the field, so with his Mom now joining us, we set forth. The wind was negligible, making it even more stifling hot in those blinds, as hour after hour passed slowly by without any sign or sound of turkeys ever having been anywhere within a hundred miles of us. Throughout the long afternoon I kept peeling off layers of clothing in order to better tolerate the heat...first my hat was jettisoned, then an outer shirt, and finally, my shoes and socks came off. I even loosened my belt and unbuttoned my trousers in hopes of cooling down, but that was, for all practical purposes, impossible...sweat poured off my forehead in rivulets as the minutes turned to hours. I noticed the same sufferings of my blind-mates Eric and Mike. We were all pretty miserable. Well, that is, we were miserable until 6:17 p.m., when yet another from a long afternoon's worth of forlorn calls on a mouth diaphragm garnered a loud gobble from directly behind us!

Almost immediately, I could hear the tom drumming as he closed in on our position, and although our two blinds were practically touching, the sound of his feet shuffling in the leaves behind us made me fear that he was going to try and squeeze in between the two of them in order to reach the decoy spread out front! Thankfully, at the last moment the tom swung wide and came around the right side of the other blind...so close to Carol that she could've reached out a window and slapped him as he went by!

On he came in a bee-line towards the silhouette jake decoy stuck 22 yards in front of us, but I didn't bother letting the lovesick lothario get all the way there before I whispered to Eric that he was free to shoot whenever he felt comfortable. Seconds later his shotgun roared and the turkey collapsed. However, I immediately took note that the tom's head remained upright, so I quickly threw the blind up and over our heads as I sprinted out to get a boot on his neck. Then, after the tom was subdued, the celebration commenced.

As Doug, Carol, Eric, and I danced around whooping and hollering, Mike exited the askew blind with a wide grin across his face, all the while proclaiming, "Y'all ain't gonna believe this footage!" He then proceeded to play back the video on his camera's monitor for all of us to enjoy. In it, everything went according to plan right up until the tom went down, and then, after a flurry of jostling about and blind materiel briefly covering the lens of the camera, you saw a bareheaded, barefooted fat man sprint into the frame to stomp on the turkey's neck, all the while struggling to hold up his unbuttoned pants with one hand. We laughed until our bellies hurt!

The next morning we tried to replicate our good fortune of the evening prior, but I only succeeded in calling in a single jake. I told Eric that he was a perfectly legal turkey to shoot, but do you know what this young man who was dying of a terrible disease told me in response? He said, "That turkey ain't ever gonna get big if I kill him when he's little." I almost choked up and cried right then and there.

In the Fall Carol called to tell me that Eric wanted to shoot an alligator. I put them in touch with my good friend Bill George, who does quite a bit of gator hunting, and in short order the arrangements had been made for Eric and a buddy to be taken out on the adventure of a lifetime. By the time they arrived in Florida, Eric had lost quite a bit of his mobility, but he still had enough strength in his arms that he could fire a long gun if he looped the index finger of both hands through the trigger guard and pulled them back in tandem. Bill rigged up a spear gun with a rifle stock to accommodate this limitation, and then he strapped Eric into the seat of an airboat.

That night they had an epic adventure, and Eric ended up taking an alligator almost 13 feet long. He really wanted to have it mounted in a full-body pose, which as I remember cost upwards of $300 per foot, but Doug and Carol saw to it that their son's wishes were met. That alligator was one of Eric's most prized trophies of his short lifetime well-spent as a hunter of nearly every game animal found on this continent, as well as a few from Africa, and when he passed away at the age of 25, that gator, his Osceola gobbler, and about a bazillion other mounts had to compete for space in a *packed* funeral home. Eric had touched the lives of a multitude of people by then, and the church for the funeral was also filled to overflowing. At the end of his services the lights of the church were turned off, leaving all of the mourners in total darkness. Then, in through the front door walked six of Eric's best buddies fully adorned in their coon hunting gear, complete with rifles on their shoulders and headlights to illuminate the way, as they came to carry their friend's casket back out to a waiting hearse. By that time there wasn't a dry eye in the place, and even today, I can't recall even a fraction of that scene without choking up and shedding a tear or ten.

Eric Corey and his folks Doug and Carol

A beautiful dark-winged Osceola tom from Green Swamp WMA

Kenny Dorman won our 2007 Annual Beetlenecker/ Cracker Green Swamp Invitational Golf Tournament, defeating Bill George, me, Doug Pickle, and Buster Brown. I crafted the trophy.

It was another five days of tough hunting on the grounds of Green Swamp WMA before I finally killed a tom of my own, and several more days after that before I could fill the seasonal bag limit of two. By then I'd spent 19 days in total hunting the wild and foreboding swamps of Florida. Every single moment had been an absolute blast, with great weather and very few bugs to ruin things. The good times shared in camp had also been exemplary, with many, many laughs and stories told 'round the campfire. Florida is one of my favorite hunting destinations anyway, but those special times spent with folks I love like family, as well as the Corey's and all the others I'd met at the handicapped event put everything in perspective and helped me to fully realize just how eternally lucky I was to lead this life that I'd chosen. How could the season ahead ever fail to warrant awe and amazement after such a wonderful beginning?

Well, the next six days in South Carolina tried my patience. The camaraderie was certainly good, with Larry Sharp's clan from Kentucky joining me there along with Brenda and Shirley Morris from West Virginia, and Allan Stanley from Delaware. However, the turkeys were very quiet and uncooperative that spring. I only heard gobbling on half of the days and shot just a single tom, despite working hard and putting lots of miles on my boots. I wasn't even finding much sign, leading me to believe that the flock numbers were way down from previous years. Sumter NF had always treated me well, but what I was failing to find now made me question whether it might be time to venture out in coming years and work on other states needed to whittle down my second U.S. Super Slam. I never did like to get in too much of a "rut" anyway, so I saw the troubles of 2007 as a sign to seek greener pastures (or, since I dislike hunting field turkeys so much, maybe I should use a term like "more fertile woods") in coming years.

The next state on the 2007 itinerary may come as a surprise to my readers, because going there even surprised *me* at the time! But, as stated in my last book, immediately after killing my first Delaware tom I had quite suddenly and shockingly considered going back again. And so, during the winter I'd put in for their lottery and subsequently been awarded another tag for Redden State Forest. The very first time I'd hunted there, the seemingly simple act of finding turkeys had been an extremely difficult proposition, but subsequent years had seen a veritable explosion in their population. A local wildlife biologist whom I'd befriended early-on (Joe Shockley) had kept me apprised of how good the local flock was flourishing, and his intel was so encouraging that I was now almost looking forward to the trip.

My South Carolina tom from the Sumter National Forest

When I showed up 24 hours before my six-day hunt was to begin, I was initially discouraged by running into people just about every place I wanted to scout. But, on opening morning I went back into the area where I'd called in a couple of jakes the previous season, and at dawn I was rewarded by the sound of a bird gobbling really well. It ended up being a quick hunt, and shortly before 7 o'clock the tom strutted up in front of my gun barrel. I figured that it was probably one of those same jakes from before, now one year older, but the long, hooked spurs on his legs indicated otherwise. After slinging him over a shoulder, I told myself that *this time* I could leave my least favorite state behind (it's so full of people, trash, congestion, and bustle...everything that I despise about human nature) and never come back again. Stay tuned to see how that turned out...

The first state in which I had ever killed a tom other than Indiana was Virginia, way back in 1987, and I'd wanted to go back there ever since. My pursuit of a second Super Slam gave me just the motivation needed to do so with a trip to Quantico Marine Base, near Washington, DC. Doug Pickle had invited me to come up and hunt there with him. He's one of my great friends from our Florida turkey camp, but despite a couple of days at the base and another six days hunting some of Doug's leased ground and a few other prime private honeyholes supplied by Doug's good friend Ken Greene, I failed to fill even a single tag. We had multiple close encounters and exciting hunts every day, but something always seemed to go wrong.

Delaware in 2007

Despite my great fondness for Doug and Ken, that week in Virginia left a bitter taste in my mouth. You see; I'm basically a solo hunter by nature, and always feel my best and hunt my best without an audience. My truest, most heartfelt view of turkey hunting is that it's a sport which ought to be conducted on a "one-on-one" basis. My friends, of course, wanting only to help me out and share in the thrill of the hunt, didn't know this, and they hadn't ever set me out to "do my own thing." We had hunted the whole time together, as a unit. Basically, that left me feeling like I'd been hamstrung in conducting the hunts as I best saw fit. The three of us are all very accomplished turkey hunters, but we didn't always agree on methods and strategies. In my mind, I thought that the indecisiveness of too many opinions often resulted in us making the wrong moves, at the wrong times. There's an old saying that goes, "too many chefs spoil the soup," and while I left for home deeply appreciative and grateful beyond measure for all that these guys had tried their hardest to do for me, I was at the same time dissatisfied with how the soup had turned out.

Returning home to Indiana sure felt good! The regular gang was all back in place at Tea Mountain, and we spent the first few days at Tom Foley's beautiful, rustic log cabin smack-dab in the middle of those 1600 acres of prime Brown County turkey habitat. Spirits were high, and good times were had by all in attendance. Unfortunately, the turkeys didn't share in our glee, and they abused us unmercifully. Don Foley and I gave it all we had out on "the fingers" (our

Doug Pickle with a 2007 Virginia gobbler

traditionally-hunted portion of the property), but the only successes we found came in the "what if" category. Then, after Don had gone back home for work commitments, I shot a great tom on the third day of the season, taking exquisite joy in rushing out to a pay phone to call and tell him how all it took was getting rid of his dead weight slowing me down in order to put a tom on the ground. The two of us never miss out on an opportunity to take jabs at one another, but that's just the way we show our love.

Venturing down to Jefferson County, I next took Frank Emert and his wife Nancy on a hunt featuring a whole plethora of exciting happenings…multiple toms heard, multiple toms boogered, multiple toms shot at and missed, and then multiple toms killed. It was one of the most intense, action-packed hunts of my life, with nary a dull minute before we finally had two big gobblers flopping in the leaves side by side shortly after 9 a.m. Of course, I was a nervous wreck by the time this hunt ended, but it left all three of us grinning like village idiots!

Set on vengeance, I then headed back to Virginia. However, this time I didn't go nearly so far east as before, and instead, stopped off at a rather intriguing place called Fairystone Farms WMA, in Patrick County. The kill totals and overall turkey population in that county were five times higher than up where Doug and Ken lived, and besides that, it was terrain which just suited my eye for what turkey country ought to look like; mostly deciduous forests with far fewer pinelands. I would also be hunting alone and in control of the show, so there would be only myself to blame if things went wrong. They didn't.

*Frank & Nancy Emert with their
Indiana double kill*

Once I'd put boots on dirt, I killed a great tom on the very first morning. Then, I shot another on the second day. I could've and probably should've filled a third tag on Day 3 (a tom which slipped in on my weak side unannounced), but I declined to take an "iffy" crack at him. That was just as well, though, because I certainly didn't want to cripple and lose a turkey. There's nothing worse. It's always better to error on the side of caution, rather than run that risk, so I let him walk away to live and battle another day. The turkey soup from my return to Virginia (as opposed to the tag soup sampled during the previous trip) tasted *much* better!

A Fairystone Farms victory from Virginia in 2007

With Virginia now successfully in hindsight, I traveled over to New Jersey's Delaware Water Gap area. This place had piqued my interest greatly the first time I'd ever hunted there, and I was eager to check it out again. According to my understanding, this whole region had been relegated back in the 1970's to be dammed and flooded as part of an enormous hydro-electrical generating plant, but environmental concerns and protests had indefinitely put the project on hold. However, the Federal Government had already bought up most of the land by then, leaving many old farms and homesteads abandoned in the process. It is really a beautiful area of rolling hardwood hills seemingly perfect in design for raising turkeys, and I was hoping to find them in numbers sufficient for holding my attention.

That certainly proved to be the case when I killed a tom on the very first morning. My original plan had been to shoot one bird and get out so as never to again feel the need of returning to New Jersey, but a strange thing happened during this trip: I'd found the ground to be so beautiful and compelling that I decided to stay for a while. It was legal to buy all the leftover tags you wanted until they were sold out, so I acquired one for the next hunt period and spent another five days there. Although I didn't kill any more turkeys, I did find the area to be a fascinating place chocked full of history. Some of those old abandoned farmhouses dated back into the 1700's, and descendants of Revolutionary War heroes like the Rosecrans family still lived there after refusing to sell their land to the government.

New Jersey gobbler from the Delaware Water Gap

My next stop was in Pennsylvania, where Jon Pries had invited me to come and hunt on his beautiful farm near Williamsburg. Being a traveling turkey hunter too, Jon was out of town chasing after gobblers someplace else at the time, but he'd granted me permission to hunt on not only his farm, but a neighbor's 250 acres. There were an additional 6,000 acres of state land beyond his fence line, which Jon also claimed to hold birds. Unfortunately, a truck pulled into the driveway and parked next to my van just prior to gobbling time, and then two fellas dressed in camo hopped out and began gearing up like hunting the farm was a normal everyday occurrence. My presence didn't seem to bother them or alter their plans, in the least.

They ended up being a father/son team. Doug was the elder fellow's name, but I forget his son's. Both of them were so friendly that my initial annoyance at their arrival was overlooked, and when Doug suggested that we all walk down to the woodline below the farmhouse to await first gobble, I acquiesced. He wanted to let the turkeys heard dictate a plan where we wouldn't mess each other up.

The first bird to pipe up was back behind the barn where we'd parked, and then several others began hammering it in the woods directly below where we were standing. I don't like feeling crowded when I'm turkey hunting, so I "asked permission" to make a play at the solo bird. Doug-and-son eagerly agreed, and as I hiked back uphill the woods where they were headed exploded in frenetic gobbling. It was hard walking away from that ruckus, but what else could I do?

My only option now was to stay the course and hunt the little slice of woods behind the barn while these unknown guys had their run of at least four toms in the prime spot below Jon's house. To be honest, I wasn't particularly happy about the whole situation and felt like I'd been basically edged out of what I'd anticipated being a great opportunity to score my second Pennsylvania gobbler. Jon hadn't mentioned anyone else coming into the farm, and in fact, had been rather adamant that I would have the whole place to myself. When I subsequently heard heavy wingbeats from the vicinity of all the gobbling and looked back in that direction to see two big black birds sailing out over the treetops after being boogered by the other guys, I must admit that I felt like justice had perhaps been served.

The tom I was after had actually roosted on another neighbor's property where I couldn't hunt, but he wasn't very far into it. Choosing a big oak tree as a setup spot 40 yards from Jon's barn and 40 yards from the property fence, I anxiously

Wearing a hat of Hunter Orange in Pennsylvania

awaited another gobble to assuage my growing fears that I might've already spooked the bird. The spring woods weren't as yet showing the first hint of greening buds which might've helped to cover my approach, and despite the other distant turkeys hitting it hard, this closest tom had only gobbled twice before clamming up. When he failed to answer my first cutt/yelp series of calls on a glass, those fears seemed validated.

Five minutes later I cutt harder on my call, and the targeted tom ripped it from about 150 yards away. A tree to my left with more ground cover surrounding its base looked like a better setup spot, so I hustled over there and got nestled in. Ten minutes later, without any more calling on my part, I saw a hen approaching. She never said a word and was soon thereafter busily scratching in the dry, crackling leaves like she'd found a motherlode of June bugs or something else delightfully delicious. My eyes strained from watching so intently for the tom which I hoped to be following along behind her, but it wasn't until another 15 minutes had passed before I spotted just the very tip of his white-crowned head peering out from behind a tree on the other side of the property fence.

The old boy was a wary one, spending long minutes fully erect and gazing intently, but eventually he'd fuzz up briefly and advance a few steps. Then, he'd repeat the whole painfully-slow routine. It took him *forever* to cross the fence line, and even more time to get in tight, but finally I lined up his head just above the triple sight beads on my Benelli M2. Just as I was about to squeeze the trigger, the hen alerted and putted once. This caused the tom's head to arise even taller than it had already been, and I took that opportunity to end our chess game of life and death consequences.

Doug and his son came back to the house around 8:30 and told me their tale of woes and heartbreaks, having boogered not only the initial two birds that I'd seen fly away, but several others, as well. Then, they laughed and invited me to come out to their 7,000 acre lease to get a shower and attend a trout-stocking party. I spent the rest of that day hanging around with these guys and their friends, and we had a *large* time of it. More than a few beers were consumed,

A young Trevor Bays with a gobbler almost as big as himself

and numerous friendships were formed. I ended up regretting ever thinking any bad thoughts at all about how the morning had begun.

Connecticut was the next place where I intended to hunt, but the following day was Sunday. Since that state doesn't allow Sunday hunting, I made a pit-stop of sorts in New York, where young Trevor Bays and I had a fantastic hunt with lots of action. We ended up being in amongst turkeys from first gobble at 5:06 a.m. until Trev pulled the trigger at 8:47 a.m. It had been obvious from our very first days afield back in 2003 that Trevor was destined to become a turkey hunter, and each year thereafter only further convinced me that he was also bound to excel at the sport. Even at his young age, the kid was performing like a seasoned pro.

The results of a great 2007 hunt in Connecticut

Hustling on up to Connecticut, I spent the first couple of days hiking far and wide but finding nothing of note. A phone call to the wildlife biologist then propelled me into exploring Tunxis State Forest, and boy, am I'm glad that I did, because the very next morning I heard my first gobble of the trip. Soon afterwards, I was standing on the bird's neck. This is another state that doesn't allow camping on their public lands, so I'd been forced to sleep in Walmart parking lots every night and commute to the hunting areas each morning. That routine was quickly getting old and stale, and besides, the black flies were threatening to eat me alive, so I decided to forego the second tag in my pocket and go someplace where I was free to set up camp and relax. Vermont seemed to fit the bill for what I was seeking.

The Green Mountain National Forest is a vast area, and they allow camping. However, I didn't hear any gobbling for the first 4- 1/2 days. During that time span it also rained practically non-stop both night and day, leaving me soggy and discouraged. And yet, the particular area where I'd set up camp had been recommended in a phone call to another wildlife biologist, and I had subsequently found quite a bit of physical turkey sign there...droppings and scratchings aplenty in the hemlock-dominated forests along a real pretty babbling brook that looked like it ought to be loaded with native trout.

When the rain began subsiding during late morning of Day 5, I found myself once again already out in it and fairly-well soaking wet. I hadn't heard a thing at dawn to give me any hope, but finally, a loud yelp on a mouth call generated that glorious sound which I'd been so anxious to hear for nearly a week...a vibrant gobble! The tom ripped out another one all on his own before I could move the five yards needed to reach a good setup tree, and then within minutes of getting settled-in, I spotted the bird angling down the steep slope in front of me. A second tom accompanied him. Without any more calling on my part, I watched anxiously as both birds slipped and slid their way to the bottom of the hill before climbing up onto the short ridgelet where I sat in wait. They came right on in, too...passing behind numerous large hemlock trees which allowed

A rainy-day tom from Vermont in 2007

me ample opportunities to swing my shotgun's muzzle ahead of their path. At 28 yards I squeezed the trigger, and the second Vermont gobbler of my life piled up pretty as you please.

When you've been cramped up in a van for five straight days and nights of rain, everything you own eventually gets wet. There's just no escaping all the moisture. By that time I was *really* ready to dry out, and with a forecast of (what else?) more rain for the foreseeable future, I decided to head on down the road. The Vermont gobbler that I'd come here to find was now packed away in my cooler, so the one turkey tag still remaining in my rain-drenched wallet was unceremoniously forfeited for the promise of a warm woodstove in Jake Bays' New York deer camp.

This welcomed change of scenery and the chance to dry out all of my gear also brought with it an uptick in turkey encounters on the remnants of the once-bustling Bays dairy farm, which was now completely devoid of cows. It seemed like everywhere Trevor Bays and I hunted that spring, we found lots of turkeys and plenty of good luck, and in only a matter of days I'd filled both of my tags. Trevor, as well, finished out his bag limit with a second tom.

Ownership of the farm and exactly who would get what was still in limbo following Tony's death the year before, but at that point it looked like Jake

A beautiful New York gobbler in a patch of ramps

would end up with a sizeable chunk of the ground. He was also in the process of building a big lake down in the "beefer pasture," where I'd had so many good hunts in years past. Hunting on the farm would of course never be the same again, but at least things were beginning to feel a bit closer to some sort of "new normal."

With a whole week of the season remaining, I still had time to try and squeeze in one final state before returning home in time to make Jen's birthday party on June 1, so I then pointed my van towards Michigan. Some random spot in a random State Game Area served as my starting point, but heavy thunderstorms and pouring rain rolled in during the early morning hours. However, by 5 a.m. it was only drizzling when I stepped outside the van, and immediately thereafter, a distant thunderclap was answered by a gobble. A second rumble caused another one, but before I could sally forth in pursuit, the skies opened up into a torrential downpour. At that point I merely stepped back inside and crawled into my sleeping bag. I was road weary, the rain was relentless, and the turkeys could wait.

It was 9 o'clock before the downpour ever began to subside. By then I'd already arisen refreshed from my "catch-up nap" and begun cruising around the area. I was hoping to see turkeys out in the fields. Unfortunately, the only ones found were some hens on private ground, so I returned to the spot where I'd heard the bird gobble twice at dawn's thunderclaps. During a short scouting hike, I found two sets of big gobbler tracks in a wet, sandy pipeline.

That would prove fortuitous the next morning when I called in what I can only assume to be both of those toms. The first visual contact I ever had with them was when they stepped out of a thick tangle of blackberry vines at six yards, and I'd had to let them walk on past before shouldering my firearm for the shot. One of the two was noticeably bigger than the other, but both had thick, heavy beards. When I clucked on a mouth call to stop their departure, the "lesser" tom was the only one to raise his head. That was a bad move on his part, so I shot him.

It had been a quick and successful trip to Michigan, and I'd thoroughly enjoyed my time there. In fact, the only problems encountered were the weather, a horrendous number of mosquitos, and the lack of even a single morel mushroom found. The potential of picking gobs and scads of those tasty fungi had been a driving force in my choice of hunting area, but alas; I'd been too late in my arrival and they had already come and gone.

My Michigan tom from 2007

Despite a few problems nearly unmentionable because of their unimportance, the 2007 season had been a tremendous success. I'd hunted a dozen states for the second year in a row and had managed to knock off seven needed towards fulfilling my goal of a second U.S. Super Slam. That meant there were now only 17 remaining on the list. I'd also reduced my magic number of states necessary for the public land version to only three. The 72 days I'd spent hunting were also the second highest seasonal total of my life, and as most of you know, it's the actual time spent hunting which is the single greatest measure of how I view success. The year of 2007 most-certainly fit all of my criteria for being regarded as a great year!

2007

A typical feather shrine to one of my fallen adversaries

Chapter 2

2008

Zane and I had once again set ourselves up to guide some hunters on a pair of private landholdings, both of which were commercial sod farms. The first of these properties was about half a square mile, and the other was approximately one mile wide and two miles long. On opening day Zane took two guys out on the smaller property where we had guided in years past, while I headed down south about an hour's drive to explore our new and larger piece of ground with the first of my clients: Travis Cline and his lovely wife Megan, who was there only to observe and photograph the experience.

The Resmondo Sod Farm was an interesting place...two mile-square sections of green grass stacked north to south. There weren't very many trees within the confines of the farm itself, but it was surrounded by typical Florida habitat of cattle pastures mixed with hardwood and pines. You couldn't drive around on the farm without seeing turkeys here and there, but it was a challenging place to hunt because of the paucity of any cover.

However, there was a conglomeration of trees in the southwestern corner surrounding the headquarters and implement shed, and that's where the farm's foreman (Gary-Lee) suggested that we start. A deep, foreboding, almost moat-like ditch ran along the property line there, and then it turned with the corner to border much of the farm's western edge. Gary-Lee told us that turkeys typically roosted in trees on the other side of the creek and would pitch down to spend their entire day wandering around in the sod. Then, at dusk they would reverse course and fly up to roost across the creek. However, by mid-morning of most days, this "south flock" could be found hanging out in the shade of the trees near the shop.

Our initial opening day setup in that copse of trees produced nothing more than a confirmation of Gary-Lee's observations. The tom and a buddy gobbled early, often, and close-by, but then flew down into the sod with nine hens and began wandering away to the east. Anticipating their route, I realized that we could cut the distance to the flock by quickly circling back through the trees and getting set up on the opposite side of the grove. Once our dekes were set out, it was only a matter of minutes before the first pair of hens came in yelping and carrying-on like they were among old friends. Three others soon followed behind, but the rest of the flock stalled out at about 150 yards and refused to budge an inch closer. I felt sure that they would eventually come to us, and we were perfectly willing to wait patiently for that to happen, but by 10 a.m. we were still idly twiddling our collective thumbs while the gobblers held pat out there in the middle of all that grass.

Suddenly, we spotted Gary-Lee's white pickup truck slowly approaching the flock from the north, and from where we sat, it certainly looked like he was trying to herd the turkeys in our direction! Now, Gary-Lee was anything but a turkey hunter, and I'd already picked up on the fact that he was rather bemused by anyone wanting to shoot a bird which he viewed as being stupid as a stick. In all fairness to him, the turkeys on that farm showed very little fear of Gary-Lee or any of the other hired hands working in the fields, so his opinion seemed somewhat valid when viewed from that perspective. However, I had tried to impress upon our host the importance of my clients wanting to *hunt* these birds in a fair-chase manner, rather than just driving up to a tom and killing him with a tennis racket (as Gary-Lee suggested). It was now obvious that my point about fair-chase had been misunderstood!

Well, the turkeys didn't take any more kindly to Gary-Lee's shepherding attempt than we did, and they skirted out around the truck and moved rapidly away to the north. After failing in the turkey rustling game, Gary-Lee drove over to tell us not only what he'd been trying to do, but what he'd been witnessing around the farm all morning...multiple other gobblers parading around in full splendor. Feeling like it was time for a little meeting, Gary-Lee and I went for a walk, and when we returned I felt much more confident that our host had a firm grasp on how this hunt was to go down.

Taking us far to the north and dropping us off at another section of the farm, we set up with intentions of making a play on a pair of toms Gary-Lee had spotted earlier. According to his story, he'd driven up so close to the fighting pair that "I couldn't see them over the hood of my truck." Exiting the cab, he'd walked around to find the toms engaged in a vicious battle with necks intertwined, pushing and flogging each other ferociously. At that point he "had to kick 'em apart so they wouldn't hurt each other!"

Gary-Lee's size 14 boots must've persuaded the toms to vacate that particular area, because we saw nothing during the rest of the morning hours. After hitting a local diner for lunch, we came back for the afternoon hunt fully refreshed and ready to make something positive happen at a spot along the western edge of the farm about a mile north of where we'd started the day. Three big live oaks grew just inside the farm's border at that spot, and far out into the sod from there we could see a tom and his accompanying hens. Gary-Lee told us that this group of birds liked to roost in the oaks, so we used his truck as a shield to keep the flock from seeing us erect a Double Bull Blind in their shade, and then the three of us slipped inside while Gary-Lee drove away. Several hours later the whole flock began easing in our direction, and then the tom quite suddenly broke away from his ladies and walked directly at us.

At that point I thought the gobbler was on a path to destiny, but before he got close enough for Travis to kill him, the silly bird took flight and flew into the tree under which we sat...landing on a limb about 15 feet straight up above our popup blind! Pieces of tree bark rained down upon us as he paced back and forth for a few minutes, and then he just as suddenly decided to pitch back down to earth, landing out of range and walking towards another oak tree a hundred yards northwest of us. That's where he roosted for the night.

The next morning we were right back in our blind and anticipating the tom pitching down and walking out into the sod via a dusty two-track that ran right past our blind. Instead, he flew out and landed 75 yards away without ever gobbling even a single time in the tree, and then he immediately began moving to the north at a steady pace, gobbling frequently as he went. Multiple hens did come by us, though...and every single one of them walked the path precisely where I'd thought the tom would travel. However, now they were hurrying to catch up with their departing boyfriend, and all we could do was sit listening to his fading gobbles. I was in the process of calling hard on a glass call to try and turn him back around, when suddenly, I heard the very distinct "chump" of a tom going into strut at close range. One glance out the back window of the blind put us all into scramble-mode, as there was a big gobbler already squared up and just about to peck the head of my strutter decoy at 24 yards! I have no idea where he came from, but Travis capably and permanently put a stop to his shenanigans.

Travis and Megan Cline

I now had some time to hunt before my next guiding assignment, and I wasn't the least bit surprised when those efforts produced absolutely nothing of note for the first couple of days. That's just the way things normally roll at Green Swamp WMA. However, when I typed the word "nothing" in that previous sentence, I truly meant *nothing*...not a single gobble heard, or even any sort of visual contact made. But, as so often happens in this sport, things have a way of changing rapidly, and the very next day I experienced a fantastic hunt after finding myself at dawn surrounded by not just one, but two toms absolutely ripping it in an old favorite area that had produced regularly for me in years past. One of them subsequently rode back to camp in my van as an honored guest.

After blanking again the next day, it was time to serve as a guide at the handicapped hunt put on by "Hunters Without Limits." Formerly, this event had been held under the directive of the NWTF's "Wheelin' Sportsmen" program, but they were no longer running the show. I have no idea what happened to create the division, but I'd successfully guided at this event for three springs in a row and I was very much looking forward to continuing with my commitment to their noble cause.

My assigned hunter in 2008 was Jared Bronner, a U.S. Army veteran who had suffered severe injuries when his Humvee had been blown up in Iraq. Being able to help this guy sort of re-discover himself in the wilds of Florida was an honor and a privilege which I took very seriously. Me, Jared, and his friend Jan worked hard the first day without success, but on Day 2 we finally put it all together and walked away with a fine Osceola gobbler and lasting memories to show for our efforts. My good friends Charlie Parrish, Craig Morton, and Bill George had also guided during the weekend, and the entire event was a resounding success in every possible regard. There were even a few turkeys killed, although that didn't really matter. Our "victories" couldn't be measured in feathers brought to bag, but in the smiles and laughter shared between participants and guides alike.

Jarrod Bronner's Osceola

Hunters Without Limits group photo

Green Swamp gobbler at a hiking bridge on the Florida Trail

Our 2008 golf trophy went to Bill George's house

I stayed in Florida for another week before heading elsewhere. As usual, the good times had by me and my friends in our turkey camp were memorably fun, but one afternoon in particular was mentionable: I'd brought down a bunch of pheasants from a fall trip to South Dakota, and this resulted in an epic meal where I deep fried about 15 of those tasty game birds to go along with whatever everyone else contributed to a collective feast. There were about 20 of us in camp at the time, and after stuffing ourselves full as ticks, we sat around all afternoon telling stories and laughing. It was a blast, but then again, we *always* have fun in that camp!

My final guiding duties in Florida that year were with a fellow from Michigan. Despite fervent effort over three days, the hunt ended in abject failure when he not only missed a turkey, but a second one, as well! The way I run my hunts is to guarantee the client an *opportunity*, so I had certainly done my part above and beyond any expectations. In short, I'd earned his money. Still, I felt really bad for Brandt because of how good a guy he was, and I vowed to help him kill an Osceola the following spring, no matter what it took...grenade launchers, claymores, or perhaps tying one up to a tree before his arrival. I know Brandt felt really bad about the misses, but I probably felt just as bad *for* him!

For now, though, it was time to hit the road, with Louisiana being my next destination. Five days of hunting at Jackson-Bienville WMA later, I'd only heard one single gobble. At that point I was badly in need of a change in scenery in order to change my attitude, so I ventured over to Texas intending to make a play for an Eastern bird in the hill country of the Angelina National Forest. Subsequently, I missed a tom on Day 1 when he flew down from his roost directly at me and I panicked in trying to shoot him out of the air as he swooshed by overhead at about 25 feet in elevation. However, I then made amends two days later after calling in the same bird good and proper. He was a big, gorgeous, chestnut-tipped Eastern, taken on a real pretty hardwood ridge, but even more importantly; this East Texas tom left me only one bird shy of a Public Land U.S. Super Slam.

A Texas Eastern from 2008

Intent on extracting revenge for the earlier beating Louisiana had given me, I stopped off in Natchitoches for a delicious meal of mud bugs (boiled crawfish) before venturing out into the Kisatchie National Forest. Maybe it was just a matter of being on a hot streak of "one in a row" that did the trick, but soon thereafter I found myself standing on a tom's neck. Truth be told, it was probably just the fact that I was now hunting in an area which actually held a decent population of turkeys, although the place was also overrun with other hunters. Then, I came close for the next four days in a row without any additional kills. By the time I finally got out of there, I was beginning to question if I would ever again kill a turkey. That's how it goes in this sport...one day you're up, and the next you're down. The only way to alter that is to keep fighting through the bad times, because as I've mentioned numerous times, things have a way of turning around in the blink of an eye.

There's more to love about Louisiana than just boudin

After a fairly short road trip, I found myself in Mississippi. The first time that I'd hunted there, it had taken me 12 days before finally pulling the trigger. I fully expected things to be just as difficult this time around, but instead, it ended up being a wonderfully productive trip with three toms shot during the six days. Each of them re-taught me lessons I already knew.

The first bird was an example of success gained through patience. It was a little after high noon before I pulled the trigger on him, despite starting the day within 75 yards of his roost tree. This tom had a number of hens surrounding him all morning long, but by biding my time and being generally coy with any calling, I was able to eventually assume the role of that one remaining girlfriend still hanging around after all the others had wandered off to lay their eggs. Bingo!

The second tom was a product of keen observation. I'd found some big, bold, and fresh scratchings at the bases of trees and fallen logs in a new area scouted during the afternoon, and although I heard nothing fly up at dusk, I came right back there for the morning hunt because my interpretation of the sign was that it had been made by a tom. Ballistic gobbling greeted me at dawn, and I was able to sneak in and set up close while the bird was still tree-bound. It was below freezing, and my fingers were numb when I tried to chop into the tail end of his next gobble with a little cutt series on a glass pot. The calls sounded shrill and too high pitched. I knew better than to use a friction call in cold weather, before the material (and my hands) had a chance to warm up, so I switched over to a diaphragm and tried to put some emotion into my next yelps. The tom fired right back in response, and then he went silent. Now; I've experienced that situation so many times that I knew it was most likely due to one of two scenarios...either he was busy strutting for real hens, or else he was sneaking in on my position. A few minutes later I got the preferred answer to that question when I heard a low, dull drumming sound which always excites me to the very center of my soul. Not long after that, the tom strutted up within easy killing range.

The third Mississippi gobbler of the year was a product of paying attention and not being afraid to make adjustments in my setup. Early-on I'd thought that I was hearing a distant dog barking, but my ears told me to move a hundred yards closer for verification. From there, I could tell that the sounds were actually a far-off tom with a rather peculiar, stop-and-go gobble. He was reluctant to answer my calls initially, but warmed up a little bit as the morning progressed. Still, the old boy refused to budge towards me, so I began a series of lateral movements in re-setting up every 40 yards or so as I tried to give him the impression that a real hen was doing normal hen stuff. The tom became more and more vocal with every new calling location, and his gobbles began to take on a desperate tone. In no time I could tell that he was closing the distance between us. Rushing over to find this departing hen didn't work out very well for the gobbler, and it wasn't long before I had him under foot.

I'd drawn an Illinois tag slated to begin on April 18, so I next headed back to a Pope County spot which had treated me very well once before. I had every confidence that it would produce good results again. However, there were already a couple of fellers set up in tents at the primitive campground nearby, and I was contemplating moving elsewhere to avoid crowding them when they waved me over and offered me a bowl of hot venison chili and a cold beer. Well, I can't say no to offers like that, and after we'd talked for a while, they insisted that I was more than welcome to share camp with them.

This little campground served as an access point to a large chunk of Shawnee

Mississippi's got a lot of cottonmouth moccasins, but some of these, too

National Forest land, and although I abhor hunting near other folks, I figured that I could walk far and gain some separation from my new friends the next morning. Then, at dusk, another group of three guys pulled in and set up their own camp nearby. At that point it was too late to go find somewhere else offering more solitude, so I decided to strike out extra early the next morning and walk far away. This is my general modus operendi anyway on public land, but it was even more crucial now that things looked like I'd be hunting in a crowd. If it didn't work out I could always make a move elsewhere after the morning's hunt.

Well, everything *did* work out…splendidly! I never saw another human after leaving camp, and instead, found myself surrounded by three hard-gobbling toms at daylight. The one I shot was only on the ground for four minutes before taking a permanent dirt nap, and then I commenced a nice, leisurely stroll back to camp with a fine old gobbler safely tucked into my hunting vest. On the way I began picking morel mushrooms, and by the time I'd reached my van there was almost as much fungal volume in my vest as turkey flesh! I never even heard another gunshot during the entire morning and had no idea what all those other hunters were doing or where they were at, but I was long gone and on my way home before any of them returned to camp.

Illinois turkey hunting can be awesome

I've written about Tea Mountain, in Brown County, Indiana on numerous occasions. This property was a magical place where I spent the opening few days of turkey season all throughout the 1990's and the first decade or so of the 2000's. Comprised of some 1600 acres of private landholdings owned by Tom Foley, it was a wonderland where Tom's nephew Don Foley, along with Bruce Wilson, brothers DeWayne and Russell Feltner, and me chased after gobblers with wild abandon. Tom didn't care about turkeys at all, but he really enjoyed searching his ground for morels, so while our crew got after the gobblers, he and his friends scoured the ground for tasty fungi. This little gathering was an annual tradition greatly enjoyed by all of us.

Donnie and I always hunted together, and we were known for giving each other a nearly-continuous ration of false-grief...all in fun, of course! The truth of the matter is that we both really enjoyed each other's company on these hunts, and we shared many a laugh and good time. Originally, our partnership had been one of "hunter" and "triggerman," and I often reminded him of just exactly who was whom in that arrangement. But, as time progressed, Donnie gained more faith in his abilities and become more of an active participant in the strategies and calling. Going into that 2008 season he let it be known early-on that it was now time for him to "take the pebble from Doc's hand" and become the guide.

Opening day weather was perfect: clear skies, mild temps, and no wind. The first bird to gobble was roosted over on Rattlesnake Ridge, and he gobbled *hard*.

However, getting to him entailed crossing a substantially steep and deep hollow, and many years of experience told us that other turkeys should eventually start gobbling on our side. Sure enough, one soon did from out on what we called, "the fingers" (a series of seven parallel ridges running north to south). This was where Donnie and I spent most of our hunting hours anyway, so we eased out towards the gobbling and were soon set up at the tip of the westernmost ridge (Finger #1). The tom(s) were actually across a big hollow north of our position, but for some reason they gobbled at one or two of Donnie's screeching chicken-scratchings on a Cane Creek Glass Call that I'd given him a few years earlier, and before too much longer they appeared to be headed our way.

It was at this point that I asked for permission from my "guide" to call just once, and Donnie most graciously acquiesced. I can't even begin to describe the look on his face when neither tom answered my yelps on a diaphragm, but believe me, it was priceless! Holding out his hand with palm upwards, he ordered, "That's it...you're done...give me your call." I hung my head low in mock shame, emphatically spitting the call out into my own hand before handing it over to Donnie. "All of them," he insisted, and I took my diaphragm call case from a chest pocket and tossed it down in the leaves between our feet. Then, I reached into a vest pocket to withdraw my own glass pot and do likewise with it. We laughed, then laughed some more, and when Donnie's next shrill, squawking yelps elicited ferocious gobbles from both birds, I thought that my guts were gonna split wide open from laughing so hard. How two idiots yucking it up in the woods didn't scare those turkeys clear into the next county is a mystery to me still, but they continued to gobble on their own as they closed ground rapidly.

These two toms were on a suicidal death march, and I told Donnie that if the chance presented itself, we should try for a double kill. He agreed. However, I'd been around my friend long enough to anticipate him not actually pulling the trigger when the time came...thereby letting me take the blame for meat-hogging him when only one tom piled up. And so, when both gobblers were standing tall at 22 yards, I counted down for our duel trigger-pull before hesitating with my own until *after* I'd heard the report of Donnie's gun. I was actually surprised when he shot, but just as soon as his bird fell, I killed mine, too. Thus, we ended up with a classic and memorable double. It was a great hunt, with a wonderful friend, and the both of us gained tons of mileage out of the humor from my "forfeiture" of the calls and Donnie usurping my title of "lead guide." I had no intentions whatsoever of killing a bird when the day started, but boy, I sure am glad that I did.

Don Foley and me at Tea Mountain in 2008

Another memorable story from that year involved our annual dinner held the night before opening day. I think it was Bruce who brought the elk ribs to be cooked over an open fire. As the afternoon progressed and meal preparations were well under way, Tom imbibed in quite a bit of amber colored liquid. Two sheets into the wind and eager to eat before the ribs were ready (they were slow-grilling to perfection over hot coals), he then commenced pouring lighter fluid on the hot embers directly underneath the meat. When the dinner bell was finally rung, those heavenly-looking elk ribs tasted pretty-much like pure kerosene. However, since it was our gracious host who had done the dirty deed himself, we all silently ate that meal and acted like we enjoyed it. I swear: I could still taste lighter fluid the next day whenever I burped! All of us have recollected back on that episode in living color many times since, and we still laugh about it just about every time we get together.

Tracy Deckard and I have been great buddies since we were freshmen in high school and we've hunted together countless times. Both of us love turkey hunting above anything else, with waterfowling running a close second. Tracy's youngest son Levi is every bit as serious about his ducks and geese as we are, but turkeys were never quite his thing. Oh, he certainly enjoys hunting them, but being a farmer, spring has always been a hard time for him to get away.

Well, in 2008 the three of us had an opportunity to share a hunt which resulted in a fine old gobbler for Levi, but the most memorable part occurred while the

Would you like seconds, Bruce? Russell Feltner serves up a rib with Pete Wilkerson and Bill Louderback in the background

Levi and Tracy Deckard at the 2008 tick nest

tom was still creeping in the final few yards and taking his own sweet time doing it. Levi was 15 yards in front of his Dad and I, and unbeknownst to us both when we sat down, we were situated in a huge nest of ticks. We couldn't move for fear of spooking the tom, as literally hundreds of tiny "seed" ticks crawled up our pant legs and all over us. It was like a damned horror movie! Just as soon as that shotgun went off, Tracy and I jumped up and headed for the truck, where we used balls of wadded up duct tape sticky-side-out to remove gobs and scads of those hated arachnids. YUCK! I itched for a week, just thinking about them!

The next day I headed out to Rhode Island for a visit with my good friends Mark Plante and John P Smith. These two guys are as good as humans get, and their mere presence makes hunting in this armpit of the nation tolerable. Rhode Island is *not* an easy place in which to kill a tom on public land, and I stated some rather frank opinions about its negative aspects in Volume 1. Since then I've found no good reasons to change any of those views, and 2008 ended up being an 8-day struggle before I was finally able to experience a wonderful hunt full of suspense, intrigue, frustration, and ultimately, jubilation. After killing my second-ever Rhode Island tom, I felt like I would indeed never be coming back again, but of course, that was before I decided at a later date to go for a third Super Slam. It's funny how perceptions and circumstances change over time…

My great friends John P Smith and Mark Plante in New Jersey

From Rhode Island, I next ventured up to New Hampshire's Pisgah State Park. This was a place which I had simply picked nearly at random on a map, and when I heard gobbling while standing in the parking lot of a trail head the very first morning, I never had the need to go any further. I came real close to killing that bird initially, and then I got it done the following day. That quick victory allowed me to make a welcomed escape from the vast hordes of biting gnats which were already about to drive me crazy, and I got outa there just as soon as I could get my wheels turning! I certainly don't mind the hardships, trials, and tribulations encountered in the turkey woods, but bugs in quantities like that really bug me. On the plus side was the scenery. New Hampshire is definitely in the top tier of the most beautiful places on this entire continent, and I always enjoy visiting there. I'm not real crazy about their noon quitting-time regulation, or the expensive cost of a hunting license, but other than those minor inconveniences, it's all good.

An historical old house foundation in New Hampshire 2008

Next stop: New Jersey. My previous trips to the Delaware Water Gap had been fun and successful, and I was hoping for more of the same in '08. Things certainly looked to be headed in that direction when I called in three red-headed birds on the first day. I was sure one of them was a jake, but both of the others had rounded tail fans, and it was only after I'd walked up to my fallen gobbler that I discovered his beard didn't even project past the breast feathers. Oh, he was an adult tom alright, but all except for about a half-dozen strands of his beard looked like they'd been sheared off with a pair of scissors. Many people call this beard rot, but that's not correct. The strands have merely broken at a weak line of melanin deficiency caused by malnourishment or illness at an earlier time of the bird's life.

During the rest of the week I came close to killing a bird every single day. Something always seemed to happen at the very last minute to keep them safe from my dastardly plans, though. It was frustrating to some degree, but I was having so much fun being smack-dab in the middle of turkeys every day that the negative outcomes didn't bother me even a little bit. By noon of Friday I'd decided to drive on over to New York and hunt with Trevor Bays for the weekend, then slip on up to Maine before coming back for another go at filling some New Jersey tags.

Most of those plans went almost exactly as I'd intended. The only departure from the script was Trevor missing his bird on Sunday. After working hard all weekend to get that opportunity, my little buddy didn't take his failure very well. Yes; there were even a few tears shed in anguish and angst. Of course, I understood perfectly well what kind of frustration Trev was feeling, because I'd been there so many times myself. I did my best to console, assured him that we would make up for this minor hiccup upon my return later in the month, and then I headed on up to Maine.

I'd never been to the Vernon Walker WMA before, but when I pulled into a remote access lane at midnight, my headlights illuminated turkey tracks in the muddy road just beyond the gate! That seemed like it might be a good omen of things to come, and despite cold, rainy conditions with lots of wind, I managed to find several birds the next morning. One of them strutted up to me on the second day and became the final bird needed to complete my Public Land Super Slam (or, as close as I could get, since North Dakota doesn't allow non-residents to hunt on their public ground). Furthermore, he left me only ten states shy of completing a second U.S. Super Slam.

I still had three days of New Jersey's very last 5-day hunt period in which to kill a tom, and I'm sure glad that I went back, because I shot turkeys on Wednesday, Thursday, and Friday! Added to my previous success there, that gave me four toms in only eight days of hunting. I really enjoyed my time spent in the DWG, even if everything hadn't all been daisies and roses. For instance: it wasn't legal to camp, I ran into too many competing hunters, and you had to quit by noon. One other regulation which seemed at first to be a positive was allowing hunters to buy as many leftover tags as they wanted (very cheaply, too). However, by the time I left the state I saw this as a terribly misguided way in which to run a turkey management program. There was nothing to keep a good turkey hunter from stacking up incredible numbers of birds, and in fact, I met one guy who told me with great pride in his voice that he'd legally shot eleven during the season. Several of my own friends boasted of killing six. As the fifth smallest state in the nation, what's the point in having basically an unlimited annual bag limit unless the goal is to wipe out your turkey population? I left for New York torn about my contrasting feelings for New Jersey. Yes; it had been very good to

This cool tree serves as a backdrop to a 2008 New Jersey tom

Another DWG tom in front of a house built in the 1700's

me, but I felt like the resource itself had suffered from my having visited.

The next day was Saturday, so Trevor Bays was free from school to go hunting with me and try to make amends for missing a bird the previous weekend. Eager for revenge, we went right back to the same farm where that had occurred, and before the morning dew had dried off of the alfalfa fields, I'd called in a pair of big gobblers. Trevor smote the left-hand bird, and then we headed on over to Trevor's family farm to butcher the tom at their deer camp.

Just as I was about to make the first incision on that turkey with a sharp knife, I yelped real hard on the diaphragm call in my mouth and a real hen cutt back at me from the far side of the pond behind the camp house. When she cutt again, a tom 75 yards behind her gobbled. That year almost all the birds anyone had seen on the farm were jakes, but this one sure didn't sound like any squawking juvenile!

Forgetting all about the task at hand, I grabbed my gun and vest, and then Trevor and I circled around to get in position on the unseen hen. The old girl was by now really agitated and fired up, so it was easy to get in tight. Then, before we could even hunker up against a good setup tree, she suddenly broke into a furious cutting sequence and followed that up with a gobble. At first I thought it might've come from the tom heard previously, but then he ripped out one of his own. Yep: the hen had definitely gobbled, alright!

Several years earlier I'd witnessed a California hen gobbling three times, so I knew that they could do it. Even still, hearing this one was totally unexpected and it caught me by surprise. After recovering my composure and interjecting some sharp two-note yelps into her ongoing diatribe, the old hussy practically turned herself inside-out with more staccato cutts as she tried to assert dominance over me. Then, she stomped up to about 15 yards away and stood there glaring at us while alternately cutting and gobbling in an attempt to locate the brash upstart hen (me) which had pissed her off.

This went on for several long minutes while Trevor and I made ourselves small and stared in disbelief. The hen was throwing an absolute hissy-fit, complete with frequent gobbling, which fired up the tom behind her even more. Anticipating his arrival on the scene, I was waiting with gun in the ready position atop my right knee (I shoot left-handed) when he quite suddenly appeared standing there statue-still at about 40 yards. I didn't even need to move my gun a fraction of an inch, for he was perfectly aligned with where it pointed. Waiting for him to come a few yards closer, I was surprised when he abruptly turned around, putted two or three times, and retreated out of sight. Since neither Trevor nor I had moved at all, or given the gobbler any reason to spook, I was at a loss to explain the sudden downturn of events.

However, the hen wasn't alerted in the least. She continued carrying-on right in front of us practically non-stop with sharp cutts and perts, agitated purring, and a regular litany of gobbles, and before too long the tom calmed down and piped up once again. I knew right then that we were still in the ball game, and when the hen then decided to move back towards her boyfriend, I broke my silence and whined on the mouth call to get her attention. I followed that up with a little 3-note cutt, and she went ballistic!

Rushing back to stand even closer to us than before, the hen threw everything she had into her efforts to make me sound off and show myself. In between standing tall and burning holes in the brush with her evil-eye in trying to find her antagonizer, she cutt, yelped, and gobbled...a *lot*. Each gobble was accentuated by throwing out her neck exactly like a tom or jake would do, and while the sounds produced weren't the melodious, chest-rattling shout-outs of an old Eastern tom, she had me convinced that they were the very best that she could muster. Her efforts were commendable, and she was obviously proud of every gobble leaving her throat!

Well, the real tom couldn't stand it, and he began regularly answering with gobbles of his own. Following another long display of the hen's auditory talents right there in our faces, she then decided to move on to our left and away from the tom. This was a good thing, from my perspective! I let her keep right on going without uttering a peep, because this time I didn't want her coming back. It was almost a certainty that the tom would soon follow along behind, and that would put him in very, very grave danger.

Sure enough, it wasn't but a short spell later before Trevor whispered that he could see the tom dancing towards us in full strut. Immediately thereafter, I saw him, too. When he closed the distance to 34 yards, I let the old boy have it upside his head with a load of number 5's.

After gathering up the tom and sitting back down at our setup tree to rehash the hunt, I explained to Trevor what an incredible event he had just witnessed. I told him that there were most likely not a half-dozen living turkey hunters who had ever even heard a gobbling hen, and how lucky we were to have witnessed probably close to 100 of them from that crazy old gal. Many of her best efforts had been produced in plain view of us and from well-under 20 yards in distance. And then, as we were sitting there letting everything soak in, it dawned on me that we each had been carrying video-capable cameras or phones in our pockets the whole time, and yet, not even once had either of us even thought about pulling them out and capturing the events for posterity.

I was fine with that. My young protégé and I had witnessed an amazing event, and had shared yet another unbelievable day of turkey hunting together. That was plenty good enough for the both of us!

A young Trevor Bays and our delayed double of 2008

Trevor and I switched to a new farm the next day and I shot a great tom during yet another fantastic hunt. The deaths of Tony and Evelyn Bays had set their three adult children to battling for ownership of the farm, and now things were a damned mess. Since 1989 I'd been free to hunt all of the Bays landholdings, but with Jake and his siblings no longer even talking to one another, Trevor and I had been outlawed from hunting on any ground now controlled by the eldest brother, Jim. That's why we had been forced to seek out new properties. I guess that worked out ok for us in the long run, since we picked up permission on a couple of "banger" new farms, but the whole situation was rotten from the inside out and didn't sit very well with me. The warm, fuzzy feelings which hunting in New York had always produced were definitely waning, and to be honest about it, some of the appeal was beginning to ebb away. I missed Tony and Evelyn terribly, I missed the way things had always been on the farm, and I missed the sense of family and togetherness which I'd always found in ending my annual turkey season in New York. Turkey hunting is about so much more than simply the killing of the birds. Oftentimes, that's not even the most important part.

My second NY tom of '08, taken with Trevor Bays

Seeing as how it was still only May 26, I decided to break away early and squeeze in one more state, and after a 15-hour drive, I found myself at the Barry State Game Area of Michigan at around noon. My old friend Ron Ronk and his wife De had already been there for a day before that, so over a delicious fried fish lunch at a local diner, we talked about how many turkeys they'd been hearing and seeing. Fresh Intel is invaluable when hunting a new place, but as a solo traveler on most of my trips, that's not something I get to benefit from very often.

The afternoon hunt produced a little bit of turkey action, although no feathers in-hand. However, the following day was a thorough enjoyment, culminated by a dented primer and a great tom brought to bag after a long feud featuring many ups and downs. The two of us had battled as if our lives depended on it, but of course, that was true only for my opponent. Through shear persistence and perseverance, I eventually came away victorious. This was a great way to end my own personal turkey killin' for the year, leaving me with one more fantastic memory to recollect upon for the next nine months before spring season might came back around and rescue me from the turkey hunter's doldrums.

De had seemingly been stuck in a turkeyless funk ever since her 5-year-old daughter Susie had shot her own very first turkey earlier in Indiana's season. Since then, Momma had not only boogered up several toms, but missed a couple others, as well. Now, we hoped that having me around would help to change all of that, since I was riding along the crest of an incredible lucky streak…having called in 13 toms during the past nine hunting days, and killing eight of them. Unfortunately, I underestimated the power of the bad juju which had clutched a stranglehold on De's psyche, and despite calling in a couple of different toms for her on the final day, she didn't shoot either one. Unlike my own memories made during 2008, De would have only haunting images to disturb her sleep after the season ended.

Personally, it had been an incredible run for me; a year when I could seemingly do nothing wrong. During 68 days of hunting, I'd called in 73 toms to under 40 yards and shot 19 of them myself. Furthermore, there were another half a dozen birds shot by people whom I'd been guiding. I'd also tallied 12 states for the third straight year, and extended my out-of-state success streak to 40 trips in a row. There were other notable goals met and already mentioned, too. For instance, I had now killed turkeys in every state needed for my "Public Land" version of the U.S. Super Slam, and I was also just 10 states away from completing that second overall Slam. As I said, it had been one helluva good year and I was mighty proud of the numbers recorded, but there was so much more to be thankful for, as well…the sights seen and memories retained, the great friendships and laughter shared with other like-minded and tormented souls, the incredible meals eaten along the way, and all of the many other intangibles which made my lifestyle such a wondrous way to spend three glorious months in a row.

For me, New York is famous for turkeys and trilliums

Chapter 3

2009

Zane Caudill had moved up to Alabama the previous year, and he was so busy making a life up there that coming down to Florida in the spring wasn't a high priority for him. Hence, we had decided to split up our guiding partnership. This made sense for a number of reasons, not the least being that it allowed me to run the operation as I best saw fit. Zane could be a little headstrong and opinionated; one of those people whom you either loved, or not so much. I was definitely in the former category and considered him a great friend, but he'd already rubbed a couple of clients the wrong way. Our business arrangement had always been based more about him supplying the land contacts anyway, as he was a native Floridian and knew a lot of people. To be honest, the majority of our clients were folks who wanted to hunt with me specifically, and for that reason alone it just made more sense to fly solo. Still, it was only with Zane's blessings that I took over the operation.

A lot of our clientele came from the turkey hunting forums which used to be so popular on the internet, and the first ones for the 2009 season were, too. David and Marjie Calhoun hailed from Louisiana. On opening day I put David in a blind on the northern edge of my best property, while Marjie and I set up about 600 yards south of him and hidden from his view by a series of cypress heads. Turkeys habitually used and/or passed through the western third of this half-section sod farm, and although we heard no gobbling at dawn, a goodly number of hens were seen headed towards David. He later claimed the figure topped 75, but not a single gobbler was among them!

At about 8:30 I spotted two toms in our pasture, and once they saw the strutter decoy with two hens in front of us, it didn't take them long to close ranks. In fact, they ran the whole way. Once they were in the decoy spread in full strut, I yelped to try and make at least one of them crane up a neck, but instead, they gobbled in unison. Marjie didn't need any more of a signal from me, and she forthwith laid the smack-down on her first Osceola. Rather than run the risk of spooking any turkeys near David, we stayed on our side of the farm taking pictures until it was time to go eat lunch. The afternoon hunt was a basically a wash.

Whereas we'd witnessed only those two gobblers on our initial outing, Day 2 was much more productive with multiple toms heard and seen. However, it wasn't until 2:30 in the afternoon before I was finally able to call a tom in close enough for David to make good on his shot. Once that big Osceola hit the sand, we all headed back to camp grinning like opossums chewing on briars. We'd had a ton of fun hunting together, and created a friendship that has lasted strongly to this very day. David and Marjie are fine people, and both of them have a profound love and respect for the wild turkey.

Marjie Calhoun in a dry cypress pond with her fine Osceola

Next up to bat was Brandt, the fella from Michigan who had missed two birds with me the previous season. This time he brought along a brand new Benelli Nova pump gun, with assurances that it already had been patterned. I'd acquired

David Calhoun's "half-buzzard" tom, sported multiple black wings

a new property prior to the season, accessible only by boat, and it looked to be a doozy of a turkey-killin' spot! Small and isolated, the ground bordered an unhunted cattle pasture where turkeys were regularly visible. At various times of the day they would wander down into the gorgeous oak hammock where we had permission to hunt.

Despite a weather pattern of perpetual drizzle, we heard two or three birds gobbling up along the edge of the pasture at dawn, and soon thereafter a huge tom could be seen strutting for all he was worth about 300 yards away. However, he was quite content to stay right where he was at and wait for his hens to arrive, and that is exactly what happened when at least a half-dozen came out of the woods to join him. It wasn't until 8:30 before a different tom approached our oak hammock, and without any gobbling or strutting on his part, he was soon standing 28 yards away from us, with his head run up high into the perfect, "kill me now" pose. Brandt missed.

Not only did he miss, but he missed so badly that the tom merely took a couple of steps and stood tall in the same posture as before. "Kill him again," I whispered. This time, I could see the pattern of Brandt's shotgun hit high against a huge cabbage palm frond directly behind the tom. Unbelievable as it sounds, the bird was so unimpressed by this display of errant marksmanship that he just flew about 10 yards and came right back down to stand statue-still again! "KILL HIM," I insisted.

At the third shot, the obviously bullet-proof tom merely wandered away into the cabbage palms, looking highly confused. It was as if the loud thunderbolts, the hiss of streaking pellets, and the smacks of those same projectiles slamming into the flora surrounding him weren't anything of which to be overly concerned. And, in reality, why would he be worried? Not a single copper-coated pellet had struck turkey flesh or feathers! I was flabbergasted, and Brandt was nearly inconsolable in his dismay and embarrassment. An immediate return to camp for a session at the patterning board was called for, and the results pointed out that his gun was shooting about a foot high at 30 yards.

The next morning was one of those days when you'd think every bird in America would've gobbled their proverbial genigonadelia right out through their beaks...and they did! Heck, I think even crows and buzzards must've been gobbling too, since I could discern *at least* 11 different toms hammering it hard to greet the dawn. Much earlier than I'd expected it, five of them pitched down into the cattle pasture about 250 yards away. This bachelor group then spent the next hour perfectly content to wander around out there in the middle of the pasture while sporadically gobbling at anything or nothing. Then, I spotted another tom way off to the side. This one never uttered a peep or strutted, and when all of the longbeards began moving in his direction, he immediately turned and *ran* away from them. One member of the group then left his buddies behind and chased the bashful interloper clear out of sight, which was a distance of probably 1200 yards. I suspected that this satellite tom might've been the one Brandt missed the day before, although I had no hard and fast data to support that theory.

I'd been occasionally gobbling on a tube call all morning to try and elicit a jealous response from this gang of hooligans, and while they did gobble back every single time I did it, they never showed any inclination whatsoever to leave the pasture. However, a couple of late-arriving hens took notice, raising their heads to stare for long spells at the oak hammock where Brandt and I sat waiting. When I eventually began cutting a little bit on a diaphragm, they answered with similar calls of their own and began jogging our way. The toms followed dutifully along like lovelorn puppy dogs, and soon, the whole flock was filing into the oak hammock. Moments later, every single one of the toms was strutting 20 yards away from us.

Unfortunately, they were all knotted up tight together, and if Brandt had taken the shot during those first few minutes, he would've killed (or, missed) the whole group. However, he chose wisely and held fire until one tom had moved off to the side a little bit, and this time, when the Benelli Nova roared, a big 'ole Osceola gobbler piled up into a heap. Brandt had finally killed his first Florida turkey, and while we were both extremely happy about that, I think the overwhelming initial feeling was a sense of *relief*!

Brandt Detmers finally connected in 2009

With four and a half days available to hunt on my own before the next two clients were due to show up, I headed out into the highly pressured public lands of Green Swamp WMA, where I got my butt handed to me on a platter. People, people, and more people everywhere I turned seemed to be the common denominator in every failure. In fact, the only things I called in were a few hens and some honyawks in camo. There is a stark difference between public and private land hunting in Florida, and my long string of failures left me wondering if I might never kill another WMA bird. I was bumming, but there was more to it than my bad luck in the turkey woods; I'd also built a nine stroke lead after ten holes of our annual golf tournament, only to then completely forget how to swing the clubs and lose by five. Things were not going quite as smoothly in Florida as I'd planned, and it wasn't over, just yet…

Todd and Dave from Pennsylvania arrived in time to hunt during the afternoon, and promptly at 6:44 p.m., on my old standby land where Zane and I had been guiding for several years, Dave missed a gobbler from a whopping range of 24 yards. Now, the way I've always set up these hunts is that once the trigger has been pulled, my obligations as a guide have been fulfilled and payment is due.

Brandt had understood that, and so did Dave. However, I take the act of helping my folks kill their Osceola very seriously, and it rips me up inside to see them fail. Thus, so long as the bird hasn't been hit and crippled, I will usually try to get them another chance. That's the way it had rolled with Brandt, and it just seemed like the decent thing to do for Dave. Besides that, he only had a couple more days available to hunt, while Todd's vacation time was flexible and he could stay longer.

Well, to make the story a little shorter, I failed in my efforts to get another tom in close enough for Dave to kill. Oh, we had several of them skirt by us during the next two days; ones that we *might've* been able to scratch down, but that isn't the way I do things. Either we would have an up-close and personal turkey encounter, or we would let the birds walk. Dave was perfectly fine with those conditions. He was also painfully self-aware of how badly he'd blown an absolute golden opportunity on the very first morning, and now he was simply grateful in getting to spend some more time experiencing the wonders that are Florida Osceola hunting.

Todd and I had struck up a close friendship upon our first handshake, and I really wanted to take him to the new property where Brandt had found success. Once Dave had caught his flight homeward bound, I shared the details of this place with Todd, and when I mentioned that it was accessible only by boat, he immediately began whistling the tune from the TV show, "The Love Boat."

Our method of delivery the next morning was an airboat ride, which added a bit more excitement to the proceedings. However, the real thrill was when two different toms started their morning salutations within 40 yards of our initial setup! Despite a bevy of hens calling all around us and then pitching into the pasture about 60 yards away, the gobblers couldn't focus their attention on anything other than my strutter decoy practically underneath the roost, and that's where they both hit the ground. Todd had his Osceola laid out good and proper before the airboat's plane engine had cooled down, since Captain Billy was waiting on the lakeshore for the report of a gunshot.

Things had finally turned around for the positive in Florida, and the following morning that good luck continued on in the same trajectory when I experienced a magnificently tough and thrilling three-hour battle with a pair of wary toms back at Green Swamp. It was one of those hunts which leave a feller feeling satisfied on any number of levels, and I was very proud to check in an excellent Osceola.

Todd Banning's "Love Boat" gobbler of 2009

A Florida limbhanger from 2009

Something else had happened the night before that was worth mentioning. I'd found a bobcat in the middle of the road which was so fresh that I wasn't totally positive of his mortality. But, wanting to save the skull for my girlfriend and give the pelt to Bill George, I picked him up and put him in the back of the van for the 10 mile drive back to camp. The whole way there, I half-expected the still-warm cat to revive and jump me!

A few days later I shot another public land bird, and this one was an authentic stud well-worthy of attention. He weighed only 14.5 pounds, but his spurs measured a very wickedly sharp and curved 1-3/8 inches. That fine tom served as a fitting capstone to my time in Florida...a trip which easily ranked as one of the best ever. I'd called in 22 toms during those 17 days, and seven of them left the woods with us. Additionally, our beloved Marie Caudill had killed a bird all on her own at the tender age of 79, and the thrill of that accomplishment had set the mood for our entire camp.

Another one of Florida's diminutive, but long-spurred toms

Heading north, I next ventured up to eastern Tennessee. This was very steep and rugged mountain country, and difficult to hunt. It wasn't until the seventh day of the trip before I had anything positive to report so far as gobblers were concerned. Oh, there had been turkey encounters enough to frustrate me, and I saw lots of elk to gaze at in wonder, but getting the drop on a tom proved to be problematic, at best. My good buddy Tracy Deckard had joined me in camp after the first three days, although neither one of us could figure out how to kill a bird in those mountains.

All of that changed on the seventh day when I finally got in tight on a roosted tom, and shortly afterward, I succeeded in calling him and a buddy right up my gun barrel. However, they had come to me through a tangle of sucker saplings, and I made a grievous error in judgement by deciding that I wanted to shoot the second tom, which appeared to be noticeably larger in size than the lead bird. Both of them had swingin' beards, so what the heck was I thinking?

Just before the targeted tom would've broken out into an opening, the closest bird alerted and began rapidly exiting the scene. That caused his buddy to turn and join him, and I had only the briefest of windows to make good on a shot at a big red and white head herky-jerking through the saplings. I saw only one bird fly away after the explosion of gunpowder, so I felt sure that I'd connected, but when I went to claim my prize, there was no dead turkey lying where he should've been! The sound of scuffling feet in leaves brought me rushing over to the lip of the shelf, and when I peered over its edge, there below me, standing tall and obviously not dead at all, was the very same bird I'd supposedly just killed. In the blink of an eye he took off in flight, leaving me so shocked that all I could do was absolutely nothing.

Sitting back down at my setup tree to try and figure out what had gone wrong, I quickly saw the answer plain as day. There, about six feet in front of my gun's muzzle, was a poplar sapling of about 1- 1/2" in diameter that was very nearly shot in two. Multiple other sapplings beyond it also showed the bright marks and splinters of having absorbed my gun's charge of pellets, and when I arose to inspect the damage to the poplar, it toppled over at the first touch of finger to wood. Damn the bad luck! But, I had nobody else to blame other than myself for not shooting the first tom to give me an unobstructed view. I had suffered through a proverbial "brain fart," and it cost me a big old gobbler.

Tracy had picked a whole mess of black morel mushrooms during his otherwise unsuccessful hunt, so at noon he was forced to listen while I bitched and moaned all during a delicious lunch of grilled venison steaks and 'shrooms rolled in crushed saltines and fried in butter. I was not a happy camper, but a meal like that tends to at least lessen an aching heart. Only a little, though.

After dinner I dragged my shattered pride back up the side of the mountain to the scene of the crime, hoping for some sort of redemption. I brought along a gobble tube, too…figuring that those now-separated toms might be anxious to regroup and willing to answer a gobble. At 2:00 p.m. I coaxed out my best rendition of a gobbler yelp on a diaphragm and then shook the tube one time.

At 2:30 I heard a gobble from up-valley; the same direction my missed bird had flown. No other utterances were made by either one of us until 4:00, when I gobbled three times over a ten minute span. Thirty seconds after the last of those, the tom gobbled again. During the next twenty minutes he gobbled four or five times, but since he didn't appear to be moving towards me, I decided to go over there. However, when I stood up, I spooked a pair of bedded deer from a shelf down below me, and they ran off in the direction of the tom. I can't say for sure whether the silence that followed was connected to the ruckus, but I heard nothing more from the bird for about an hour. At that point I gobbled once, then dropped down to set up on the deer's shelf and began making some real quiet stuff on a diaphragm and a slate call. Nothing answered, but ten minutes later a distant thunderclap made the tom gobble from much closer than he'd been all afternoon, and ten minutes after that, he sauntered into view at 27 yards. His next step put him behind a tree large enough to cover my movements to get properly aligned, and when he exited from behind that tree, he took a load of 5's to the face and died a glorious warrior's death. The gobble call had done its job, and I had, for some reason totally undeserved, been granted my reprieve.

The next morning I set out with Tracy to help him fill a tag. Despite drizzling rain at dawn, we heard multiple gobblers. Three of them were ripping it from the top of a tall, very steep ridgeline...a lung-bustlingly steep incline that took us over an hour to conquer. Even if it hadn't already been raining, our clothes would've been sopping wet from the sweat produced from our hands-and-knees assault of that hellacious mountain.

Of course, once we'd ascended to the top, it was already well-past flydown time and the birds had hushed up. But, one of them eventually gobbled from over the back side of the ridge and all the way down into the valley below. There was no way in Hell's name that I was going to leave my lofty perch after all the work it had taken to gain the upper ground, so we began looking for a good setup tree from which to make a stand. This ridgeline was predominantly covered in big chestnut oak trees, but as we gazed around, it dawned on both of us that the ground was completely devoid of any vegetation. It was just bare dirt. Bare dirt and elk droppings...*lots* of elk droppings! Then, I spied a large game camera chained to a tree, and on the top of it was a metal tag stamped with the words, "Property of Rocky Mountain Elk Foundation." We were smack-dab in the middle of an elk park!

With the tom now gobbling regularly all on his own, we set up with Tracy about fifteen yards directly below me. My first yelp got stepped on by a resounding gobble, and almost immediately, it became quite obvious that this tom was both willing and able to do all the legwork necessary to reach his newfound girlfriend (me). He only gobbled a couple more times, but I could hear him drumming loudly as he steadily climbed the slope we shared, and I knew that this was going to be one of those quick ones turkey hunters dream about.

However, there was a problem. I have really exceptional hearing and Tracy doesn't. From my position I could easily track the tom's advancement by his loud drumming, but I could also see that Tracy's gun was pointed to the left of where it was originating. The grave mistake made on our initial setup was that we were too far apart to communicate, and now all I could do was watch and hope that my partner realized the error of his alignment before it was too late to do anything about it. My hopes were in vain.

A hollow-sounding, but quite resounding, "PUTT" was the first signal conveying that the gig was up, and then I watched mesmerized as the tom pitched off the steep slope below us and glided out through the misting rain as he headed back down into the valley from which he'd just climbed. I sat there for a few seconds letting what I'd just seen soak into my brain, and then I eased my way to Tracy and leaned down to whisper over his shoulder, "please tell me that turkey wasn't white."

"Yeah, he was white."

Technically, the tom was a "smokey-gray" gobbler, but we'd just blown the chance at a bird of a lifetime. I can still see him gliding away into that foggy, misting rain whenever I close my eyes and daydream about loves lost...

Over the next four days I never again caught so much as a glimpse of that colorful bird, but I did find others aplenty. Tracy killed one, and I scratched down an additional three. Elk were a common sight, and the scenery was spectacular, although brutally rugged. Everything about east Tennessee impressed me favorably, except for the trash, garbage, and discarded household appliances and furniture strewn about. It never ceases to amaze, befuddle, and disappoint me in how people supposedly portending to be "outdoorsmen" can defile the beauty of the wilderness by tossing their refuse down as they go. No matter how far back into the woods I might venture, I find the disgusting evidence of other people's presence. I must say that my feelings are so strong about this subject that I truly don't believe it is physically possible for my hands to release trash anywhere other than where it belongs...and that sure as hell ain't in the woods! I've long entertained the perpetual question in my brain that goes something like this, "who is worse…those that throw down trash in the forest, or those who walk on by without picking it up?" Thus, my game bag is seldom empty when I return to camp, even if its contents might only be somebody else's disgusting garbage. It takes a village to raise a man, and it takes a population-wide mindset to create a norm. Please: try to do not only your own part, but someone else's, in making this world a better place. Ok; rant done.

Steep ground and long spurs for my TN "redemption" bird

Hard work pays off once again in the mountains of east TN

Tracy Deckard climbs back up after scoring on his TN tom

Over the next couple of weeks I hopped back and forth between Indiana and Kentucky, struggling mightily in both to either kill birds myself, or guide others to success. Part of the reason for my difficulties in Kentucky was that they had been the recipient of a freak storm back in January which coated every surface with 3-1/2 inches of ice. Countless trees were toppled due to the added weight, and come turkey season, it was a monumental task just to walk around in the tangled mess. I've never seen anything like it in my life. Kentucky looked like it had been hit by a massive hurricane. The plus side is that the storm created millions of acres of "rabitat," so bunnies, songbirds, and a plethora of other critters both big and small benefitted tremendously. I did eventually get both of my Kentucky tags filled, and a Hoosier bird, as well, but each of them had come about only after long, laborious, and intense hunts...to be honest, just the kind that I like the best! The downside is that I hadn't called in even a single bird for anyone else in either place.

With my tail-end smarting from getting whupped so thoroughly, I was eager to make a return to one of my favorite destinations...the Loess Hills of Iowa. It's a uniquely beautiful place, and holds such a good population of both turkeys and deer that I became enamored of her charms the very first time I'd hunted there. If Iowa wasn't so greedy in charging a non-resident over $200 for a single tag, then I would return there more often, but that's a worthless "if." They are, so I don't.

My 2009 Indiana tom featured a paintbrush of a beard

A marathon gobbler from Kentucky in 2009

In 2009 I didn't hunt Iowa very well. I boogered countless deer and turkeys seemingly every time I took a step in the woods, and it took me four days before I finally got things right. But, the picture I took of that tom is one of my favorite images of all time, so I'll share it here:

Iowa's Loess Hills region is charming for all the right reasons

The Burr Oaks of the Loess Hills are incredible

Three days in Montana's Custer National Forest earned me my first Merriam's of the year, and a couple days after that I got in tight on another roosted bird, figuring to kill him just as soon as his feet touched earth. I would've, too...if my shotgun shell hadn't gone "poof," instead of "BOOM!" That was the first time I'd ever had a factory-loaded turkey round fail to fire, and after pulling the trigger, I actually watched the load of shot sprinkled down to the ground about halfway to the tom standing at 30 yards. Afterwards, I picked up the wad 7 yards from where I'd been sitting.

Although alarmed, the tom hadn't appeared to be terribly spooked. Yes; he did fly "reluctantly" away, but I was fairly hopeful of getting on him again. I just didn't know that it was going to happen so quickly! Twenty-nine minutes after the initial misfire, I made amends and smacked him upside the head with a round that definitely wasn't a dud!

White-tipped tail fan and Ponderosa pines from Montana in 2009

I first hunted the Pine Ridge region of Nebraska back in 1995. It was a gorgeous place back then: miles and miles of statuesque Ponderosa pines, with lots and lots of turkeys. What I found 14 years later couldn't have been more shockingly different. A couple of huge wildfires had ravaged this region in those intervening years, and what had once been unbroken vistas of trees, trees, and more trees, were now rolling hillsides of long-ago burned stumps and brown grass. The only remaining roosting spots were found down along the creeks and rivers, or in isolated stands of pines which had somehow been spared from the flames.

I wasn't at all sure if I could even find so much as a songbird in that sterile-looking habitat, but low and behold, I almost immediately began seeing turkeys while driving around. I also heard plenty of gobbling on the very next morning, and in the following three days I succeeded in filling all three of my tags. I'd

Fire has forever changed the Pine Ridge region of Nebraska

Only isolated pockets and groves were spared from the flames

But, despite the destruction, there are still turkeys to be found

been very pessimistic upon my arrival, but what I'd found in the intervening timeframe made me feel much more optimistic about the region's future potential. Yes, it had indeed been devastated by fire, but like a Phoenix, there was promise and hope rising from the ashes.

Dropping down into Kansas, I hunted on some public land where I'd never been before. It was an isolated and rather hard-to-reach property, and when I first drove up to the gate I could see a gobbler strutting on a high ridgeline about 400 yards away. As you can imagine, I took that visual as a good sign! Over the next couple of days I shot not only that bird, but another as well, and although I hadn't even intended to do so while planning out the season beforehand, those two Rio's gave me yet another single season Double Grand Slam. The trip had also supplied lots of "bonus" wildlife sightings such as quail, pheasants, and Prairie Chickens. Doves were thick as ticks on a dog's back, and both ducks and geese abounded. Of course, there were also a bunch of deer, and I even saw a bobcat up close.

Kansas was good to me in 2009

The last state hunted in 2009 was Michigan. This was my third year there in a row, but each time I'd tried someplace different. It didn't matter, though; Michigan public lands were really loaded with turkeys back in those days, and it hadn't taken much of an effort to fill a tag. That held true in '09, too.

As I reflected back on the year, I realized that it had been another great one: all the way from Florida and onward until the very end. In fact, I'd been so efficiently successful everywhere I hunted that I'd reached every single one of my goals quickly and had come home on May 20. The new girlfriend wasn't overly happy with my wandering turkey hunter ways anyhow, and with her birthday falling on June 1, it was probably a good thing for our relationship that

I came home early. I look back on that decision now and wonder what the heck I was thinking, but at the time it seemed like the right thing to do. Funny how our perspectives change as the years roll by...

I'd hunted in nine states during 2009 and tallied 58 days afield. Between me and the folks I'd been guiding, we'd been able to bring 24 toms to bag. Those were all decent numbers, but again, with being so efficient, I'd fallen short of my main goal, which every year was to get in at least 60 days of hunting. I vowed to do better in 2010, and then I filed the 2009 season under the "Highly Satisfactory" category before heading home.

A fine Michigan tom in '09

Chapter 4

2010

We started out the 2010 season with another cruise on The Love Boat. Opening weekend was a total wreck weather-wise, with heavy downpours that drenched us time after time, but Todd Banning's buddy got his first Osceola on Sunday morning, and Todd himself missed one that afternoon. They had to leave for home shortly thereafter, but before we parted ways, Todd made sure to reserve his spot for the following year. Our secluded little honeyhole, reachable only by airboat, was just too much fun to resist!

I had next scheduled a rather difficult guiding project…four guys at the same time. No longer having a partner to help me out made it logistically problematic, but of even more concern was the dearth of turkey sightings or sign, or even gobbles heard, in the week spent scouting beforehand. None of the properties where I'd been guiding for the last few years looked promising at all, and I was extremely pessimistic about whether or not I could find enough turkeys to fulfill the expectations of my clients. In other words, I was a nervous wreck.

Kevin was the "point man" for the group, so after placing two of his buddies in a previously-built "log cabin" blind on a cattle farm and a third guy in a similar blind on an adjoining sod farm, he and I headed over to my best prospect; another sod farm where I'd seen a couple of toms early in the week. Those birds obliged by gobbling early, but they were deep into the neighboring ranch. Then, a far distant black dot about a thousand yards away turned into a strutting turkey when viewed through binoculars, and Kevin told me that he could see the bird thrust out his neck in song whenever I called. We couldn't hear the gobble from that distance, but the turkey could obviously hear me, and he rapidly closed the distance between us by gobbling, sprinting 50 yards, gobbling again, and then repeating. In no time he'd gotten close enough to shoot, although long before then I'd realized that it was a jake. Kevin had specifically told me early-on that he wasn't interested in spending the kind of money I was charging for the hunt to shoot a youngster, so the jake was safe from harm. Well, at least he had been, until within spittin' distance of our blind. At that point, Kevin abruptly changed his mind and surprised me by putting the jake down for keeps!

The three other fellas had little good news to report for that day, other than a few far off gobbles heard, and the following morning didn't start out much better. Then, things took a turn (not for the better) when Donnie missed a bird at around 8:00 a.m. He was bummed, and so was I, because that trigger pull technically obligated him to pay for the hunt. I can only guarantee my clients an *opportunity*; I cannot guarantee their ability to hit what they shoot at! However, as I've said previously, I hate to see anyone go home empty-handed, so I vowed to give him another chance after the remaining guys in their group had found success. And, that's exactly what happened when in early afternoon I called in a brute of an Osceola for Tommy, and followed that up with another for Brad a few hours later. With three more days remaining until they had to head for home, the odds of Donnie gaining redemption looked good, but alas, we failed. As time passed I kept thinking back on an old adage which I've come to embrace fully over the years, and I'll paraphrase it here: in turkey hunting, you've got to take advantage of every opportunity which presents itself, because you never know when, or even if, you might be given another.

Once that foursome had headed for their Kentucky homes, I turned my attention to Green Swamp WMA, where I was now free to wander around for a while before heading out west. The first four days were a dismal failure, even though that felt like standard operating procedure out in "The Swamp." Then, I got on an uncharacteristic lucky streak with successful outings four days in a row. A pair of these birds I took myself, while Bill George and his son William shot the other two. An attempt to make it five days in a row with Bill's daughter Belinda fell short, but that little setback didn't affect my attitude in nearly so negative a manner as did the act of somehow losing my camera while fighting my way through the nearly impenetrable swamps of Green Swamp. Thus, I ended up with no pictures of my Florida experiences in 2010, including photos of the turkeys my clients had taken. After a thorough but fruitless search I went out and bought a replacement, although that was shallow compensation for the photos forever lost.

Water had definitely been a major factor to contend with in 2010: a year hugely different from four of the five preceding ones, when I would've needed to pour drinking water from a Platypus bottle if I'd wanted to get mud on my boots. Wet years are starkly different than dry years, and not nearly as enjoyable for one *very* major reason…the bugs! Wet years produce lots of skeeters, gnats, and deer flies, and only by erecting a mesh tent in camp could we gather for our traditional afternoon gab sessions. Florida public land in those days didn't allow hunting past 1 o'clock, which wasn't a bad thing, since it gave our camp crew an excuse to sit around and yuck it up.

I know that I've mentioned in stories past some of my friends in camp, but here's another partial list of the "regulars" who were there in 2010: Floridians Zane Caudill and his wonderful folks David and Marie; Charlie Parrish and his lovely bride Cathy; Bill and Suzie George and their kids Belinda and William; Kenny and Cindy Dorman; Arlys and Marilyn Talbert; Rick Brown; Timmy Tanner; talented callmaker Tim Sandford, and my ex-girlfriend Robin McCormick. Others who annually filled out our camp included the legendary bowyer Eddie Parker, as well as Virginians Doug Pickle and Betty and Willard Reedy. However, a few of the crew weren't present that year, and we missed them for their absence: Craig Morton from Pennsylvania had taken a new job and couldn't get away; Royce McCalister had recently undergone back surgery; Steve Fincher (affectionately called, "Sasquatch" due to his gargantuan size-18 feet); and Zane's ex-wife Laurie. Still, we had a great time, ate many a fine meal, and shared countless stories and laughs. I would never dream of living in Florida full-time, but I absolutely love the month or so that I spend there every spring. A great deal of that enjoyment comes directly from all of these (and others unmentioned) great friends. I regard them more as family, except that we don't fight and argue.

Leaving all of them behind, I began making my way out west. The first stop was in Louisiana, where I got my butt kicked for eight days straight. Then, on the ninth morning, I experienced one of those "dream hunts" where everything went exactly as how I might've envisioned it in my fondest dreams: three big longbeards drumming and gobbling in my face from short range. Their presence presented me with the perfect way in which to make a graceful exit from the trials and tribulations endured for so long, and I did not fail to capitalize on that opportunity. The tom I took had strange-looking spurs which hooked almost all the way back to his leg bones.

Then, I spent two glorious days traveling around in the southern part of the state and eating boudin. Some of you know that this is one of my favorite foods. On the internet, there's a webpage called boudinlink.com. The creators of that site have rated many boudin makers with school grades (A+ thru F), and my mission on this trip was to sample as many of their A+ selections as possible. If I liked a particular brand, then I would buy two or three additional pounds to keep in my cooler and over the next week or so I ate a couple of different links several times each day. This allowed me to do my own comparisons and write my own reviews. I definitely came up with several favorites, and immediately began planning for the next time I would be hunting in Louisiana so that I could further expand my "studies." YUM!!

Louisiana was tough in 2010, but eventually gave up a good'un

Pulling into New Mexico's Lincoln National Forest at about 5 a.m., I stepped outside the van to a mercury reading of 29 degrees, with heavy snow pack covering most of the ground within eyesight. That was quite a difference from the last month, when I'd been hunting in Florida and Louisiana! But, I heard a gobble almost immediately and took off toward that beautiful mountain music. It wasn't until I was knee-deep in snow that I realized things might be more of a challenge than anticipated.

Then, before I could even work my way through the snowfield, heavy rains rolled in and put a severe damper on the ardor of both the tom, and me. It wasn't long before I'd crawled back into the van to catch up on some much-needed sleep following the all-night driving session I'd endured to get there before gobbling time. Thunderstorms serenaded me while I slept, and it continued to rain hard for the entire day. By the next morning the weather was even worse, with an amalgamation of strong winds, rain, sleet, hail, and finally, heavy snow. Charming conditions for turkey hunting!

Once that mess finally broke up, I was finally able to get out and hunt. Nothing much came of my initial efforts, but at dusk I heard multiple toms gobbling in a canyon far below me. It was too late to try and push the issue before dark, so I decided to sneak in there the next morning. I'm glad that I left the van early, because it was a long, steep descent to the canyon bottom, and the whole time I kept thinking to myself that it was gonna take some herculean efforts to get back up to the top. Heck; the slope was so rugged and treacherous that I worked up a sweat going *downhill*.

Of course, the first gobbles of the day made me temporarily forget all about those future hardships. Although the first couple of birds sounded groggy, as if they'd just woken up, things soon thereafter turned into a proverbial shouting match with at least twenty toms absolutely ripping the walls apart. Their gobbling rippled back and forth in waves. I'd never in my life heard anything like it!

At the bottom of the canyon was a posted property line fence, and while most of the gobbling was within the boundary of the private land, there were numerous toms scattered along its perimeter. Unfortunately, I made a mess of the first few setups, since I couldn't seem to concentrate on any one particular bird long enough to get him killed. Instead, I kept flitting around like a kid in a candy store too eager to sample all of the goodies at once. Still, I knew that I was into something very special down in that dark canyon, and I was confident that it was only a matter of time.

On the other hand, I kept gazing up at the rimrock far above me and thinking about that long, steep pull which I would eventually have to make. Considering my options carefully, I decided on a rather odd game plan: I would bide my time and savor being in the midst of so many turkeys, but then I was going to pick the right moment and kill two toms with one shot. The reason for that was because I just couldn't foresee coming back down in there the next day, so I might as well fill my bag limit and get out.

That's exactly what happened, too, when I finally convinced five toms to slip under the private land fence and snake their way towards my setup on a flat shelf down low on the canyon wall at about 4:30 p.m. The trailing trio definitely looked bigger than the leading pair, but I most certainly wasn't looking to carry out any more weight than necessary. Once the flopping was over and I'd started making my way uphill, I then found an elk shed...the first one ever...so I just *had* to bring that along, too!

Two and a half hours later I literally pulled myself over the rimrock edge on hands and knees before sprawling out gasping and huffing for air. Never in my life had I taken my body to its absolute brink of physical exhaustion, and it was more than an hour before I could rise up on wobbly legs to try and make my way back to the van. That night, every muscle in my body cramped non-stop for hours on end, despite nearly continual rehydration efforts. The decision to never venture down into that canyon again had been the right one (see: my next trip to New Mexico), but carrying out two dead gobblers and an elk shed might not have been the brightest of brainstorms!

My 2010 Lake Dorothey gobbler in Colorado

My next stop was Colorado. I had drawn a permit for the Lake Dorothey unit, which is a rather unique spot. Most of the good turkey habitat lies about eight miles from the trailhead, and I believe that the vast majority of people who hunt there, do so via horseback. Well, I didn't have a horse, so it looked like I was destined for a long hike. However, there were a couple of fine fellas camped at the parking area, and they told me that there were a few birds nearby and I might not have to trek all the way to San Miguel Canyon to find one. They were right, and that very afternoon I called in a bird which came in screaming at me like he thought that I was the only hen left alive in the whole state. I was quite happy to put his charge to a stop with a load of 5's upside the noggin, thus saving my still-shaky legs from the exertion of a long hike the next day.

There's a public land spot in Colorado where I've been a few times, and because I've never seen another turkey hunter anywhere near it, I am most definitely not going to divulge its whereabouts in this book. The only thing I will say is that birds have always been there, up around 9400 feet in elevation, and the aspens are usually decked out in snow when I show up late in the season. It's a spectacularly beautiful place, and while I've never been just covered up in turkeys, there are enough. In 2010 I found exactly one, but he was willing to play the game to perfection.

Colorado high country tom from 2010

Nevada offers an extremely limited number of non-resident public land tags which are distributed by lottery, and I had been lucky enough to draw my second one in 2010. However, on the day of scouting before my permit became valid, I didn't hear anything in the canyon where I'd shot my tom in 2004. Checking with the guys at the BLM office, they suggested another area altogether, and on the way there I just happened to run into a fella who operated a big game guiding service. He claimed that four toms wintered in the canyon where I was headed, with only one having been killed so far.

I arrived at around 3 p.m. and almost immediately discovered a feather pile where someone had cleaned a bird. However, that was the only turkey "sign" found. I also didn't hear any gobbling at dusk, so my mind was filled with worry all night. That was simply wasted energy, because promptly at 5:07 a.m. a tom began gobbling from the canyon rim. I'm pretty sure that he'd been messed with during the first season though, because despite a willingness to gobble at my calls, the tom proved wily and wary enough to never come within gun range. I finally spooked him by making a tactical blunder in early afternoon, and while that was disappointing, it gave me the perfect opportunity to head on back into town to stock up on groceries and ice. The long battle with this tom had seeded a determination to stay out in the boonies until the matter had been settled to my satisfaction, and when I got back to the canyon as the sun was settling low on the horizon, I found the tom strutting along the same narrow ridgeline below his roost site where he'd spent so much time during the early morning hours.

Our next duel at dawn was a wonderful chess match of moves and countermoves. He only gobbled four times from the roost before pitching out and gliding over to another ridge entirely, and after picking up a hen, he continued to hold his ground while we feigned and jousted. Then, I slightly spooked both birds while attempting to sneak in tight. The good part is that I hadn't scared the holy bejesus out of either bird, and I felt sure that they would soon calm down and return to their usual activities. An hour later, a gobble signaled that our game was back on, once again.

This time I was much more cautious in my approach and able to slip in close to where the tom was hammering out infrequent gobbles all on his own. The previous day's results indicated that I'd perhaps called too much, so now I utilized the more subtle tactic of rhythmically scratching in the sand and leaves like a feeding hen. Despite the low volume of those sounds, it wasn't long before I could tell that the tom was advancing towards me. His drumming was absolutely booming in volume, and I could even hear the tips of his wings furrowing through the sand. At about 50 yards out he began loudly clucking to try and make me divulge my position, but all I did in return was continue to periodically scratch like a disinterested hen.

Our "winner-take-all" battle was conducted in a stand of very thick and dense willow-type ground cover, with poor visibility. We were so close that I'd liken it to hand-to-hand combat. The drumming was all-encompassing and everywhere, so I never knew exactly where the tom was standing...that is, until I saw his shadow passing over the brush directly in front of my gun barrel...the wily old rascal had snuck around and come in the back door! Luckily for me, he didn't see anything amiss and eventually circled out front. When he stepped clear of brush at 18 yards I was already locked onto his head and neck, and when he stood tall two steps closer, I lowered the boom.

My second Nevada public land gobbler came in 2010

This quick kill in Nevada afforded me some extra time before an Arizona permit became valid, so I drove on over and hunted in California for a week. The trip started out bad and just got worse, since I was spending my time up in the Mendocino National Forest on ground that quite simply doesn't hold a lot of birds. The weather was also atrocious, with perpetual rain and heavy winds. In fact, it was raining so hard on the second day that after getting soaking wet at dawn, I'd called it quits. Once I had changed into dry clothes and begun cruising around on forest service roads, I was stopped at a crossroads checking my maps when a truck with "Town of Upper Lake" printed on the side pulled up beside me. The two fellas inside it were real friendly, but the driver's first question sort of startled me. "I see you're dressed in camo," he said. "Are you a turkey hunter, or growing pot?"

When I confirmed that I was, indeed, a crazy turkey hunter from Indiana, Joe (the fella's name) told me that I would be hard-pressed to find turkeys up in these dense National Forest lands. However, if I got tired of trying, I should come down into the valley and give him a call. As he handed me his business card I thanked him for the offer, but I didn't really intend to take him up on it. Being the sort of hard-headed, obstinate man that I am, I figured that if there were any turkeys around these parts, I was bound and determined to kill one right where I was at.

Well, four days later I'd had enough. The only turkeys found so far were a couple of hens and a lonely jake, and while I had seen some impressive Tule elk bulls, they weren't what I was after. It was high time to make that phone call, and by the very next morning, was I ever glad that I did! The valley of which Joe had spoken was basically agricultural and/or cattle and horse farms...*far* different than the dense, steep, and turkeyless mountains where I'd been hunting. The fertile valley was also *full* of birds! Joe had grown up in that area, and he had access to lots and lots of places...every one of which, as near as I could tell, would qualify in my mind as veritable turkey hunting zoos! I left California three days later with three turkey's worth of meat in the cooler and a new-found admiration for its wow-factor.

Snow was a common occurrence in California

King's Canyon's giant Sequoias should be on everyone's bucket list

There is nothing in this world like those awe-inspiring Sequoias

Once again, I found lots of turkeys in the Arizona zone for which I'd drawn a tag. However, the wind blew like a zephyr for the first two days. *I hate wind*! My hearing is by far my strongest physical attribute, and when 40 mph gales are whipping the tree limbs, it seriously affects not only my ability to kill turkeys, but my attitude. Fortunately, the third day was everything that the beginning of the hunt was not, and I probably heard close to a dozen gobbling toms. By 6 a.m. I had already wrapped my tag around the scaly leg of a good'un and was heading towards Utah with a wide grin on my face.

This was the first year when Utah offered a state-wide license sold across the counter instead of by lottery, and after purchasing mine at a Wal-Mart, I opted to hunt the same area around Cedar City where I'd been once before. Huge flocks of Merriam's winter in the private lands below there, but once they've dispersed and begun climbing up into their remote National Forest summer grounds, finding them can sometimes be tricky. These wandering devils can venture more than 40 miles, or more! With snowpack still quite deep when I arrived, even getting around (either by van, or by foot) was a challenge, too.

It took me three days to finally locate the right elevation on which to find the birds, but once I was on 'em, I was on 'em *good*. A plethora of tracks spotted in the snow along a gravel road had first alerted me to their presence, and despite my generally poor record when it comes to Merriam's, I was then lucky enough to make short work in getting one's neck under foot. After a quick stop in Salt Lake City to see my sister, I then headed towards the final three states planned for 2010…Idaho, Washington, and Oregon.

A rarity in my life…an easy Merriam's from Utah in 2010

There are some states where I struggle mightily, and some where things have always gone smoothly. Idaho can definitely be categorized in the latter. It's not that her turkeys are any easier or less wary than those found elsewhere, and I've certainly worked hard for those successes, but the particular circumstances have always seemed to fall neatly into place and filling my tags has simply come at a quicker-than-normal pace. That's exactly how it happened in 2010, when all it took was three days to put me headed towards Washington with a pair of fine birds riding along in the cooler.

Hell's Canyon makes for a dramatic and beautiful backdrop

My Mom's younger brother Jack was one of my favorite relatives as a child, and he lives near Vancouver, Washington. He's only eleven years older than me, and we both grew up hunting squirrels with my Dad. Even still to this day Uncle Jack tries to come back to Indiana on or near our August 15 squirrel season opener because of the memories the sport holds for him. Knowing that I was going to be in his home state during the spring of 2010, we made plans to hunt turkeys together. Jack had never been, but I knew that he'd get a kick out of it and I hoped to call in a first bird for him.

Over the course of three days we tried to find turkeys close to his home, but only achieved a modicum of success. I think we heard one or two gobbles in total. By then I was ready to head back over to eastern Washington, where I had access to a tremendous piece of ground located within the Colville Indian

Reservation. Unfortunately, Uncle Jack's foot began hurting real bad and he declined the invitation to accompany me there. I thought about offering to carry him on my back, because I knew fully-well that the horse ranch where I was headed bordered on the unbelievable.

This place was amazing...2500 acres of prime turkey habitat, with another 2000 acres of accessible leased ground, and I had the whole thing to myself. Killing two turkeys wasn't so much a question of "if," but rather, "when." The only bad part was that the temptation to get it done quickly was so strong that I couldn't resist the urge. By 8 o'clock of the first day I'd already heard at least a dozen gobbling toms and filled each of my tags. I should've taken my time and milked it out longer, but that old adage of never letting an opportunity pass by kept running through my head.

A fine day's results from hunting in Washington during 2010

My arrival in Oregon during the late afternoon was met with cold temperatures, heavy wind, and snow. Then, it turned even worse overnight, with mercury readings plummeting well below freezing. I heard zero gobbling and didn't even see a single bird all day long. I knew fully well that I must surely be hunting in a good area that held birds, because the district wildlife biologist was camped just down the road from me. Why else would he be hunting there? His words of encouragement kept me from going elsewhere, and I decided to stick it out and hope for the best.

Well, my thermostat at dawn showed 23 degrees, but at least the wind had completely died off during the night. Sunshine even broke through the clouds several times throughout the morning hours, even if the temperature never did rise above thirty. However, despite the bitter cold, I heard two different toms gobbling before the sun came up, and things just got better and better as the day progressed. By the time it started snowing around noon, I'd heard no less than eight different gobbling birds and been in constant contact with turkeys ever since they'd flown to ground. Then, ten minutes after quarter-sized snowflakes began drifting lazily down from the heavens, I finally succeeded in calling in three hens with two toms. A few minutes after that, one of the gobblers lay completely covered up by the rapidly increasing snowfall. I sat there for a long time soaking it all in; the beauty, the hunt, the stillness and solitude. It was a special moment in a long history of memorable hunts, and one that I will always remember fondly. By the time I got back to the van there was at least two more inches of white stuff turning my surroundings into a winter wonderland...in late May!

More snow...this time in Oregon

For the next few days the weather remained rather volatile, to say the least. It frequently snowed, and every other day the wind would howl at insane velocities. But, sunshine occasionally poked through the cloud cover often enough to melt off some of the accumulated snow, and on the days when the wind didn't blow, the woods were still as a graveyard. The only constant seemed to be the temperatures, which hovered quite low. During the entire week that

I was there, I don't think they ever climbed above 40 degrees, and frequently bottomed out in the low 20's at night. This made for some tough turkey hunting as I tried to fill my second tag, but eventually, I caught a tom in the right mood, at the right time, and in the right spot.

Rather than call it a season (after all; it was only May 25), I decided to angle home via Michigan. In hindsight, that was a big mistake because of the terrible pocket of hot, humid weather which had parked itself over the Great Lakes region for nearly a week prior to my arrival and was predicted to remain. All four days of my trip saw temperatures rise well into the 90's, and the humidity was absolutely stifling. Turkeys don't like those conditions any more than I do, and I only heard four gobbles in total.

So ended rather ingloriously an otherwise glorious spring, and I was soon headed back to the "reality" of summer and a dreaded *job*. I'd hunted in 12 states overall and tallied 63 days afield; calling in 58 birds to less than 40 yards. Generally speaking, things couldn't have gone any smoother anywhere along the turkey trails, unless you were to factor out the amount of time it took to score a kill in Louisiana and the brief Michigan debacle to end it all. Snow had certainly been the weather event of the year, as I'd been forced to endure that stuff in all nine western states visited. However, despite the level of discomfort which frozen rain administers to the hunter, it hadn't seemed to affect the turkeys themselves all that much.

After ruminating about the season just passed, I realized that I was now only a single state away from completing my second U.S. Super Slam! I was also within reach (22) of a heretofore unmentionable and seemingly insane *third* Slam, and plans were already in the making for taking care of as many of those as possible in 2011. The biggest difficulty would be in choosing which states got left out of the rotation, but that's the way it goes for me every year. As always, I found myself caught in the dilemma of too many good places to hunt, and never enough time!

Several of these were spread throughout the west in 2010

Chapter 5

2011

Ahhhh...Florida! She is always like a breath of fresh air to me after coming from the cold and damp of an Indiana winter. I like to arrive about a week early in order to get my private lands scouted out for the clients I've scheduled, but some rather extensive vehicular repairs had me running late in 2011 and I arrived only one day prior to the opener. Still, I found four or five toms on a couple of my farms, so confidence was running high.

My first two clients were a father and son team whom I'd befriended on an internet turkey hunting talk forum. The Dad (Tom Noren) was a physician from Michigan, and his son Scott lived in New Mexico. Both of them were top-notch guys and we had big fun, although the hunt itself ended up being a rather short one. By noon we had two great Osceolas in the cooler and opening day of the following year already reserved.

My next client was a friend of Dr. Bill Powers from Indiana, who had hunted with me and Gary Shepherd several years prior. We struck out in our initial hunt on The Love Boat property due to a trespasser messing us up, but shortly before noon Captain Billy relocated us to the Resmondo Sod Farm, where, if you recall, I'd previously guided hunters in the past. Billy was now managing that farm and told me that he'd regularly been seeing a big tom near the grove of trees where the farm implement shed was located, but by the time we got there all I could see were two hens out in the sod. Ignoring the hens and running them off, I then erected a popup blind in the shade of the live oaks and placed a strutting tom and two hen decoys out in the grass.

Scott Noren and his dad, Dr. Tom in the swampland of Florida

It wasn't even five minutes after we'd settled into the blind before Don spotted a turkey far off in the distance. My binoculars confirmed that it had a red head, but although a loud yelp on my glass call made him thrust out his neck in song, we couldn't hear a thing. The bird immediately began moving towards us. However, long before he could reach the dekes, I'd determined that it was a jake. When I conveyed this news to Don, he simply told me that he'd be just as happy with a young bird as he would with a world record tom. Don had previously told me of his plans to have the bird mounted, so I was quite surprised when he then shot this jake right smack dab in the middle from very close range, shattering both wings and both legs and sending adrift in the wind a tremendous number of body feathers! Don didn't seem to care in the least... he was happy as a clam!

The next day would feature our annual golf tournament, and that year we had a couple of new players to contend with in Bill George's grown children; Belinda and William. We had made it a stipulation early-on that any invitation to participate would be predicated upon killing their first turkey, and Belinda had finally fulfilled that requirement a few days prior. Subsequently, both of these kids thumped the collective field of their father, Doug Pickle, Kenny Dorman and me like red-headed stepchildren. Belinda took home the trophy after firing an 82, and her brother shot 83. The rest of us failed to break 100. Obviously, some rule changes were in order to level the playing field. Perhaps in coming years we could force those two to tee off from the tips, while we old timers used the red women's tees?

Following five days of dismal hunting results in The Swamp, I surmised that the moon's celestial location closer to Earth than it would be in the next 40,000 years had a great deal to do with the bad luck. Or, maybe it was just because that place is so often one of the hardest spots in America to consistently kill turkeys. For whatever the true reason, I took a whoopin' there almost as bad as I had during the golf tournament. Then, Captain Billy proffered an invitation to come and hunt at the Resmondo Sod Farm, where he'd consistently been seeing that same old tom hanging out near the implement shed. He didn't have to ask me twice!

For many years I'd been cogitating on how best to effectively kill "field turkeys," and this situation presented the perfect opportunity to try out some new ideas. One of those dated from way back in the mid-80's, when I'd considered painting the image of a giant turkey tail on a five foot tall piece of 1/4" plywood, adding carrying handles and a gun rack on the back, and then simply crouching behind it as I walked directly at a flock of turkeys out in an open field. I felt positive that this would work, but I'd never actually tried it. Of course, now that there are so many negative reactions being heaped upon the "reaping" crowd these days, I'm overjoyed that I didn't ever follow up with the scheme. I would not want my legacy in this sport to be known as the grandfather of the reaping movement! But, you also must realize that this particular story originates from 2011, long before any of that stuff had ever gotten started. How to deal with turkeys in a wide open space was, and had always been, a daunting and formidable task. Two-inch tall sod doesn't leave a feller much of a hiding spot!

Instead, I decided to try another novel (at the time) approach that I'd also been considering, but which at the time seemed equally as radical as the oversized tail. The next morning I simply walked out into the sod farm well before daylight and put up my Double Bull popup blind right smack dab in the wide open, with three Dave Smith full-bodied hen decoys set up 25 yards away. I felt as exposed as a big red zit on a baby's asscheek when daylight broke, and my confidence of success was questionable, but I was bound and determined to give it a whirl. Back then I didn't have the benefit of hindsight and experience telling me that turkeys will basically ignore any monstrosity such as a blind unless it's moving. However, I *had* taken careful note of how these sod farm turkeys paid very little attention to the trucks and field workers moving around in their midst, so maybe they'd do the same with a big, boxy blind.

Well, the tom which roosted across the moat-like ditch gobbled early and loud, and at flydown time four of his lovely ladies that were sleeping nearby pitched out and then splashed down in the middle of my decoy spread like ducks. It had rained hard the previous night and there was a thin sheet of standing water across the entire farm. The tom, however, veered off to the side and landed 75 yards away, immediately fuzzing up into a full strut. He then answered any and every call I made, but refused to budge even one inch towards me. In fact, he turned and began easing directly away to the north, and it wasn't long before the real hens beside me hustled off to join him.

Now I found myself in a quandary: I obviously couldn't reposition or make a move to get 'rounders on the flock without being seen, and yet, as they drifted further and further away, it was obvious that I was being left behind in a place where they no longer had any inclination to hang out. And then, an idea popped into my head...

Standing upright and lifting the blind off the ground a few inches, I began easing over toward my first decoy. None of the turkeys seemed to give that initial movement the slightest notice, so when I got to the decoy I lifted the blind up and over it. Once that was done without spooking the flock, I put the deke and its stake in a sack on my back and then headed over to the next decoy. When that one was likewise gathered and bagged up like the first, I repeated the sequence a third time. From the turkey's point of view my blind was now the only thing out in the middle of that huge expanse of short green grass. Then, I began walking directly at the flock, which was already some 400 yards away. I tried my best to keep the bottom edge of the blind as near to the ground as possible, so the birds wouldn't see my feet and realize that I was some sort of strange looking predator.

As I got closer and closer, I noticed how the turkeys paid absolutely no attention whatsoever to me, and once I'd closed to within about a hundred and fifty yards, I set the blind down, took out a decoy, and mounted it on its stake in the dirt at my feet. Then, I lifted the blind up and over it in a reversal of my previous actions. Keeping the blind between the decoy and the flock of turkeys, I moved a few yards towards them and repeated the procedure; then again. Once the final deke was set, I moved off to the side so the faux hens were now visible to the birds, and when I called on a diaphragm, the tom gobbled in response as all of his ladies craned their necks to gaze at these new gals in their vicinity who hadn't been there only moments before. Four of the dozen or so real hens comprising the flock came straight to my spread in a trot!

Unfortunately, the tom continued to strut in place as the remaining hens just went right back to pecking and scratching in the dirt where they were at, and when all of them began moving off to the north once again, the few hens standing beside me turned and hurried to catch up with their departing friends. I let the whole group of them get another 400 yards away before I began repeating the entire process; this time setting up only about a hundred yards from the flock, but receiving very similar results.

By now it was mid-morning, and the sun was beginning to beat down unmercifully on my blind. Inside, I was sweating profusely. Furthermore, the wind had begun picking up, forcing me to exert a lot of energy by physically holding the blind down in order to keep it from blowing away. I was in a bit of a pickle so far as making this strategy work, but what else could I do? The charade needed to be maintained if I had any hope of getting the drop on that stud of a tom.

Long story short: I continued to repeat this crazy stop-and-go sequence until around noon. By then I'd relocated multiple times, and I was not only hot and sweaty, but wearing out. It looked like all of my efforts were bound for failure when the flock took up residence on a sandy mound out there in the middle of the sod farm and began preening and loafing around. Sensing that the time was right for trying something radical, I decided to just keep on walking at the birds instead of stopping short to try and call them in, like I'd done every other time. My intentions now were to either creep within shooting range, or run the birds off for good. I'd had enough!

The wind was blowing so hard that the blind rocked wildly from side to side as I walked towards the flock, and yet, they didn't panic. Closer and closer I got, as my hopes began to rise...

Eventually and unbelievably, I found myself within about 40 yards of the loafing flock before they began getting antsy and started to ease away in a semi-alert manner. The tom trailed behind all of his girls, and since they were separated by a few yards, I decided that the time for action was at hand. It was now or never. Setting the blind and decoy sack down, I swung the shotgun off my shoulder and prepared to make a shot through the only open window. By the time I'd gotten ready and born down on the tom's white-topped noggin, he was nervously eyeballing me from about 45 yards away. That's longer than I normally like to shoot, but certainly within my Benelli's effective range, and when I touched finger to trigger he piled up in a wad.

I'd done it! It had entailed hard work and utilizing some rather unorthodox tactics, but the efforts had paid off big time. I was proud as a peacock of what I'd accomplished. Not only that, but the tom's long, sharp, and wickedly curved spurs of 1- 7/16 inches added yet another degree of satisfaction gained from an ordeal fraught with difficulty. I was pumped up!

Osceolas tend to grow long daggers

Two more fruitless days at Green Swamp brought me right back down from the lofty elevations to which that hunt had propelled me, and then my final pair of clients for the year arrived from Texas. Dave and Scott were good-natured guys and a blast to hunt with, and right from the very first instant it was obvious that they were here to enjoy themselves during this once-in-a-lifetime adventure. Our hunt lasted for three days, and every morning, just before leaving the van, each of them would place three beers and some ice in a gallon ziplock bag to carry in the game pouches of their vests; not because they were out to get drunk on the hunt (something to which I would have never abided), but just because they liked beer. It was their water, so to speak, and throughout the day they would sip on a cool beverage while we sat in blinds awaiting turkey action. Three beers over the course of a long day does not a drunkard, make!

Most of the Florida properties that I've acquired throughout the years are not very big. Many are under a hundred acres, and very few are comprised of greater than half a section (320 acres). Besides that, they are either cattle pastures or sod farms...open ground dotted with cypress ponds. Being located in Polk County, they are also flat. That means you can generally see for a very long ways, and so can the turkeys. Hence, I've developed methods of hunting them that are very low impact. Specifically, that means I prodigiously study the ground and how the local turkey flock uses it, and then we hunt from blinds placed at strategic locations; either man-made pop-ups, or what I call "log cabin" blinds made from fallen logs, tree limbs, and Spanish moss. The run-and-gun method employed by so many turkey hunters elsewhere works very well, but it also spooks untold numbers of turkeys that the hunter never even knew existed. As I said, my properties are small, and I can't risk scaring all of my turkeys onto the neighbor's ground.

Additionally, I use decoys. Not just one or two, either. Over the years I've found that turkeys are very much social animals, with one of their strongest instincts being to hang out with other turkeys. They are flocking creatures by nature, and they can hardly resist the urge to interact with any other flocks seen. Every turkey on the planet is also on a never-ending quest to climb the social ladder, which is done by fighting to establish dominance. They do this not only with turkeys in their own flock, but with other birds encountered during the day. What this means in practical terms is that I strongly believe in putting out rather large spreads of decoys. We quite regularly employ 6-8, and I've been known to utilize as many as sixteen. One or two stutters are usually included in the mix, along with up to three jakes and numerous hens in various postures. These aren't just any decoys, either; they are all full-bodied fakes made by Dave Smith. Not only does that brand look the most life-like (in my opinion), but they are American-made in Oregon. In addition, the material they're crafted from can absorb a tremendous load of shot pellets and still show very little evidence of the hit...an added benefit of which I've been painfully forced to learn during the many years of taking out clients who get excited and pay no attention whatsoever to whether any of my beautifully painted fakes are in a direct line with the real tom who is the sole focus of their shot string!

The properties themselves (being flat and open grasslands) are also a major factor in my ability to operate in this manner, because I can drive right out to my chosen spot in the middle of the night (long after the turkeys have all gone to roost), erect my blind(s) with comfortable chairs for the hunters and myself, and then put out the decoy spread before driving back to camp. Then, in the morning, we can park further away as needed and walk in under cover of darkness carrying a minimum of gear. This process makes for long hours for yours truly, but it minimizes the impact on our turkeys.

Dave and Scott knew the game plan beforehand, so they were quite content to sit in their blind sipping on brews while awaiting the turkeys to show up. I had erected a second blind right beside theirs in the interest of maximizing comfort, so occasionally throughout the morning I would hear a soft "pffft" as one or the other of them opened up a new refreshment. But, despite knowing that there were at least four gobblers on the property, the morning hunt was a total bust…not a single gobble was heard, nor any turkeys seen.

After going to town for a delicious lunch at Granger & Sons BBQ, I decided to split the party up in order to increase the odds of making an afternoon kill. Putting Scott in a log cabin blind on another nearby property, Dave and I returned to the place where we'd hunted in the morning. That was a mistake of sorts, since Dave and I subsequently had three toms come in to our decoy spread at about 4:30, despite winds that were howling so hard I had to hold the blind down. The way these birds came in would've been an ideal situation for a double kill, and I was regretting my decision until I got a better look at the birds through binoculars. One bird had decent spurs, the second tom had only one spur, and the final gobbler had absolutely *nothing* on his legs!

Once Dave smote the normal-spurred tom mightily about the head and neck with a load of shot pellets, an interesting thing happened. Both of the survivors came back and began traumatizing their fallen buddy. It was a particularly vicious battle, with lots of kicks and wing floggings, eye pecking, and head/face skin-in-beak grabbing and pulling, and it went on for forty five minutes! Of particular fury were the attentions administered by the no-spurred tom, and as the battle began to wane, he did something which I had never witnessed before. For want of a better descriptive term, he got down and violated the dead bird's face! Then, he abruptly stood up, stared down at the expired tom for several long moments, and walked away with his new best friend beside him. Anthropomorphically, I could envision the thoughts going through that spurless tom's head: "You've beaten my butt since the day we hatched from eggs, and I've never had any chance to retaliate because of my spurless legs. Well, take *THAT*," (hip-thrust added for emphasis)!

During the rest of the afternoon it rained, and then it poured buckets all night long with lots of lightning. It calmed somewhat by dawn, but just long enough for us to get settled into our blind. Then, the *real* weather event began with the blast of a squall line and subsequent intense thunderstorms which drove us running from the field despite having a tom within sight at the time. The entire day afterward and on through 9 o'clock was a bust because of wind, heavy rain, lightning, and even a nearby tornado. Some days are just best experienced from the safety of substantial shelter, but we made do in our tent camp, instead. Fortunately, we lived to tell about it!

The storm cell blew out overnight, and the next day was beautiful. However, our field was flooded, and despite the gorgeous weather, we heard nothing but tree frogs croaking and peeping all around us. That's the way it goes sometimes after a major storm...the turkeys seemingly need an extra day to acclimate and return to normal. Long hours of nothing followed, and by 11 a.m. I was bored and ready for a nap. Dave and Scott in the other blind were content to sit on this field until lunchtime, as I had told them there were turkeys around, and they trusted me. After making a few more loud cutts and yelps, I stretched out on the wet ground for a little shut-eye until it was time to go eat.

I hadn't been asleep for more than five minutes when a loud gunshot startled me awake. A gobbler and two hens had run into our setup unbeknownst to me, and Scott had capably put the non-gobbling gobbler face down in a puddle. The boys got a good laugh out of their guide sleeping through the kill, but that just made for a better story in the end.

Dave and Scott give the "Hook 'Em Horns" sign over a wet tom

Six more days of mounting frustration were to follow as I tried to kill a second Osceola for myself. Green Swamp (as she so often does) abused me unmercifully while giving up only a bare minimum of opportunities, and I failed to capitalize on any of them. Truth of the matter is that I was only "in the game" once during that spell, and most of the time I was just riding the pine. It's hard to be the hero of any contest if you never get to play. When I was eventually forced to leave Florida by a tag soon to become valid in Delaware, I was aggravated at the weather, the turkeys, and with myself for how poorly I'd performed…especially-so on the day before I left, when I'd given up at 13 minutes till 1 o'clock (legal quitting time) and promptly boogered two unseen hens that were heading into my setup. Although I didn't see him, I was quite certain that their boyfriend who I'd been battling with for the last two hours was tagging along behind.

I'd now spent 20 days in Florida, and while part of me was ready to head north out of the heat, bugs, and non-cooperative turkeys, another part of me was reluctant to leave it all behind. I felt sure that with another week or two of hard effort I might kill one more gobbler…

A 4-foot tall hand painted concrete turkey found in Waldo, FL

When I arrived in Delaware on Friday it was windy and raining hard, and the forecast called for more of the same on the 'morrow. This state's public land regulations are kind of goofy. If you're lucky enough to draw a tag in their lottery, then your particular season segment starts on a Saturday. You can't hunt at all on Sunday, and the remaining portion of your permit runs from Monday thru Friday. That's it: six total *mornings*, because quitting time also ends at 1 o'clock each day.

In driving around all afternoon I located nine toms and six jakes on or near public property, plus a bunch of hens. This was as good an initial scouting venture as I could ever hope for, and so very different from what this state offered up during the first couple of times when I'd hunted there. Back then, it was extremely difficult to find *any* turkeys, whatsoever!

Two of the toms and three of the jakes had been spotted in a small hidden field of public land where I'd found turkeys in years past, so I opted to start right there. But, seeing as how the weather was going to be perfectly miserable, I decided to carry in a chair, a blind, and some decoys. These are items that I use extensively when I'm guiding, but not nearly so much as when I'm flying solo. Blinds especially make me feel confined, and they limit my hearing. My personal tendencies are generally more Spartan in approach, but on that day I even brought along a blanket. It was cold and I was tired from having arrived early enough to beat out my competition to the parking area, so I figured that I might as well stretch out and nap before daylight.

Nothing gobbled as dawn gloomed in, but with the steady rain, that didn't really surprise me. I knew turkeys would eventually make their way out of the woods and into this field, and sure enough, it wasn't long before a lone hen had saddled up against one of my female decoys and begun aggravated-purring at her. Then, a trio of jakes came onto the scene, and the dominant one immediately took to making amorous moves with another of my hen decoys while his buddies ganged up on the one next to it. The pair's courtship rituals were too aggressive though, and they knocked her over. The other jake was gentler, but driven, and he soon climbed up on the decoy's back and began treading. Then, he started breeding it!

About then is when two adult gobblers rushed out of the woods. They totally ignored the jake having his way with my decoy, and instead, began chasing the other pair of youngsters all around. The real hen even got involved in the skirmish, and for several minutes there were five turkeys juking and jiving in tight quarters while the other jake continued to do nasty things to my decoy. I'd already stuck my gun barrel out the window of the blind by then, and I was waiting until one of the toms separated from the other turkeys. However, when that finally happened and I tried to take aim, I couldn't see any color whatsoever on my Truglo Magnum Gobble Dot sight!

All season long I'd been struggling with my poor eyesight, and now, here inside a darkened blind *and* with leaden clouds and rain removing any hint whatsoever of the sun's potential, I couldn't see for squat. Every turkey in the setup other than that one breeding jake was rushing around hither and yon, and that in turn also created an ever-growing sense of anxiety in me. I should've just backed off and regrouped, but I panicked. Aligning the tom's head with where I *thought* my gun was pointed, I fired...and missed.

None of the turkeys seemed overly alarmed by the loud report of my shotgun, although the two adult toms did move far enough away that the thought of touching off another round never crossed my mind. The love-sick jake, though? He never even broke stride and continued breeding my decoy without missing a beat. When I then cutt hard on a diaphragm, all five male turkeys within eyesight gobbled! But, the mood had definitely been broken, and before too much longer the lover-boy jake hopped down and all of the turkeys began wandering away in different directions.

Sitting there aggravated and disappointed, I kept staring at the hen decoy still upright...the one which had been sexually assaulted all morning...and even though my vision was blurry, I was pretty sure that there were white streaks up her back. When the 1 p.m. quitting time finally arrived, I went out and confirmed that my suspicions were true; the jake had successfully passed his seed onto my decoy! I took a picture as proof for the Dave Smith Decoy company that their product was truly lifelike.

When I walked up to my van carrying all the gear I'd hauled out into the field early in the morning, there were two conservation officers waiting for me. I greeted them by holding up my abused hen decoy and pleading, "I hope you've got a rape kit in the trunk, because I want to file charges against the jake that did *this*." We all laughed, and then they proceeded to check me as thoroughly as I've ever been checked. They looked at everything I owned: hunting license and permit, my shotgun to make sure that the barrel wasn't too short and whether it was plugged, individual shotgun shells to verify that they contained only legal-sized pellets, inside my van and coolers for anything illegal, and even my decoys. I mean to tell you; they were *diligent*!

Delaware rules prohibit the use of any real turkey parts being used on a decoy, and even though I'd correctly employed a fake tail on the strutter, I wasn't operating totally within the strict letter of the law. You see; the old Dave Smith strutters had slits in their sides to facilitate the addition of primary wing feathers for maximum realism. I hadn't used them because I knew the rules, but I did have a set of feathers in my decoy bag. After explaining this to the officers, they cut me a break and didn't write me a ticket. Allowing for how minutely they'd checked everything else I owned, I would bet good money that they had already been watching me in the field with binoculars and knew that I hadn't utilized the feathers. Otherwise, I probably would've gotten fined. Of course, maybe it was simply my cooperative and friendly attitude or the attempt at humor which kept me off the hook, but who knows? I never mind getting checked by law enforcement, anyway. In fact, I actually *like* to see that they're doing their job. I try my best to abide by every rule and regulation particular to the state in which I'm hunting, so why should I care? Let this be a lesson to everyone else, though: ignorance is no excuse for breaking the law. I should've known not to carry those feathers. Period.

The next day being Sunday, all that I could do was scout. I was still bummed about Saturday's miss, but then in early afternoon I found something to brighten my spirits; something which put a silver lining around the gray cloud of having blown a golden opportunity. Spotting two toms and three hens on private ground that was very close to public, I looked them over with binoculars and discovered that one gobbler was wearing jewelry. Yep; he was banded on both legs! I then spent a couple of hours checking out how best to access the public land options nearby, and then I tossed and turned all night in hopes of perhaps seeing him again, although in line with my gun barrel.

Everything that shines in Delaware isn't necessarily scrap metal

Morning eventually dawned, and brought with it a tremendous hunt involving four different hard-gobbling toms and multiple hens. After passing on the chance to shoot one eager bird early, I was rewarded for that questionable judgement in late morning when the next tom called into gun range hopped up on a spoil pile at 24 yards and gave me a good look at him. I was fairly confident before ever pulling the trigger that his beard had that same peculiar twist as the bejeweled gobbler, and when I subsequently walked up to my fallen adversary, the first thing that I saw was the glimmer of aluminum around his ankles. What a thrill!

North Carolina's Uwharrie National Forest was a difficult hunt. One day I pulled back into the remote campground where I was staying and was immediately approached by a neighboring camper who said his truck was in need of a jump start. As I was helping him out, he inquired about what I was hunting, since I was fully decked out in camo and all of my other hunting gear was plainly visible in the floor of the van. When I told him that I was turkey hunting, he replied that he was hunting too, but hadn't had any luck. He then offered me his business card and explained that what he was after were Yeti's. Yeah: Bigfoots! This guy was the producer of a TV show dedicated to the search for Sasquatches! I told him that I couldn't really help him on that matter, as I hadn't seen any of them, either.

A couple of days later I sort of succeeded. Not in finding a Bigfoot, but in finally hearing a gobbler and calling him in. It was a magnificent hunt full of intrigue, beguile, and intricate chess moves resulting in a nerve-wracking conclusion that had my blood coursing and my knees shaking. And then, I missed. This was my second screw-up of the year, and to say that I was frustrated and disappointed would be a very, very grave understatement.

After five days I'd had enough of the Uwharrie and ventured out for new territory in the Nantahala National Forest. I needed a change of scenery in order to change my attitude, and boy, was I ever glad that I made that move! The very first morning I heard six gobbling toms and killed one. Two days later I filled my other NC tag, and shortly thereafter I was leaving the state with a whole new outlook on life. Ain't it funny how little things like actually hearing and seeing turkeys can triumph over the negative vibes stemming from previously hiking mile after mile in a seemingly turkey-less desert? The killing of those two toms also boosted an ego previously bruised from missing a couple of others. Just like that, I once again felt confident that I could hit what I was shooting at.

This 2011 North Carolina tom put the smile back on my face

My next adventure was a terribly unsuccessful trip to Illinois. Now; I've had many great hunts in that state, and have killed some absolute brutes. I've also picked morel mushrooms by the bushel basket while there, and few things in life make me happier. However, nothing good happened in 2011. A low-pressure cell had parked itself right over top of the entire southern Illinois region where I'd drawn a tag, and the danged thing stayed there unmoving for the entire duration of my 7-day license. I nearly got drowned by vertical flood waters every time I ventured out into the woods, which was every single morning from before dawn until noon, since I only had those seven days to get things done. It was a horrendous hunt overall, and I left for home cursing Illinois turkeys, the state itself and how they run their hunts and overregulate everything, and myself for having not hunted hard enough or well enough to change my luck. I was not a happy camper when I crossed over the record-flooded Ohio River bound for home.

Some distressing news greeted me at Tea Mountain. After spending the first few days of turkey season there for the last 20 years, Tom Foley had decided to sell off the entire 1600-acre property to the Nature Conservancy, who would later transfer ownership to the State of Indiana so that the land could be run as a Fish and Wildlife Area open to the public. All of us who reveled in the tradition of hunting there (me, Don Foley, Bruce Wilson, and the brothers DeWayne and Russ Feltner) were shocked, to say the least.

The weather also interjected a tangible feeling of angst amongst our group, as it rained so hard that none of us even attempted to venture out on opening day. Instead, we went down and ate breakfast together at the Gatesville General Store while reminiscing about all the good times and laughter we'd shared on that amazing piece of real estate. Then, the rain finally let up. In the afternoon we were joined back at camp by Tom's buddies Bill Louderback, Joe Harrod, Steve Baker, Pete Wilkerson, and Tom's son John for our annual dinner cooked outside over an open fire pit. The menu that year included elk ribs, venison, and fried turkey, along with green beans and corn, hot bread, and fried morels. Then, the feast was capped with pecan pies crafted by Miss Vickie (Bruce's wife). The food was phenomenal, but a palpable feeling of sadness and finality hung in the air.

The area's turkeys must've picked up on the vibe, because the next day proved to be a total bust. Donnie and I never even heard the first gobble. Somehow, that seemed like a fitting way to end our time on Tea Mountain, but then again, it would've been more appropriate if twenty toms had sounded off all around us. That was closer to the way things had always been, and now, the end of an era was at hand. When we all packed up and left, I'm quite sure that mine were not the only damp eyes.

Missouri is a state that I haven't hunted very often. I don't really know why, other than to say that I always figured on getting the hardest places out of the way first, and then I could come back and take my time enjoying what, for many years, had been one of the top turkey hunting states in the nation. Case in point was that year of 2011, when my friend Neill Prater invited me to stay with him and hunt either the nearby Harry Truman Reservoir, or some of his accessible private lands. It didn't really matter which, as there were plenty of turkeys available on both. I filled my tags in only three days, and when I told Neill of hearing on average 12 birds per day, he apologized for the bird numbers being "really down." Seriously?! The first tom I shot that year also completed my second U.S. Super Slam.

In looking back through my notes, I realized that it had been since 1991 that I'd hunted in Missouri: twenty years. My last trip there had been when Ron Ronk and Steve Seramur accompanied me, and then that fall Steve had suddenly and unexpectedly died. I'm quite certain Steve and I would've had many a great time, shared a barrel full of laughs, and stacked up who-knows-how-many toms in the intervening years, so before leaving the state I lifted a cocktail in toast to both my dear departed friend, and The Slam just completed.

My good friend Steve Seramur was quite a guy

Iowa is one of my favorite states. Not just because they have a lot of turkeys, but for many other intangible reasons. Being basically a rural state, it's not too crowded and the people are nice. They also have pheasants, and I *love* hunting those birds! Furthermore, the scenery where I turkey hunt is some of the most unique and fascinating ground in America. Unfortunately, the bag limit is only one bird and the tags are expensive and distributed by lottery. Despite these negatives, it's a great place to hunt. I always breathe easy when I arrive, knowing that I'm soon going to be into turkeys, and most probably in a very big way!

Just as I'd anticipated, it didn't take long to be surrounded by gobbling toms. The bad news stemmed from subsequently doing something yet again that had been a frequent occurrence all spring long. No, I didn't miss another bird. I only scared the bejesus out of one with an ill-time movement. At that point in the season I couldn't even count how many toms I'd boogered. This was something I've always focused on avoiding at all costs, and the frequency with which it was happening in 2011 was both alarming and utterly maddening. I knew that a big part of the reason was my worsening vision, but I hadn't taken the time before the season to go and see a doctor.

Well, the rash of boogerings (and the latest one, in particular) needn't have bothered me too much, because despite strong winds all day, I ended up hearing seven gobbling birds in total and calling in two. The second one was promptly cut up into parts lovingly placed into (2) one gallon ziplock bags and packed in the ice of my cooler, to be later consumed in a variety of ways. I do love hunting wild turkeys, and I especially like eating them!

When you buy a turkey license in Kansas they give you an atlas of WIHA properties around the state. This acronym stands for Walk-In Hunting Areas, and these are private lands which have been leased to the government for public access. It's a wonderful program, and I've had many excellent hunts on these types of ground over the years.

For the first part of the trip I hunted up in Marshall County, in the northeastern section of the state, and while I didn't kill any turkeys there, I did have some exciting hunts. However, by the third afternoon I was ready for a change of scenery. Even though I'd heard that the turkey population in the southeastern corner had taken a nosedive in recent years, I just had to go see for myself. My last time there had been a wonderful experience when I'd finished up my first U.S. Super Slam on a place called Mined Ground WMA, and I couldn't imagine not being able to find a bird or two there, now.

The first thing I noticed upon arrival was the temperature. It was brutally hot! Despite that, I did hear three turkeys ripping it hard throughout the morning's hunt. Unfortunately, they were all far into inaccessible private lands, and I never heard the first bird on the same public ground which had previously treated me so well. Thus, I was forced to cruise around with the air conditioning on and seek out turkeys the lazy man's way, and sure enough, shortly after noon I stopped on a road running alongside a State Wildlife Area and, using a mouth call, coaxed out a gobble back beyond their fence. I couldn't hunt that property without non-toxic shot, so I then had to travel far and wide in search of some. Finally, I located a single box of Winchester Heavy Shot 2- 3/4" 6's in a small sporting goods store 50 miles away, and then I raced back to Neosho. I didn't see or hear anything else during that last hour of hunting time, but at 8:13 p.m. I heard one distant gobble. That lone pronouncement only gave me a general idea of the tom's roost location, but that was good enough to make a play for him the next morning.

At dawn that same tom was eager to gobble, but he wasn't exactly what you'd call, "over-eager." He only blasted out a half-dozen or so while in the tree. But, thanks to his lone gobble from the evening prior, I began the day pretty close, and long before he pitched down I was hunkered up under a nearby oak tree. The tom's flight path to ground took him right overhead at an elevation of probably 25 feet, and then he landed out in a bean stubble field 100 yards behind me. Once on the ground his gobbling pace really picked up, and the tall, wispy brown grass between us allowed me to crawl closer undetected. Slithering to a small oak on the edge of the field, I gradually eased up into a seated position only 60 yards away from where the tom was spinning around in circles in full strut, and then it only took a few light yelps to bring him far too close to my gun's muzzle for his own good. Those baby magnums performed admirably.

My old buddy Tracy Deckard pulled into camp at about 4 a.m. the next morning, and the first thing I said to him was, "Would you *please* pick these damned ticks off of my back?" The cursed little buggers had been eating me alive for days, and after Tracy had removed a dozen live ones and counted over twenty additional welts along my spine, I felt quite a bit of relief. It takes a mighty good friend to drive all the way from Indiana to Kansas in order to pick ticks off another man's back in the middle of the night, and I thank my lucky stars for a buddy like Tracy. Later that very same day I discovered the miracle of permethrin, and my life has been a wonderment ever since. Few things in life are more satisfying than watching ticks crawl up your pant leg and then rolling over and dying.

One more day of not finding any turkeys on the vast acreage of public lands around us made the decision to try some place new an easy choice, so we drove up to Washington County to hunt more WIHA lands along the Nebraska state line. The next morning I filled my final tag with a bird which started his day in the safety of another state altogether, but simply couldn't resist the sweet yelps coming from my Bear Hollow diaphragms and an Andy Kaiser glass call made from Hawaiian Koa wood. He died a glorious warrior's death with his feet firmly planted a hundred yards south of the Nebraska state line, making him the first (and only) bird I have called from one state to another.

Later that afternoon, while guiding for my old tick-pickin' buddy Deckard, I watched from a few yards behind him as he miscalculated the distance to a tom strutting with a half-dozen ladies. Every turkey in the bunch (tom included) flew away unscathed at the shot. Two days later, in the same pasture, he missed what was most likely the very same gobbler, but it wasn't because of any ranging error. This time the tom and a jake had been standing bolt upright, in the perfect "kill me now" pose, at a whopping range of 21 yards! With the weather forecast to get progressively worse than the biting cold and wind-spitting snow we'd been hunting in since noon, we then opted to call it a day and make an exit out of Kansas.

Tracy headed for home perhaps a little bit more than depressed from his two misses, while I opted to travel up to Michigan and hunt with my precious old friend, Christene Gerace. It had been many years since she'd killed her first tom with me back in Indiana, and during the intervening decade or so she had moved back to Michigan in order to be close to her father during his last years of life. Everything Christine does is done with great passion, and in becoming a fanatical turkey huntress up there, she'd acquired lots of great ground on which to pursue the King of Gamebirds. One such piece was only 19 acres in size, and yet, it was what you might call, "in the right spot." Although drizzling rain kept the birds quiet in the roost and inspired us to seek turkeys elsewhere for most of the day, we headed back there during the late afternoon hours confident of making something good happen. After all, she'd seen a flock of 18 turkeys there only a week prior.

Well, things got very hectic soon after our arrival, with hens, jakes, and toms at one point surrounding us on all sides and mouthing off in a virtual cacophony of exciting turkey music. When the moment for the hunt's culmination arrived, I had no less than seven adult gobblers from which to choose. They all looked good to me, so I just shot the first one in line. It was only after I'd rolled the 23 pound tom onto his back that I found out he didn't have *any* spurs! I preach the gospel that you can't eat beards and spurs, but every time I shoot a bird without hooks of any sort, I just can't help but feel a little bit disappointed. Not terribly so, but it does smudge just the slightest bit of sheen from the overall joy of winning at this game.

Two weeks later I rolled into Bill George's family "camp" in western Pennsylvania at about midnight. I was too jacked up with excitement to drift right off to sleep though, and it was probably close to 2 a.m. before the sandman finally paid a visit. Despite my tiredness, when the alarm went off at 4 a.m. I arose bleary-eyed to greet everyone else down in the kitchen of Bill's 3-story, 9-bedroom and 13-bed farmhouse. Bill had convinced Charlie Parrish to ride up with him from Florida, and they'd picked up Doug Pickle in Virginia along the way. Craig Morton lives only 25 minutes from camp, so he was there to hunt with us, too.

Pennsylvania during the last week of May can offer quite variable conditions. Sometimes the weather hasn't yet turned spring-like at all, with the woods still barren of leaf cover and looking as if snowpack has just recently melted. Other times it already feels like summer, with trees fully leafed out and tall ferns carpeting the forest floor. Both conditions offer their own unique challenges, and neither lends itself to making the turkey hunting easy. In 2011 the woods were hot, humid, and sticky, with such advanced flora that it made the time spent afield feel more like a challenging chore. Even hearing birds was problematic, as the sound of their gobbling was being absorbed by all the vegetation. If you heard one, you knew that the tom was close.

I didn't fully grasp that reality until I'd gotten too tight and run birds out of the trees a couple of times over the first three days. Hey; by this late in the season, that just seemed like par for the course, anyway! However, my companions were suffering similarly, and Charlie even compounded the collective frustration when he missed a tom from a whopping range of 14 yards. That was it, though...when all was said and done, some of the best turkey hunters I know had struck out completely to end the season with zero gobblers having their pictures taken while hanging from the camp's dinner bell.

In a nutshell, 2011 had been a brutally tough year for me. The weather could certainly be blamed for most of that, with hot temperatures and frequent rain, wind, and even tornadoes seeming to follow me everywhere I went. However, I didn't feel like I'd hunted particularly well, either. Oh; I'd persevered and made things happen in eight of the ten states hunted, but there had been too many days when it felt like I was just going through the motions. Not just a little of that stemmed from what had been going on back home, where my "obsessive turkey hunting" had taken a heavy toll on my love life with Jen. We'd broken up (for the first time...there would be many others ahead) mid-season. Then, when all these frustrations and aggravations had mounted to a certain boiling point, I'd gone and done something never even considered before...I quit early and went home on May 14. Although I did sneak back out for that doomed four-day hunt to Pennsylvania, I probably would've been better off to just stay at home.

Thus, my season totals and statistics were greatly reduced from the numbers to which I'd grown accustomed. Usually tallying in the high 60's or low 70's in days afield, I was down to only 57. Between myself and the folks I'd guided, we had been averaging almost 24 toms during the last six years, but that had fallen to a mere 16. Gobbles heard and gobblers called in were both drastically reduced, as well, and in every category of which I keep track, I had recorded numbers at or near the bottom.

Yes; my 2011 season had seen some trials and tribulations, but at the same time I was quite proud of several things...not the least of which was simply persevering through all of the difficulties encountered and soldiering on. I'd also completed my second U.S. Super Slam, and so far as I knew, that was the first time it had ever been done. I had to admit that this felt pretty darned good, but even that accomplishment needed to be kept in perspective, for I knew fully-well that I was extremely lucky to be where I was at and not having to be home working for a living every day and all year long. Being able to turkey hunt for three months straight was how I defined success for myself, so in those regards alone it had been a great year.

With only twenty states remaining in my quest to complete a third Super Slam, and a number of them being located out west, 2012 was looking to be a fun, action-packed adventure. I was definitely looking forward that!

Bill George, Charlie Parrish, Craig Morton, me, and Doug Pickle

Chapter 6

2012

My 2012 Florida turkey season was a wild rollercoaster ride of emotional highs and lows, with never a dull moment. Whereas the previous year had been extremely wet and bug infested, featuring frequent heavy thunderstorms and even an occasional tornado, 2012 ended up being dry as a popcorn fart. Because of that, I probably didn't tally more than a handful of mosquitos seen or swatted the entire time that I was there. This simple fact alone made the whole trip a rousing success, but that didn't mean it was all smooth sailing. I actually began the year with quite a bit of worry: most notably, I was concerned about my eyesight. I was having a lot of trouble seeing things clearly, and I had a strong premonition that this would cause me some troubles ahead. I just had no idea that it would happen so soon...

Everything started out great when my four clients all killed their birds during the first three days of the season. Jen and I (yes, we had reunited) had come down a week early to scout, and we'd kept a watchful eye on nearly a dozen gobblers, so those successes hadn't really come as much of a surprise. I knew the birds and their particular idiosyncrasies well, and had merely capitalized on them expeditiously.

After completing my guiding duties I then switched attention to hunting at Green Swamp, and the very first morning there I called in a bird that should've gone back to camp with me. Instead, when the time of reckoning arrived I couldn't see both him and my gun sights clearly, so I never pulled the trigger. It didn't take that sharp-eyed rascal in front of me very long to figure things out, and he was soon exiting stage right in a rapid manner. Two days later I called in the same bird for a second time, and despite once again struggling to see him standing tall at 32 yards in the dim swamp woods, I went ahead and let 'er rip. The next few minutes were a blur of frantic chasing and panic-driven exertion, as the wounded tom outpaced me in the tangled fallen limbs and cypress knees before making good his escape. I was just sick about it, too. I spent the entire day looking for him without ever finding so much as a feather. Missing a gobbler is bad enough, but crippling one is the absolute worst feeling imaginable. I was so overcome with dread and remorse that I wanted to puke.

The next day I did the same thing again! Never in my wildest of horrendous nightmares could I have imagined such a terrible occurrence, and the emotions of frustration, exasperation, and depression which I felt afterwards left me physically shaking in my boots. I couldn't even write it all down on paper until I'd had a sleepless night in which to calm myself to the point where I wouldn't rip the pages from my journal in anger. Another long day was then spent diligently and fruitlessly searching the area for any hint of the bird's whereabouts. In the end I concluded that this tom would probably live through the ordeal, since he had gathered himself after tumbling to the ground and flown away. I'd only found a single neck feather at the point where he'd been standing prior to the shot.

Bill George had also missed a turkey. The day after that, during a late afternoon "property tour" with Jen, Bill, and his daughter Belinda, we had watched his missed gobbler fly up to roost only 50 yards from the road, giving us the perfect situation in which to help David Caudill (the beloved and frail patriarch of our turkey camp) get a bird. The following morning, Bill had built a little brush blind beside the road and gotten David tucked into it, and then he'd walked out and used his boot heal to scratch an "X" in the sandy road. Returning to David's hide, he whispered that the gobbler was going to land *on* that very spot. And, lo and behold, he was right! David was tickled to no end by the way in which the demise of that turkey had come about.

After failing to hear anything the following morning in a favorite spot known as "The Hole," I returned to the site of David's kill and headed north of there, towards a bird Bill had heard gobbling frenetically on the day of his own miss. It was 11:30 before I got there, and the temperature had already risen into the uncomfortable range, so I was shocked when a far distant tom answered some loud cutting on a glass call. Despite the late hour and blazing climatic conditions, he began gobbling on his own quite regularly as I hustled to close

David Caudill and Bill George with the "X" tom

the distance of nearly a mile in between us. Heading towards the tom in a trot, I just about ran over another gobbler as I rounded a palmetto patch, and then I heard a second bird sounding off in another cypress head around which I'd just traveled to get where I was going. From that point on it became one of those flash hunts involving a perfect setup and only three or four yelps on a diaphragm call before the targeted tom was standing statue still at 20 yards. At high noon and with bright sunshine sufficiently illuminating both the target and my shotgun sights, I didn't miss this one.

Later on, while I was hanging around camp with all the regulars, Bill came back from hunting and asked where I'd shot the tom. I told him the name of the main road where I'd been, but wasn't any more specific than that. When he then asked me to step over into a sandy spot and subsequently inspected my boot prints made there, he laughed that Bill George laugh and declared, "I *knew* I recognized those foot prints!" Apparently, he'd gone back in to where I'd killed the bird after I was already gone and found enough forensic evidence to deduct that I'd shot "his" hard-gobbling tom. I, of course, claimed to have been so far north of where he'd heard gobbling that there was simply no way his practically-deaf ears could've detected the one I ended up shooting. And, as further evidence of my innocence, I brought up the fact that I'd either seen or heard two other toms closer to the road. All of this was true, but I did shoot a tom that gobbled a bunch, so it's possible that "Bill's" bird and mine were one

Craig Morton and David Caudill are legendary turkey hunters

and the same. We still and often laugh about those boot tracks.

It would be another five days before I scored again, but Craig Morton shot a great bird while hunting with David. They had been friends and hunting companions ever since their guiding days at Fisheating Creek back in the late '80's and early '90's, and both of these gentlemen are consummate story tellers. I could sit and listen to them talk turkey all day, every day. Besides that, I hold each of them as belonging right there at the top of any list of the finest turkey hunters ever to be born, with more experience, knowledge, and skills than you can imagine. They are, and forever will be, true heroes to me in this sport, and I'm honored to say that they are also my friends.

The golf tournament was much more competitive in 2012. I played very well except for three disastrous holes and still almost beat Belinda. In fact, she won only because I missed a 3-1/2 foot birdie putt on the 16th hole and ended up losing by a single stroke. Dangit...I *so* wanted to take that trophy away from her! She would soon be playing collegiately for the University of North Florida, so the simple fact that I'd come close should've been victory enough for me. It wasn't: I wanted more!

Successfully guiding Miss Belinda in the Baird Unit of Richloam a couple of days later was the next and final notch on the camp's victory pole before it was time to shut down my Florida fun. I'd spent a total of 17 days there either hunting or guiding, and while it was not an ordinary season by any stretch of the imagination, it was nothing less than spectacular from start to finish! Besides missing two toms, I had killed a pair. Others in camp who also filled their annual bag limit included Kenny Dorman, Charlie Parrish, and Doug Pickle, while Bill George, David Caudill, Craig Morton, and Belinda George had all taken one gobbler. My four clients had also shot one apiece. Back in camp, Miss Jenny had fit right in with the whole crew and formed a particularly strong bond with Marie Caudill, who was in so many ways the heart and soul of our Florida "family." Good times and memories abounded.

Some of my Florida "family" posing behind Belinda's 2012 bird: me, Bill George, David Caudill, Jen Roberts, Cathy Parrish, Kenny Dorman, Marie Caudill, and Craig Morton

Jen and I pulled into New Orleans a couple days later and had no sooner begun walking down Bourbon Street before she suddenly squealed in delight and rushed up to hug some goofy looking dude missing most of his teeth. I didn't know if he was family, a past boyfriend, or what, but then I heard her tell him that she was a huge fan. Even after she introduced me to "Turtle Man," I had absolutely no idea who he was, because I'd never seen his TV show. It would be months later, long after those first impressions were made there on the streets of New Orleans, that I would watch an episode and thereby confirm my initial thoughts that he was some sort of a nut. I mean, who in their right mind would ever catch a live raccoon *by hand?!*

Jenny Roberts with Turtle Man and his sidekick Banjo Man

The next morning I killed a great gobbler with a beard of almost 11- 1/2 inches and long, hooked spurs. Then, I struggled for another seven days without so much as a hint that I was doing anything right. I finally reached the point where it sounded like more fun to be doing something else, so Jenny and I spent a couple days touring around the Lafayette region and eating lots of my favorite foods: crawfish, cracklings, and boudin from a number of different makers. We had a great time, and then I put her on a flight for home before pointing my van westward.

Do you remember the story of me hunting in New Mexico and almost killing myself by carrying two toms and an elk shed up a steep canyon wall? Remember how I swore that I would never go back? Well, what do you suppose I did on the very first day back in the Land of Enchantment? Yep; I hiked down into that hellhole again. Unfortunately and unbelievably, the place was almost devoid of turkeys this time around, and I eventually made my way back to the rim neither impressed nor encumbered by the heft of any turkey flesh or elk bone.

I did, however, find turkeys elsewhere, and the following day I shot one of them. Another couple days of coming oh-so-close on multiple occasions left me both frustrated, and at the same time encouraged with the numbers of birds that I was finding, but with a Nevada tag burning a hole in my pocket, it was time to get going. I hoped to return later on and fill that second New Mexico tag.

My first two trips to Nevada had produced toms, but I'd found them in rather marginal habitat of arid desert canyons with only isolated cottonwoods serving as roost sites. This time I arrived two days before my permit became valid, and in talking with anyone in the town of Caliente who might know anything about turkeys, I learned of a couple different locations where there were actually Ponderosa pines instead of just scrub cedar. When I drove far back into the boonies to check them out, I then found tracks, droppings, and scratchings enough to get me excited about the possibilities. At one of those spots I even heard a hen yelping.

The next morning I experienced a wonderful hunt, and yet, I didn't pull the trigger. I could have, and didn't. There had been at least six toms gobbling within earshot, and since it had taken a *lot* of driving to reach Nevada, I simply wasn't in any hurry to end my hunt so soon. Now that I'd found an absolutely beautiful spot with lots of turkeys and apparently no other hunters, I decided to take my time and enjoy the experience for as long as possible. My days of feeling the need to get a bird and get gone were long past. This was gonna be fun!

During late morning of the third day I found myself with three different toms approaching my cedar-bough blind from three different directions. It was a "race" conducted at dirge speed, though. None of them seemed to be in any more of a hurry than me, although they were definitely headed in to find the source of my calling. All three toms gobbled at every call I made, and it was only a matter of time to see which one would arrive first.

I could hear the sound of wingtips dragging against the hard, rocky soil when they strutted, and echoing drumming seemed to emanate from everywhere. It was an absolutely magical moment, and to not pull the trigger when presented with the chance would've been to cheat myself of the total experience. One tom had a particularly low and vibrant gobble, and he had been my bird of choice even before dancing into view. When the time was right and his head was lifted into the perfect "shoot me now" pose, I did just that and completed the circle.

The results of a fabulous 2012 hunt in Nevada

Winter snows were still blocking access into a lot of the higher elevation areas of the Dixie National Forest around Cedar City, UT when I got there, and in fact, a major avalanche and landslide had taken out a portion of the highway leading up from town. Rather than fighting those issues, I decided to venture south and hunt a region which held Rio Grande turkeys instead of the Merriam's I had intended to pursue. What I found there was ground totally different from the mountains...mostly open desert, with a dotting of scrub cedar and an occasional cottonwood along any waterway.

In "scouting" by vehicle (my permit wasn't valid for another three days), I eventually spotted some turkeys in a private field dotted with cows. When I looked the area over on a topographic map, I discovered that a narrow spit of public land abutted the private field on its western edge, and it came all the way out to the gravel road on which I'd been driving. The opposite side of the road was also public property, so I found a good place to camp over there which was hidden from the road behind a tall, sandy hill. Climbing to its top with a chair and a good book, I could thus sit comfortably and watch what the turkeys did from about a mile distance. In scouting the birds like that for the next 2- 1/2 days, I learned their patterns extremely well.

There were quite a few turkeys to keep track of, too! Every night some of them would roost in the cottonwoods surrounding an old ranch house east of the field, where nobody lived. Others would roost west of the spit of public land, in the vicinity of an occupied house tucked into a grove of trees about a mile further down the road. Throughout the day there would be a fairly steady parade of turkeys going either from, or to, each place, and quite often hanging out in the irrigated field where all the cattle lived. Gobbling could be heard basically all day long, and it came from no less than seven or eight different toms. When I drove out to a general store about six miles further down the road and made a few inquiries of its proprietor, I learned that the guy who lived in the occupied dwelling was also the owner of the abandoned farmhouse, and he didn't allow hunting at either place. He fed the turkeys where he lived, only because his wife liked to watch them.

The spit of public land in between his two properties was only 400 yards wide, and it was almost totally devoid of any sort of cover other than a group of perhaps half a dozen brushy cedars which grew about 75 yards from the cattle field. In studying the turkeys for hours on end, I learned that they quite often came dangerously close to those cedars on their daily travel routes, and a plan began to form in my brain.

A deep and raging torrent of a willow-lined creek ran right down along the opposite side of the road from my campsite, so after all the turkeys had flown up to roost that first night, I slid down the steep bluff above the creek and then spent a considerable amount of time bending and weaving willows together until I'd built a strong bridge over which I could cross the creek. Then, I hiked out to the cedars and cut down just enough of them to build a wonderful blind around the trunks of the others still standing. In the full moon's light, you couldn't even tell where a human hand had altered the grove. It looked like a perfect ambush point, whether I ever called from there, or not.

The two days before I could carry a gun dragged on forever, but finally, Monday arrived. Long before daylight I was already tucked into my hidey-hole, and just like clockwork as the sun brightened the skyline, turkeys began gobbling both east and west of me. Within an hour I had three toms and a couple hens wandering past my blind at about a hundred yards, and when I offered a few yelps, purrs, and clucks on a glass call, the strutter in the group immediately turned and walked a direct path to eternity.

Remember how I had twice before vowed never again to hike those 1000 vertical feet down into the New Mexico canyon? Yep; I did it again, for the third time. Too many hunters everywhere else I ventured upon my return to Cloudcroft

Too much time to scout in Utah made for an easy Rio hunt

forced me into committing that crazy act, but unlike my previous trip, it ended up being well worth the effort. There were a minimum of six toms ripping it hard down in there, and the first one to commit to my dance invitations got a face full of copper-plated pellets, instead. His spurs were over an inch long and he had two beards, so I didn't mind the hike out nearly as much as the first couple times I'd been there. In fact, I took a longer, gentler route up and out of the canyon, and it wasn't a bad climb at all.

With an Arizona tag soon to be valid in Zone 21, I ventured on over to the little town of Alpine, from which I'd based my hunting operations twice before.

New Mexico's Merriam's make it hard on a fat guy

There had always been lots of turkeys in the surrounding Apache-Sitgreaves National Forest, but the enormous Wallow Fire in the summer of 2011 had raged through 538,000 acres of land and devastated that portion of the state. I drove mile after mile in scouting for ground which looked like it might still support turkeys, and I was absolutely flabbergasted by what I saw: very little other than soot and ash, blackened earth, and the charred skeletons of millions of pine trees. When a wildfire like that burns so intensely, it also destroys the soil structure of the forest floor, leading to flash floods and landslides when next it rains. Many backroads and numbered Forest Service roads were thus wiped out, and it was tricky getting around.

Despite what looked like utter devastation for any wildlife, the patchwork nature of the fire had left some trees untouched and I heard numerous turkeys gobbling on the first day that I could hunt. Unfortunately, every one of them ended up being inaccessible to me due to being across a river and in Zone 1. Then, in late evening I drove up on a gobbler and two hens as they crossed a paved road. There was no traffic, so I just came to a stop and watched them move up a hillside that had been burned to a crisp. With no green trees anywhere to be seen, I was beginning to wonder where they planned to roost when, quite suddenly, they all pitched up into the remnants of a dead Ponderosa pine. They looked like buzzards sitting there in the skeleton of that tree!

Well, the next day I did my best to kill that tom, or any of the other three or four which I could hear gobbling in the distance, but the burned and open nature of the terrain made for a challenging hunt and I failed. I did the same thing the following day, and the day after that. On all three mornings there had been a little gobbling to offer some encouragement, but that would end by 7 a.m. and the turkeys would vanish as if into thin air. Three days into the hunt I felt like I'd learned absolutely nothing about my quarry and was no closer to killing a tom than when I'd arrived.

Bored to tears, I'd already decided to move elsewhere following one last hunt and try to find a tom that was more entertaining. This one hadn't been cooperative, but more importantly, he'd hardly gobbled at all and I'd spent many an uninspired hour listening to the deathly still nothingness of the torched landscape. There weren't even any songbirds to keep my attention misdirected while awaiting a next gobble. I needed a new adversary.

Then, things changed. I think that was because another tom had wandered into the local bird's core area, because suddenly there were two birds gobbling where there had previously been only one. They lit it up, too, and were quite defiant of one another. I crept in between them under cover of darkness, setting up with each tom about 100 yards away, and then I played the coy hen part. Both of the gobblers ate up what I was selling and raced in to vie for the hen's affections, and when my chosen tom ran the 'ole flagpole up at 19 yards, I let him have it.

My 2012 Arizona "Phoenix" gobbler

As traveling turkeys hunters so often do, I drove all night to reach my next destination: a cluster of WIHA properties in western Kansas. I pulled into the parking lot at 3:30 a.m., and my alarm went off at 5 o'clock. Dressed and opening the sliding side door of my van at 5:29, I heard a gobble, so I shuffled off towards it like a very tired zombie. Once I'd closed the distance, I realized that there were actually three toms roosted in a line of cottonwoods on the opposite side of a relatively small disked field, and I could already hear their drumming as I crawled into a brush pile along an old fence line. I would've rather chosen a tree to sit against, but the only ones nearby were small black locusts with long, sharp spines both on their bark and littering the ground around them.

Short story shorter: the first tom flew down into the turned dirt between us and soon thereafter advanced towards my subtle yelps and clucks on a diaphragm call. Exactly one hour after the first gobble heard, I pulled the trigger. Then, I took a couple pictures, slung the tom over my shoulder, walked all of 300 level yards back to my van, and took a nice, long nap.

The "Zombie" gobbler from Kansas in 2012

My next victory a couple days later wasn't so easy, and it didn't happen nearly as quickly. The hunt took place on a different chunk of WIHA land that was quite large: approximately 2-1/2 sections, or 1600 acres. Most of western Kansas has roads that are laid out on a 1-mile grid pattern, and I originally heard this bird gobbling far to the east of me while I was standing beside an old abandoned farmhouse on a high ridgeline of pastureland 400 yards west of a north-south running road. After waiting a long time to hear a closer one so that I didn't have to walk as far, I finally gave up and started working my way towards the only turkey advertising for company. Once I'd crossed the road to my east and another mile of creek bottom land beyond it, I came up to the next north-south running road. The tom had continued to lure me along the whole way with his gobbles, and he was still going at it strong from another 1/4 of a mile to the east. That meant I had originally heard this bird from a total of 1-1/2 miles in distance. At that point I would've crossed the road and moved closer to where the tom was holed-up, except for one fact which stopped me in my tracks. There, parked alongside the roadway, was a truck with Louisiana plates. Someone else was already hunting there.

As an ethical turkey hunter there was only one thing to do, so I turned right back around and retraced my path. Re-climbing up to the high-ground vantage point and standing practically in my original footprints, I once again strained my ears to hopefully hear a tom somewhere within that big chunk of WIHA property. Unfortunately, the only thing making a peep nearby was a mockingbird trilling out a melodious tune from a brushy old fencerow.

With nothing to lose but dignity, I screamed out the loudest yelp that I could muster on a diaphragm call and surprisingly received a muted response. I would've sworn that it came from the same tom that I'd been listening to all morning, so I cranked out another call and this time I was quite sure of its answers origins...the very same bird that I'd hiked off in quest of a couple hours earlier was now responding from the same spot 1- 1/2 miles away! He continued to honor every calling effort I put out there, and it wasn't long before I could tell that he was indeed working his way down the creek bottom between us and coming closer. By the time he eventually climbed up on my ridgeline an hour later, there were nine hens tagging along behind him. Forthwith, he took the full brunt of my Winchester Supreme 5's like a champ. His spurs were wicked-sharp, too.

There is wild hemp growing all around this Kansas chicken coop

I love Eastern wild turkeys, and I love their habitat! Pulling into Pennsylvania after being out in the west for so long had me tingling like teenage puppy love, and when that first full-throated gobble greeted my ears the next morning, it resonated clear down into my very soul. And even though it was raining (the very first time all season that I'd hunted in rain), I felt like dancing in it.

Of course, six straight days of failure can change any turkey hunter's positive attitude and make a feller question whether he will *ever* be able to kill another turkey, and that is exactly what happened. Pennsylvania has the ability to wear a guy down at times, even though I've always found lots of turkeys in her beautiful rolling hills. Maybe it's because they're Easterns, or maybe it's the fairly difficult topography, or maybe it's the weather, or maybe it's the hunting pressure, or maybe it's simply a combination of all the above and so much more. All I know is that every time I shoot a tom in that state, it feels real, real good. That happened on Day 7.

The following morning I ran into some unexpected interference when a nesting Goshawk chased me away from a gobbling tom by screaming and frequently dive-bombing me. However, that turkey had been gobbling a bunch up to that point, so I didn't want to totally give up on him. Before dawn of the next day I came in from another direction and set up close to where he'd been carrying-on, and sure enough, as daylight crept in the tom started gobbling nearby. I was in great position and really thought that I'd slipped in unbeknownst of the hawk's attention…that is, until she spotted me putting on a camo glove and once again began screaming shrill and incessant insults at me. After the silly wench had made it crystal clear that she wasn't about to stop until I was gone from the scene, I stood up and began walking away. I just didn't feel like putting up with her crap any more. She was really messing with my serenity, and killing that turkey wasn't worth the hassle.

I hadn't taken but a few steps when that goofy bird hit me in back of the head like a ton of bricks! The force of the collision knocked my hat about twenty feet, and while I wasn't really injured by the blow, it certainly hurt. It also made me so mad that I was sorely tempted to pull up and shoot her off the limb from which she was glaring down at me, but I knew that her death would mean the slow starvation of her young chicks. I sure didn't want that guilt trip messing up my ju-ju! Picking up my hat, I turned around to face her and then walked out of there backwards so as not to give her another chance to clock me in the noggin again!

After a total of ten tough days in Pennsylvania I called it quits. The birds were being exceptionally obstinate that spring, and particularly hard to deal with. Even getting an answer to a call was, at the least, problematic. And gobbling after 7 a.m.? Forget it! When the sun doesn't set until after 8 o'clock at night, the hopeless act of awaiting gobbling from turkeys with their lips zipped shut can turn into long and boring days of nothingness. A guy can only take so many naps whiling away the time…

Doug, Craig, Bill, and me holding up all the turkeys we (didn't) kill

Having about a week left in the season, I drove on over to finish up in New York. This is truly one of my favorite destinations of them all, and my friends up there are like kin to me. However, I hadn't visited in three years because of the bitter family land-feud stemming from the deaths of Tony and Evelyn Bays. It was just too hard to see the farm being torn asunder from what I'd always known it to be. But, I missed this place and its people terribly, and I was eager to come back. There had been many changes during my time gone, and more were taking place. For one thing, there was now a big, beautiful finished lake where the "beefer pasture" had always been. I decided to park my van down beside it, rather than staying back at the deer camp, because of the fantastic view and exceptional fishing.

This lake had been in its planning stages for many years, so seeing it there didn't come as too much of a surprise. The far bigger shock was in learning that Jake and Janice had decided to split the sheets after 28 years together. I'd been coming up to New York since early in their marriage, and my annual visits had continued as they'd begun raising two great sons. I'd been there as they'd broken ground and built a new house, I'd shared their loss and mourned right alongside them as they suffered through the deaths of Jake's folks, and I'd witnessed the bitter aftermath when Jake and his siblings had parceled up the family farm and basically parted ways with each other because of it. Now, it looked like we were in for more heartbreak and sorrow, and I felt terrible for everyone involved.

I loved all of my Bays family, but I was particularly close with the youngest son Trevor. We'd been turkey hunting together since he was a tiny weed hopper, and now, at the age of 17, he'd grown into a full-blown outdoorsman of formidable talent. During my 3-year hiatus, Trevor had become involved with a group of similarly aged guys who did a lot of filming of their hunting and fishing exploits. They called themselves the Outdoor Adventure Team, and they were very tight-knit and always sharing fun exploits together. They were hoping to get some of our hunts on film, but we struck out on Day 1. Then, with Trev's buddy Wheeler running the camera, I connected on the following day to draw first blood.

Trevor and I once again gettin' it done in New York

One thing I noted in my journal during those first few days of hunting with Trevor and his buddies was how they had developed a certain skill-set reflective of being teenage turkey hunters in a target-rich environment. Whereas I had always hunted public land and thus spent most of my time deep in the woods patiently waiting on turkeys to gobble and give away their position, the methods these kids utilized were quite different. They almost exclusively drove from one farm to another at breakneck speeds in hopes of visually making contact with the birds. They wouldn't even slow down to glass into hidden nooks or crannies. If there wasn't a big tom puffed up and standing in a plowed field, we would tear off and drive like hell to the next farm on the list of places where they had permission to hunt. Being a turkey hunter of a certain age, this made me a nervous wreck. I wanted to put boots on dirt and go find turkeys or turkey sign, because *all* of their farms looked awesome and I knew fully-well that every single one of them held turkeys…whether visible from the road, or not!

The boys also held an almost (in my opinion) crippling fear of what turkeys are capable of doing, seeing, hearing, learning, and remembering. However, I noted that this was probably a good thing, because at their age they still had a lifetime ahead of them in which to acquire the knowledge that I had gained in my 30 years of turkey hunting. To be quite honest and blunt about it, these "kids" were already far ahead of me in a comparative way, since I hadn't even seen or heard my first gobbler until I was 23. In contrast, Trevor had been following along in my footsteps since he was seven or eight, and all the while picking up turkey hunting knowledge at a rapidly advanced pace due simply to how much greater the turkey population was in New York.

Trev really wanted to call in my turkeys for me. Nobody else had ever done that before, excepting of Don Foley's lame attempts at Tea Mountain, and I'd finally reached a stage in my turkey hunting career where that was acceptable. Plus, I had a hacking cough with terrible congestion, and I was drinking cough syrup and sucking on throat lozenges continually, so I didn't want to get that icky goop all over my mouth calls. For the entire duration of this trip I willingly turned the calling duties over to my young protégé, and he did a fine job of it, too. He was a little more tentative than I would've been, and worried too much about making mistakes, but again, that was to be expected at his tender age. With me occasionally prodding him on as I saw fit, he got the job done admirably.

On May 30 we almost took our first double together. We would've too, if Trevor hadn't missed his big tom all fuzzed up at 20 yards. I had waited on the report of his shotgun before pulling the trigger on a bird slightly further away, but while mine folded up dead as a wedge, the closer one ran and then flew away. Trevor was heartbroken and nearly inconsolable, even though I told him how I had missed a virtual truckload of turkeys in my life and hoped to miss many more. It just happens. That's turkey hunting. If you haven't missed any, then you haven't shot at nearly enough. Still, there were a few tears shed as we sat on a log rehashing what went wrong, and then I told him we would make amends the next time. Next time…

Next time ended up being the very next day, which was also the last day of turkey season. Both hunts occurred on ground owned and controlled by Jake's brother, who had been very reluctant to allow me access following the family breakup. He had finally consented this year, but only for his nephew's sake, and after the mini-fiasco of the previous day, Trevor and I came back for revenge on what Trevor believed to be the very same turkey which he'd missed. I couldn't say for sure, as there were a number of toms traveling from one side of the road to another, but that narrative was fine with me.

We had, indeed, seen a tom up there in the top field during late evening, so I was confident of his roost site nearby. Turkeys had been roosting in that same spot for as long as I'd been hunting the farm. The problem was in how to hunt the bird. The roost itself was on extremely steep ground sloping away to a wet bog. I felt certain that the gobbler would thus go the opposite direction; straight upwards into a series of fields separated by thin bands of grass running along the hill's contours. The first narrow strip of field next to the trees was in short hay, yet to be cut, while the second and third fields still showed corn stubble. Arriving very early, I put three DSD hens in the hay field, and then Trevor and I hunkered down low into the eight foot wide grass strip running along the field's upper edge. The grass was taller than our heads when we were seated, so it provided us plenty of cover.

At 4:40 a.m. I heard drumming. I was sure of it. Then, I heard it again. When I told Trevor to listen close, he heard it, too. The sound was coming from slightly to our left as we faced the treeline, and with Trevor seated on that side of me anyway, I felt real good about our situation so long as we weren't too visible out there sitting in the grass. I warned Trevor not to fidget around, and then I tried to make myself small as we awaited developments.

The weather was perfect, and yet, I heard not the first gobble. Not even distant toms were sounding off. That surprised me, but not nearly as much as the tom pitching out at 5:06 and landing about 40 yards to our left. One look at the faux ladies was all it took before the tom broke into drumming so loud that it was practically booming. Then, he advanced as only a lovelorn lothario can do. At 30 yards Trevor could stand the pressure no longer and laid him out, immediately shouting, "OH, YEAH!" before we glad-handed, hugged, and high-fived like a couple of fellers who'd never done this before. It was a heck of an ending to a great return to New York.

Well, so ended a fantastic and memorable 2012 season. It was the tenth year in a row of hunting at least 9 states, and for the 17th season straight I'd packed in more than 58 days of hunting. I'd also hunted Florida for the 23rd time since that first trip there in 1988 (including the last 18), and my New York

Trevor's last-day redemption gobbler from New York in 2012

A foggy and beautiful New York dawn with Trevor Bays

tally during the same timeframe now stood at 20 trips. I'd called in 52 toms in total, and we'd carried 19 of them out of the woods. Once I'd gotten past my initial troubles (FL) of seeing the target and hitting what I was shooting at, I'd tightened up and flown straight, with the only other miss all year being Trevor's faux paus on May 30. The kill figures were somewhat down from the norm, but still formidable, and I was quite pleased overall. Hopes were high as I began the planning stages for 2013.

Chapter 7

2013

Well, 2013 didn't go nearly as I'd anticipated. The first issue was that I bought a house. I hadn't really been looking for one, but then a deal became available that I just couldn't turn down. The house itself wasn't much to get excited about, but it sat on twelve acres of land surrounded on all sides by public property loaded with turkeys. How could I say "no" to that? Besides, with interest rates at record lows, it was a total no-brainer to go ahead and make the jump. And, while the house did need lots of work before it might ever be anything special, fixing up houses was how I earned a living. Only this time, I would be doing it on a place with my name on the title!

When I failed to draw tags in the lotteries of AZ, NV, and DE, it just seemed like the turkey gods were trying to tell me something, so I decided to seriously curtail my usual break-neck spring schedule and put off most of the states I'd intended to hunt until 2014. Hopefully by then, I could get back to a more "normal" year...at least, normal for me.

Of course, when I said that I was cutting back, I certainly didn't mean cutting out, and I was eagerly looking forward to Florida. That was a place I fully intended to hunt every year for my remaining days of walking upright. Truth be told, nothing short of death could've kept me away. Besides, I had people counting on me in helping them get their Osceolas.

My first three clients were the same father/son team of Tom and Scott Noren who had hunted with me in 2011, plus Dr. Tom's grandson Austin. Jen had come down to Florida with me once again, and we had been scouting for about a week and seeing several gobblers on the ground where I planned to take them on the Saturday opener. On Friday she helped me build a wonderful "log cabin" blind that was big enough to hide me and all three hunters, who were staying in an old trailer on the opposite side of the property. I felt really confident of us killing at least one or two toms the next morning. The only issue that had me worried was whether the 40 yearling calves penned up on that section of the farm most utilized by turkeys might destroy my blind overnight. By 3 a.m. I could take the worrying no more, so I went out to check on it.

Well, it was a good thing that I drove out there in the middle of the night, because my blind had indeed been torn to shreds. And, why wouldn't it have been? After all, I'd used fresh cut oak branches in its construction because of the green color the leaves added, and then I'd draped Spanish moss over top of everything. Instead of a blind, what I'd really built was a free candy store for all the cows! Anything that they hadn't eaten outright, they'd knocked over or stomped into the sand, and I had to rebuild the entire thing from scratch. But, this time I used only the dead trunks of trees and limbs which had previously served as the basic building materials for the original blind, and I delayed adding the Spanish moss until our return shortly before dawn.

I was also employing a new decoy strategy in 2013. Since I could drive out to my blind setups late at night or very early in the morning while the turkeys were still asleep (they usually roosted on the neighboring property most nights, anyway), I decided to put out an entire flock. I'd used gangs of decoys in the past by throwing in a few silhouettes with two or three full-bodies, but this year I would be utilizing an entire spread of Dave Smith's, which is a brand of decoy featuring incredibly lifelike paint schemes. Unlike some of their competitors, they are totally made in America, too.

For this hunt I put out a strutter with a tail made from real feathers, one jake, three feeding hens, two upright hens, and a resting hen. As I stood back and looked at more than $1,000 worth of decoys spread out in front of the blind, I shook my head in wonder at the irony of a fellow who basically thought of decoy use as cheating going to such measures. But, I was certain that any turkeys within eyesight of this flock (and we were hunting a flat cattle/sod farm where visibility in every direction was nearly a mile) couldn't help but come over to investigate. Turkeys are, after all, flocking creatures by nature, and a big rival flock in their territory would almost certainly create any of several reactions favorable to the hunters in my blind. Envy, anger, jealousy, gregariousness, or the simple quest for love...it didn't matter. Turkeys like hanging out with other turkeys, and I anticipated the real birds being unable to resist the magnetism of an entire flock of fakes.

When gobbling time arrived, we could hear a pair of toms off to the east of us and another pair due north. Dr. Tom wanted to do most of the calling for his grandson's first turkey, so after flydown I held back until I felt like the birds needed to hear something more exciting than his very low yelps, clucks and purrs on a wingbone. All of the gobbling we were hearing was quite distant, but every one of those toms ripped into my strident yelps on a glass and immediately began moving towards us. When they then answered Dr. Tom's next calling sequence, I put my trusted Cane Creek pot call away.

After two toms came into sight from around a cypress head at a range of about 300 yards, it was quite obvious when they first made visual contact with the DSD's: standing very tall, they stared at them for a few short moments and then broke into a run right at us! In less than a minute they were stalking confidently amongst our flock before bowing up into a confrontational chest-to-chest posture with my fake strutter. Very soon thereafter, Austin capably dispatched one of them, and following a few anxious moments when Scott had a little trouble getting rearranged for a crack at the second bird (who never even hesitated in his aggressive attack on the decoy), he too was sent flopping in the sand. Dr. Tom's previously stated main goal of getting both his son and grandson their first Osceolas had now been accomplished in the first 15 minutes of our hunt, and we still had at least two more toms nearby!

Although the other pair had been quieted by all the commotion coming from our blind, twenty minutes later I spotted a tom with multiple hens far out across the neighbor's property line. Then, I saw more red heads with them, as well as two rounded tail fans. When I yelped real loud on the glass call, Dr. Tom through his binoculars could see a number of necks stretch out gobbling, even though from the thousand yards between us we couldn't hear a thing. Despite the distance, every turkey in the flock immediately turned in our direction, and just like with the first pair, they came in a hurry. I'd already counted three toms, six jakes, and 21 hens long before they crossed under the barbed-wire fence separating our sod farm from the neighbor's.

The entire flock was soon intermingling with my decoys while totally ignoring two dead toms lying in the sand. Telling real from Memorex (quoting an old TV advertisement which capably ages me) was a virtual impossibility, for unless somebody was actively walking around or otherwise moving, every turkey or decoy looked like every other one surrounding them. Well, all except those three toms, who were getting ready to whoop my jake's plastic butt when Dr. Tom put a stop to such nonsense with emphatic finality.

It was a long time before the rest of the flock eventually wandered away, leaving behind three long-spurred limbhangers for three ecstatically grinning turkey hunters...and their equally tickled guide. What a hunt! I'm sure none of us will ever forget that one.

Dr. Tom Noren, Scott Noren, and Austin Cayer with their Osceola limbhanger triple

The guys then stayed for a few more days and hunted Green Swamp (Scott killed a bird there, too) while I guided John Patrick, my next client. When we called in ten hens with two toms at about 11 a.m. on our first morning, the results of using the DSD flock were very similar to opening day. The real turkeys completely accepted my faux flock as if they were long lost friends, and showed no inclination to leave after one of their own fell dead; thunderstruck. Just like that, my guiding duties were done in a minimal amount of time and I was free to relax and enjoy myself at The Swamp.

However, as usually happens, Green Swamp WMA wasn't eager to give up any of her prized turkeys. It was tough to even hear a bird, and days passed by without much to show for my efforts. There also seemed to be hunters everywhere I ventured, making a tough task even more so. I'd really wanted to take Jenny hunting at some point, but there was no way that I would subject her to such a madhouse. Yes; I was hoping to "set the hook" and get her fired up about the sport I so loved, but it needed to be a special situation with plenty of quick action. Jen hadn't grown up as a hunter, and up to that point in our relationship we'd only fished, frog-gigged, or gone after squirrels a time or two.

When my landowner called to tell me that he'd just seen three longbeards in a back pasture of the farm and that I was welcome to come kill one, I felt like this was the opportunity that I'd been waiting for. However, he warned me that they'd sprayed manure on all the hay fields a couple days earlier. It hadn't been just any manure, either. It was human sludge from the waste treatment plant. Doing that is perfectly legal in Florida, and it really makes the hay grow fast. But, it stinks to high heaven!

I wasn't quite sure how this would go over with Jen, although I certainly had my suspicions. Even before turning off the highway I could detect the smell of human poop, and as we pulled into the farm lane the odor of it was overpowering. One glance at my girlfriend scowling and holding a t-shirt over her nose told me all that I really needed to know without any words being spoken, so after a quick circuit around the farm to confirm that the three toms were still lounging under an oak tree in the back field with four hens, I never even slowed down as I drove right on out the gate. A twelve mile trip brought us into camp, and that's where I dropped Jenny at Marie Caudill's trailer. They could chit-chat until I got back, because even though the situation wasn't right for Jenny, there wasn't anything keeping me from filling a tag myownself in the "shithole!"

Marie Caudill and Jen Roberts became great friends in camp

A long strip of cypress swamp separated the last two fields from one another, so I figured that I could park my van on the near side and then slip around the edge of the heavy cover, emerging at its northern tip. From there I hoped to spot the flock, and then I could decide on a strategy for making a play at them.

The entire field where I chose to park had indeed been sprayed with manure, but it looked dried up and drivable. It wasn't. Only the top crust had baked hard in the sun, and everything below that was still gooping wet. No sooner had I pulled off the raised ranch road than my van became stuck in human manure three inches deep. When I attempted to back out, my tires slung sludge all over the front end of my van and up on the side mirrors, and when I tried to pull forward, the back end got coated likewise. In no time at all my tires were only spinning freely, without moving the van so much as an inch either forwards or backwards. I was stuck as a man can be, despite sitting on ground flat as a pancake, and even branches jammed under the back tires made no difference, whatsoever.

Realizing that there was no way to free myself alone, I texted the landowner a message which read thusly: "Have you ever heard the saying, "You've gotten yourself into this shit, so now you can damned-well get yourself out of it?" Well, I am indeed stuck in your shit, and I most certainly can't get out. Please help!!" He soon texted me back that he was tied up in town and couldn't be there for about 45 minutes, but help was on the way. He also stressed that it would be *me* hooking up the chains!

Deciding to try and make lemonade out of sour lemons, I grabbed my gun, vest, and a couple of hen decoys along with the strutter. Then, I tiptoed through the manure field and slipped into the edge of the cypress swamp. After working my way around its tangled mess, I crept out on the other side where I could see the entire last field, but there were no longer any turkeys visible there. I knew that they couldn't have gone far, so after placing my decoys underneath the same live oak where they'd all been standing previously, I sat back against a cypress in the edge of the swamp. When nothing answered a few calls on my diaphragm, I relaxed and got real comfortable to await the arrival of either turkeys, or the tow.

Sometime later I awoke to the sound of drumming. At first I thought it had been part of a dream, but then I realized that the music throbbing in my ears was *very* real. When I raised my head up from off of my chest, I could see three toms aggressively posturing around my strutter deke! The cover around me was so good that I could raise my binoculars and "grade" them out, and then I shot the one sporting the longest spurs. Halfway back to my van I saw the landowner's truck pulling in, and after a quick tow-strap snatch to free me up from the muck, I headed straight to town, where I spent twelve dollars in quarters at a car wash to clean my van. Then, I paid ten dollars at a motel for a long, hot shower!

During the next week I killed my second tom at Green Swamp and guided Bill's son William to a bird at Green Swamp West, which is a "Special Opportunity Hunt." These are areas where you apply as many times as you like for $5 per pop, and then if you're drawn it costs something like $125 extra. The hunt itself is five days long, and they're conducted on limited access property that is actively managed for wildlife. This is a good way to get an Osceola if you're lucky enough to draw a tag.

Overall, I was in Florida for 15 days in 2013. It was an up and down season, with lots of gobbling heard on some days, and none on most others. Then again, that's the way it usually goes on Florida's public ground. The weather was quite dry and very chilly, too. A couple times the temperature dropped as low as 28 degrees, and several other mornings it was in the low 30's. I sort of felt sorry for my thin-skinned local friends, because they aren't used to that stuff and nearly froze to death. I, on the other hand, loved it!

Doug Pickle, me, Kenny Dorman, and Miss Marie Caudill watch Bill George frying up some alligator

After leaving Florida I headed home. That's right: you read that short sentence correctly. I went home, started back to work, and slaved on my house for three weeks before ever even dreaming of hunting turkeys again. Boy; did that ever feel strange! Talk about your proverbial fish out of water.

As Indiana's youth season drew near, my old buddy Ron Ronk asked if I would come over to his farm in Sullivan County and take his daughter Suzie hunting. She had killed her first gobbler at only five years of age, but after that, had been blanked for the next three seasons. Ron claimed that it was because she got too nervous to pull the trigger, but I figured most of the blame probably fell at her parents' feet. Both Ron and De get really worked up in the presence of turkeys, and I was certain that some of their anxiety was being projected onto their daughter.

The Ronk's own a great farm which always holds turkeys, and one 19-acre isolated field surrounded by timber is like a magnet to the birds. You're likely to see turkeys in that place at any hour of the day. It seemed like a perfect spot to start our hunt, so I put a Double Bull blind right out in the middle of the bean stubble, with a DSD strutter standing 12 yards from us and overlooking three hen companions. De, Suzie, and I then crowded into the blind, while Ron and Jen watched from a permanent deer shooting hut on the field's edge.

Initial gobbling was a long way off, and so were the next four toms that I could hear. But, like I said, turkeys come to this field regularly, and I remained confident. An hour and a half after the first gobble a hen came into the field and immediately walked over to our setup. Her behavior was quite odd: she would sidle up to a hen decoy, bump up against it with her chest, and then freeze statue-still for at least a couple of minutes with her head lowered down into an obviously submissive posture. Then, she would walk over to the next decoy and do the same thing. After repeating these actions with all of the hens in my flock, she tired of being ignored and casually wandered away. By the time she left we hadn't heard so much as a single gobble in over an hour, leaving us with nothing to do but stare at the decoys, practice with our turkey calls, and try to keep warm. The temperature had actually dropped after daylight, and my feet were freezing. Being cold-natured as she was, I was sure that Jenny was shivering and miserable over in the shooting hut, too.

Suzie, on the other hand, was all good. She is a voracious reader, and with a book in her hands and some trail mix to snack on, she was quite content to wait things out. De eventually brought out a slate call for her, so Suzie then produced a long series of scratches and squeals…perfect accompaniment to my own cutts and hard yelps from a diaphragm. Then, when a pileated woodpecker sounded off to our left, a loud gobble rattled out from behind us...*close*! In looking out the back window of the blind, De hissed, "he's already in the field...75 yards... full strut!"

As I helped Suzie get her gun shouldered with its barrel sticking out the blind's front window, I could already hear the tom drumming. Then, I saw him moving fast toward us with his head down and shoulders up. At a range of about 35 yards he swung around to my side of the blind and passed by my window mere steps away. That's about when Suzie began laughing. I knew that it was totally involuntary and stemmed from pure nervousness, but try as she might, the laughing could not be contained despite Mom's admonitions to, "Shush!" I feared that our hunt would soon end in failure, but I needn't have worried... that lovelorn tom couldn't have possibly cared less about a little girl giggling from mere yards away! And then, once he'd rumbled up to my strutter deke, he couldn't have played his part any more to perfection; glowering there in an aggressive head-to-head posture, with tail fanned and neck partially raised. I calmly told Suzie that it was time to pull herself together and kill the tom before he lit into my pretty decoy, and probably to the shock of both me and her Mom, she focused-in, stopped laughing, and smote that gobbler dead as a wedge.

"I GOT HIM," she shouted! "LET ME OUT OF THIS BLIND!"

Suzie was ecstatic and jumping for joy, and so were her parents. Jen and I were, too. It was a *great* hunt, with great friends, and the story has been told and retold by all of us a million times...so far.

Jenny and I with laughing Suzie Ronk and her tom

I had drawn a pair of tags for Illinois in their annual lottery, and now I took a few days off from work to venture on over there. That state neighbors my own home of Indiana to the west, and since I was hunting in the Shawnee National Forest in Pope County, it was only about a 2- 1/2 hour drive. Previous hunts there had provided lots of gobbling and quick kills, but this time the events took some odd twists and turns. For one thing, I spent the first three days with Brian Stone. Brian had edited my first book, which was soon to be published, and in exchange for his work, I'd promised to teach him a few things about turkey hunting. The weather for those three days was cold and rainy, substantially hindering our prospects and severally limiting how much knowledge I was able to pass on, but we had a good time anyway. After he left the weather improved dramatically, and in the next three days I killed my two toms. Both of them ended up being true arse-kickers with long, hooked spurs. The only disappointment I suffered in the trip was in not finding very many morel mushrooms. They were just beginning to emerge during my stay, whereas in previous years I'd picked gobs and scads of them.

A great Illinois gobbler from 2013

Once back home, I helped Jenny move most of her stuff into my house and then I got back to work. Actually holding down a job during turkey season was something that I hadn't done since the mid 1980's, and it sure felt weird. The fact is, that I didn't like it even a little bit! When Jen told me after work one day that there had been a tom gobbling across the road from our house, I knew exactly what needed to be done, so I slipped over there the next morning intent on killing him before heading to the job site. Unfortunately, that danged turkey didn't get the memo of how he was supposed to act, and I couldn't convince him to fly down out of his roost tree no matter how hard I tried. Eventually, I was forced to slip away and punch a time clock, but not before vowing to come back the following day.

And a second one taken a few hours later from the same spot

Sure enough, the tom roosted in basically the very same spot that evening, and the next morning found me set up about 20 yards from where I'd been sitting the previous day. When I reached into my vest for the old familiar Cane Creek glass call and discovered that it was missing, I immediately realized that it must be laying in the leaves underneath the tree off to my right. I couldn't go get it without spooking the nearby tom, so I used my mouth calls instead, and this time the old rascal hammered back at anything I had to say and quickly came to me like he was on a string.

Only after he'd quit flopping in the leaves did I walk over to retrieve my favorite call, and what I found there instead broke my heart. Something (mouse, chipmunk, squirrel, or maybe even a *beaver*) had pulled two of my favorite strikers out from the call case and chewed them in half. The third striker was still held in place by the elastic band, but its tip was completely missing. The call itself, while at first glance apparently safe in the padded case, had actually been chewed, gnawed, and nibbled all the way around its rim like an ear of corn. Meanwhile, the bottom of the call looked like it had been scratched, clawed, and otherwise manhandled by something with very sharp claws. The good part is that it still sounded sweet when played with a back-up striker, but my trusty old Cane Creek looked like it had been tied to a logging chain and then dragged down a gravel road.

Still, it had been a great hunt, and the best part was that I had walked out from my own house before dawn and then returned through that same door an hour later with a gobbler slung over my shoulder. That was just about the coolest feeling I'd experienced in a very long time.

Neither the house, the tom, nor me were much to look at in 2013, but killing a gobbler on my home turf was something special

The following week I drove nine hours up to western Pennsylvania to hunt with Bill George, Doug Pickle, and Craig Morton at the George "camp" near Tionesta. Bill's daughter Belinda was there that spring too, and she hunted with me several times, In fact, she was right by my side as a good luck charm when I was able to wrap a tag around "Stumpy," a notorious tom who everyone else had been trying to kill. Doug had videoed this tom parading around a neighboring camp yard a few days before my arrival, and we had all ogled over his incredibly long spurs easily visible on the TV screen. Belinda and I almost made the mistake on the fateful afternoon of his demise by allowing the hot and muggy weather to propel us towards Haller's General Store for ice-cream, but then we spotted a tom and several hens beside another camp house as we were driving out. Pulling on down the road a bit and slipping into place up higher on the ridge, I eventually was able to call in the hens with a mixture of yelping, scratching in the leaves, and drumming. The gobbler couldn't stand to see his girls leave him, so he followed along behind them. It was Stumpy, and his daggers were 1- 7/16 inches long!

Belinda and I in Pennsylvania with Stumpy

Two days later I sort of made amends for killing Stumpy by calling in a different bird for Doug. That was it, though...the season came to an end and we all had to go on home. Despite maddeningly fluctuating weather for the entire 7-day duration of the trip, it ended up being a fine time had by all. Everyone in camp killed at least one bird, including Belinda.

I knew going into 2013 that it would be a season unlike any that I'd known for a very long time; a year when I would not be trying to cram as many days of hunting into as many states as I could. The main reason, as stated earlier, was because of the house purchase, and while I'd done a bunch of work on fixing it up before heading for Florida, I had left home with 1/3 of the roof covered by a tarp. Once I'd left the Sunshine State, I'd rushed home to get that roofing task completed, and then I'd stayed home and returned to work at my real job, squeezing in only a couple of other states. Forfeiting most of the spring like that was a necessary evil and a huge sacrifice, but I felt like it would be worth it in the end. I certainly didn't like the way 2013 had progressed in fits and starts, with no continuity, but there was no other way. Even then, I'd made good use of every opportunity and finished up the season having hunted 32 days in four states...a decent tally for any normal working man, but figures that left me feeling extremely disappointed and craving so much more. I *needed* to be turkey hunting from March until June in order to feel like myself. That's the way I'd designed my life so many years earlier, and nothing less than that would do. If I could get enough done on the house during the upcoming nine months, I had full intentions of making amends in 2014 and never again looking back with regrets.

A pretty Florida oak hammock

Chapter 8

2014

My first client of the year in Florida was a Pakistani Muslim from northern Ontario, Canada named Asif Majid. He was a super-nice fella, and we had a great hunt. The day started out with two toms gobbling real well from deep into the neighbor's property. My confidence was bolstered when both birds answered calls on a glass pot and came towards us, but one of them turned back around and faded away. However, the second tom advanced steadily, albeit very slowly. When I eventually spied him all fuzzed up in the edge of our pasture, I understood why it had taken so long to arrive; the gobbler was limping terribly and could barely walk. It looked like he was in a great deal of pain. And yet, the old warrior remained in a full strut and hobbled steadily on towards my flock of DSD's comprised of a strutter, two jakes, five upright hens, three feeding hens, and two laying-down hens.

It took this crippled bird about 20 minutes to cover the last 70 yards between us, and I could hear him drumming the whole way. Once in amongst my flock, he postured up against the strutter decoy like he was ready for a fight despite his substantial physical liabilities and I told Asif that it was time to put the gobbler out of his misery. He folded up neat as a pin at the shot. Being a Muslim, Asif then slit the bird's throat and said a prayer over him to make the meat kosher. When that was done we headed back to camp with a trophy of a bird weighing almost 20 pounds and sporting a beard of 11- 5/8 inches. He had only a single spur, on his bad leg, but it measured a very respectable 1- 3/16 inches. The other spur had been sheared off so long ago that it had totally healed over. I wondered if this was one of the surviving toms from two years earlier, when I'd brought the beer-sipping Texas boys to this same pasture and we'd witnessed a pair of birds (one totally spurless, and the other having only a single spur) flog the bejesus out of their dead partner.

A necropsy during the cleaning process revealed that the tom had broken his knee at some point, and it had healed over with a big calcium deposit which rendered the leg completely inflexible and unbendable. His drumstick was tiny, with only scant withered muscle. The amount of damage this bird had endured left me once again amazed by the toughness and resiliency of the wild turkey. They can persevere like few other animals and totally ignore devastating injuries in their unwavering quest to breed or fight as need be.

After all of the camp crew had slowly trickled in throughout the morning hours and everyone had a chance to tell their tales of woe or victory, it was decided that a trip to town for lunch was in order. The local guys had been raving about a place that was famous for their ribs, fish, and fried chicken gizzards located in the very heart of Lakeland. Once Asif had pulled up the address on his smart phone, off we went in quest...six vehicles loaded down with 15 hungry hunters.

As we made our way into town and were nearing the restaurant I began laughing, so Asif asked me what was so funny. I told him, "Well, here we have a veritable gang of redneck turkey hunters in a caravan of trucks snaking their way through the side streets, back alleys, and traffic snarls of downtown Lakeland, Florida, all while being led by a Pakistani Muslim from northern Ontario, Canada who is taking us to the best place in town for pork ribs. The ironies are just too overwhelming." We both laughed at that, and once we finally arrived at our destination, Asif ordered the fish.

Asif and his crippled Osceola trophy tom

My next two guys were already in camp waiting for their opportunity to hunt, so by 3 o'clock we were back in a blind. Although we did succeed in working a couple of toms, they stayed with the real feathers in their company rather than leave them for the fakes in my flock. The next day also saw us struggling to close the deal, but early in the afternoon a great big gobbler was on his way to a meeting with destiny and rapidly closing the 100 yards between us when, quite suddenly and seemingly out of nowhere, a pair of uppity upstart toms came on the scene and began chasing him away. When I yelped hard on a diaphragm, both of the gangster gobblers threw on the brakes, turned on a dime, and came right to us. The big tom was timidly trailing behind them by 50 yards or so, but my guys in the blind had no intentions whatsoever of waiting for him to arrive while there were two perfectly fine Osceola gobblers cozying up to my spread of dekes. The range was 23 yards, and after a "3...2...1...SHOOT!" countdown, both of them were flopping in the sand.

David Rogers and Charlie Southworth with an afternoon double

I drove my final paying client right back in there the next morning, but inadvertently drifted off the main road and got the van stuck in some loose sand. Thus, I had to carry my blind, our chairs, and all 14 decoys the final 300 yards. When three hens and a tom then ran up to us an hour after daylight, it made me forget all about those early hardships. The landowner was more than happy to give me a little tug out of my predicament after I handed him yet another guiding fee.

Now freed up to hunt Green Swamp on my own, I struck out the first day before calling in a real good'un the following morning by using mostly voice-generated spitting and drumming, along with some barely audible "flock talk" from a diaphragm. Public land toms hear plenty of fake hen yelps from the hordes of hunters who trample that ground to death all season long, so I think it sometimes behooves a feller to mix it up and try different things. I'd been using tactics like that to my benefit often over the last few years.

I do almost all of my Florida turkey hunting at Green Swamp WMA; not because it's a great place to hunt, but rather, because I've hunted it since 1988 and I know a lot of that 55,000 acres like I know the back of my hand. There are many places in Florida that offer *far* superior hunting opportunities. In fact, I tell people all the time that if I had a son or daughter and I wanted to help them kill an Osceola, just about the last place on earth that we would go would be Green Swamp. I mean that, too!

Well, there's another WMA where I occasionally hunt, but it's one which I most certainly will not mention here by name. This secret spot is only accessible with a Quota Permit, and the only way to draw one of those is by acquiring preference points from failing in the lottery several years in a row. I only get to hunt there once in a while, but 2014 was one of those times.

In a certain hidden honey-hole of that area lays a raised trail (an old tram line) that leads back through a formidable swamp, and turkeys habitually like to parade up and down it. On "scout day," I built a beautiful cabbage palm frond blind in a strategic location which would allow me to shoot said turkeys, but when I arrived early the next morning, there was already a vehicle parked at the trailhead campsite. This development discombobulated me, because I'd been the very first guy in line and nobody else could've possibly beaten me to the spot. Then, I noticed dew on the car's windshield, meaning that it had been there overnight. Camping is outlawed in this WMA during turkey hunts, so whoever had parked there was doing it illegally. Either that, or else someone had planted a "decoy" car to make people think another hunter was already there. My morals and ethics wouldn't allow me to simply pull in beside another vehicle, so I drove on down the road a quarter mile. Then, I slipped back and stood just out of sight around a corner of the road. I needed to find out if that car's owner was a turkey hunter before I could even think about walking on in to my blind.

As dawn began cracking, I could hear someone rousing around the campsite. They were making quite a bit of racket, too. It sounded like they might even be fixing breakfast, and then I definitely smelled bacon. No self-respecting turkey hunter would be carrying on like that so close to gobbling time, so I figured that it was ok to make my move. Sure enough, when I rounded the corner I saw a big guy sitting at the picnic table, and he wasn't wearing any camo. As I strolled on by I said, "Good morning," but he didn't reply. "Sorry to disturb you." Again; he said nothing.

Well, I considered the lack of any response to be pretty danged rude, so now I certainly didn't feel the least bit bad about hunting there. Heading into the swamp, I quietly slipped into my blind which was only about 150 yards from the trailhead, and I hadn't been there more than a minute before a fairly close gobble shattered the morning stillness. I let the tom belt out three or four more love songs before I uttered a perfectly sleepy-sounding tree yelp, and he thundered back in response. His next gobble a couple minutes later was closer, and I cut it off with a short cutt sequence. When he gobbled back at that, I answered with a yelp. The next gobble a minute later came from only 100 yards out. One last cutt/yelp into the tail end of his final gobble was all that I ever intended to say, and I put my Cane Creek glass down in the leaves beside my leg. I wouldn't be needing it again.

I love the sound a turkey makes as he's walking through water. Ploop, ploop, ploop. The swamp on both sides of the trail was standing water, so I knew that I would hear this beautiful music as he approached. Five minutes later, I did. Next, I heard the crunching of leaves as he left the water and began climbing up onto my levee-like trail, and then I saw a glowing white orb as it emerged from the line of cypress trees between us. When he blew up into a full strut moments later, I had already long been staring at him over the raised rib of my Benelli and planning to pull the trigger just as soon as he raised his head to look around. Instead, he suddenly gobbled with his neck thrust out parallel with the ground, and when he just left it in that position for a long time, I laid him out good and proper.

The permit for this area allowed me to bring a guest, so the next morning I "carried" Doug Pickle in there with me. We had scouted the previous afternoon and found lots of strut marks and huge turkey tracks in a sandy road, but at dusk we also heard turkeys gobbling in two other spots far from there. For the next morning our Plan A would be the strut marks, with the gobbling birds being back-up Plans B and C.

Nothing gobbled at Plan A. Not a peep. We gave it the old college try, but when it finally became obvious that this spot wasn't going to produce, we jumped in the truck and hot-rodded on down the road to Plan B. It was 9 o'clock before we got

The cabbage frond blind can be seen over my left shoulder

there, but with Doug's persistent and excellent owl hooting, a tom finally piped up back in the swamp a good ways.

Doug does not like water, and he ain't too fond of cottonmouth moccasins, either. However, there wasn't the first sliver of dry ground anywhere between us and that turkey, so I told him to follow behind me while I broke trail through the dead limbs, spider webs, and cabbage palms of a very dense and wet swamp. After going a few yards, I looked back and saw that he was slipping along trying not to make any noise or get his feet wet...both of which were *impossibilities* in that mess! "Come on," I hissed. "That tom doesn't care about a little noise. He'll just think we're a bunch of wild hogs, and turkeys hear those all the time."

Sloshing onward, we hadn't gone another 100 yards before the tom gobbled again, and he was CLOSE! I guess that swamp had muffled his earlier gobbles and made me think that he was much further away than reality dictated. There was no place good to sit down, as we were still wading in water, so I told Doug to just lean up against a cypress tree and act like he was duck hunting in Arkansas flooded timber. The only problem was that Doug had never hunted in Arkansas flooded timber!

Now, what I'm going to tell you right here is the gospel truth. I know it as fact, only because I witnessed the events with my own eyes, and I ain't lying. One call from my diaphragm and that turkey was homed in on us like a guided missile, and he drummed the whole way. Doug was ten yards in front of me, leaning up against a tree, and when that turkey appeared 20 yards on the other side of him, the bird was cutting a "V" through a stretch of standing water in an opening approximately 15 yards across. I assumed that it was shallow water only a couple inches deep, but when Doug subsequently fired, crippled the tom, and then gave chase, he disappeared from view and floated his hat in that very same spot! Three more times he did that, too, as he would slip and fall, come up sputtering, try to run again, trip over something else in the depths of that inky-black water, fall, and repeat. By the time he'd finally crossed that pool, the wounded tom had almost gotten away, but luckily for us, he'd decided to try and hide alongside a fallen log. Only his head was sticking up out of the water at that point, so Doug shot him like a coot.

Few moments spent in the turkey woods have been funnier than watching that show, and when Doug finally splashed back across to me towing a very dead gobbler, it was an absolute tie in terms of who was the most sopping wet. But, I swear right here and now that the stretch of water where we both watched his turkey strutting was three feet deep. I don't know if he was floating as he crossed it, or magically elevating like a danged hovercraft, but Doug and I both saw him do it.

My next successful hunt was one that I'm more proud of than just about any other in my life. I've tried my darndest to convey in these books the deep

Doug Pickle and his swamp gobbler after they'd dried out

respect and love that I held for David Caudill. He was one of the finest turkey hunters I've ever known, and one of my favorite people on this green earth. The man knew more about wild turkeys and how to hunt them than could even be fathomed by an ordinary human being, and he was a walking, talking fountain of stories told about his long and distinguished life as a man devoted to gaining knowledge about our favorite gamebird. I never knew him to speak anything other than the straight truth, too. No exaggeration and no bullshit. If David Caudill said something, you could take that to the bank and get a loan on it.

As a child of the depression, David had grown up in a time when his family basically lived off of what the land could supply, and when Florida's vastness and rugged wilderness held aplenty. He was truly a monument to that era, and I never tired of listening to what he was always so willing to share. David was by all weights and measures the Patriarch of our Florida turkey camp, and loved by every single one of us who dwell there.

Two seasons prior to this story, Bill and I had put David on the gobbler which landed on an "X" that Bill had scratched in a sandy road of Green Swamp. Now, in 2014, David had a permit for Green Swamp West, which was one of those Special Opportunity Hunts. He was 86 years old at the time, and also possessed a handicapped permit which allowed him to drive on any road so marked as "Handicapped Accessible." I had the distinct pleasure and honor of accompanying David during three of those days at "West," culminating in a hunt which left both of us grinning like idiots and jabbering like monkeys. Herewith is the tale:

David and his long-time great friend Craig Morton had spent the previous hunt period at GSW without killing a bird, but they'd heard several in Unit A where their permit was valid. Craig then had to go home, so I was afforded the opportunity to serve as David's "guide." Yeah; like he really needed that! This was a man who had quite literally held thousands of turkeys in his hands (both alive and dead) during his long and illustrious lifetime as a turkey trapper and guide, and he'd already forgotten more about wild turkey behavior than I will ever learn. There wasn't anything that I could bring to the table other than a good set of ears, since David was pretty-much deaf as a stone. He was also very frail and couldn't walk far without a helping hand.

On Day 1 of the hunt we didn't hear any turkeys or see much sign where David and Craig had earlier erected a pop-up blind, but in driving around during the afternoon hours on a sandy handicapped road we eventually found a place that was littered with dust bowls, big gobbler tracks, and strut marks. Immediately, we went back and took down the blind, then returned and put it in a strategic location between the road with all the strut marks and a real pretty cypress pond extensively rooted up by wild hogs. Green, twin-leafed Pinkroot shoots carpeted the turned-over pond soil, which had also been seriously tracked up by turkeys. It was a really beautiful place and just screamed, "TURKEY" to both David and me, so we were very excited for the next day's hunt!

Long before dawn I'd already spread out ten DSD's in the Pinkroot patch and along the sandy road, but we only heard one distant gobble in the first few hours. Then, a bird piped up to the south of us and began easing our way. My hopes soared when he subsequently stepped into the far edge of the pond and gobbled at a call, but for the next twenty minutes that he was visible over there strutting, I had the distinct impression that he could see hens on the other side of him that he had no intentions of leaving. Eventually, he faded back into the heavy cover in that direction, and although he would still answer my calls, his gobbles just kept getting further and further away.

David had really been struggling during the last two days with his hearing aids. They would screech and squeal loudly all day long, and I don't think he ever did hear any of the numerous gobbles which that bird had bellowed out from only a hundred yards away. But, just seeing the tom had given my friend a tremendous boost of energy, and that had him anxious and looking forward to the 'morrow's hunt. Whether David hunted on any given day was never a foregone conclusion in those later years of his life, as sometimes he just didn't feel well, but I could tell by the excitement in his voice that we would definitely be coming back. After moving the blind a little bit closer to where the tom had reached his closest point to us (63 yards), we were ready for whatever a new dawn might usher in.

The following day was cold, starting off in the very low 30's and never rising out of the 60's. Floridians do not like cold weather, and at 86 years old, David *especially* didn't cotton to it! But, Bill and I teamed up to make David comfy as a bug in a rug. First, I decked him out in a warm jacket and a fleece balaclava. Then, I brought along the thick camo comforter that I use on my cot, and wrapped it around him like a cocoon. Finally, the piece de resistance...Bill supplied a propane powered heater which made the blind warm as toast bread.

As mentioned previously, David's hearing aids had been acting up. After determining back at home that the adjuster was missing, he'd scrummaged around in a drawer and found an old pair that had originally cost him $140 (new ones were $4000!), and they seemed to work quite well. In fact, we had a lively conversation while driving to the hunting area, and I didn't even need to yell or repeat myself a single time. Then, at 7:11 a.m. a crow flying due south of the blind and about 200 yards away cawed loudly, in turn causing a turkey directly below it to gobble…a beautiful sound which David actually heard! He was obviously thrilled by this development, and the excitement in his eyes made them glimmer even in the darkened blind.

Not long afterwards, a hen near the tom yelped real lightly and David heard that subtle sound, too. We had spoken just the previous day about his inability to pick up hen talk, and he'd told me that it had been a long, long time since he'd heard one. I could tell that this was a painful admission from a man who loved the wild turkey and all of their varied vocabulary so much, and now, knowing that he could hear sounds which hadn't graced his ears in forever made my heart swell with happiness for him.

Over the next few minutes I detected several other hens making real light tree talk in the roost, and David heard every single one of them. Each time my radar ears picked up on another note of turkey music I would glance over to see David cocking his head or leaning closer to the windows with a look of wonder and excitement on his face, so I knew that he was receiving the full audio of the morning's hunt. He even perked up when a vireo warbled out a melodious little tune right beside the blind, and commented several times about other songbirds in our vicinity, as well.

At 7:20 I saw a turkey pitch down. Up to that point I hadn't said anything, but now I sent out a few light yelps. Then, I followed that up with a sharp two-note yelp and a louder five-noter, and the tom hammered out a gobble in response. I didn't want to be too aggressive with my calling for fear of running the tom's hens away from any perceived competition (me), but I most certainly wanted them to know that some other girls were in the neighborhood. After all, I had once again put out a 10-pack of decoys, and that many turkeys would naturally be saying *something* so early in the morning. It was unlikely that I could pull the tom away from the real feathers surrounding him anyway, so I needed to gently work the hens and bring them over. During the next twenty minutes the girls and I exchanged morning pleasantries several times, and the tom gobbled sporadically at whichever of us most tickled his ear.

It was so beautiful where we sat! That lush green carpet of pinkroot highlighted against the black rooted-up soil and gray dwarf cypress trees on the other side of the pond rising up through a thin layer of ground fog which hung in the air between us was absolutely enchanting. The view was totally mesmerizing, but not nearly so much as what was soon to follow, for immediately after I'd just heard my first drumming of the morning and turned to tell David about it, he excitedly whispered back, "There he is!" Looking out the blind's window, I saw the tom all fuzzed up and spinning in circles about a hundred yards away. Onward he came, as the drumming grew louder and louder, until suddenly David turned to face me again with his eyes wide as saucers. "DOC," he gruffly rasped, "I JUST HEARD DRUMMING! I HAVEN'T HEARD THAT SOUND IN 30 YEARS!"

If our hunt had ended right at that very second it would've already been the highlight of the year and a tremendous success. However, things were just about to get even better. Once the tom spotted my male decoy, he lowered his head, raised his shoulders, and came on a steady march until he was face-to-face with the fake strutter. Then, he fuzzed back up into a posture which absolutely no one could mistake for anything other than pure aggression. Intimidation didn't work out very well for the tom at that point, though, because David was already looking at him down the vented rib of his shotgun, and when the old boy periscoped up his head to survey the next move from his hated adversary, he caught a devastating load of shotgun pellets upside his noggin.

David was thrilled beyond measure, and so was I. As we sat there rehashing and recounting every glorious detail of the hunt, David confided that this was the first time anyone else had called up a turkey for him. It was also the first time he'd ever seen a tom come in to a strutter decoy, and that had impressed him immensely. He then said that if he thought his life's longevity warranted the investment, he would go out and buy one that very afternoon, but that he didn't really know if he would be around the following spring, or, if alive, whether he would still be able to hunt. That was a very sobering thought for me to absorb on such a wondrous occasion, but then we rehashed the hunt one more glorious time before walking out of the woods grinnin' and jabberin' just like I said in the opening paragraph.

Calling in that bird for David had been a watermark moment for me, but my main concern was in how it might affect *him*. Perhaps naively, I was hopeful that the excitement it generated might serve to rejuvenate his spirits and give him a reason to look forward to planning for the following spring and dreaming of additional battles with the wild turkey. I wanted my friend to once again

David Caudill's last turkey...one of the proudest moments of my life

live for the thrill of the pursuit, and be optimistic about what the future might hold. Yes; my reasons for inspiring Davod might've been somewhat selfish, but he had been in a steady rate of decline for quite some time, and to be perfectly honest about it, I wasn't ready to say goodbye.

However, time slows down for nobody, and my deep-down fears that our first and only bird taken together might also be the final tom of David's long and illustrious life eventually came to be when he passed away two years later. I'll offer more about that in the appropriate chapter, but for now I will say that I continue to wear our 2014 GSW hunt proudly on my sleeve as a badge of honor; a day when I was not only the first, but also the last person to call in a tom for this great man.

Georgia was up next, and I started out by hunting in a place where I'd never been before called Cedar Creek WMA, in the Oconee National Forest. There were certainly turkeys to be found in that area, but most of those heard during the first part of my trip lived (and stayed) on private land adjacent to the public. I probably should've been more demoralized than I was following a long string of failures, but my attitude remained good and I stayed hopeful in believing that sooner or later the luck would turn in my favor. And then, it *finally* did on the afternoon of the ninth day. That's when I fired up a hen which came right up to me and hung around scratching and pecking at my feet for nearly half an hour, while far behind her I caught sight of a strutting tom. The old boy was very wary and alert, but the hen's enthusiastic scratching eventually broke down his resistance and he slipped in to stand tall at short range. I was more than ready and able to capitalize.

A dandy Georgia gobbler with 1- 1/4" hooks and an 11" beard

Five days later I managed to scratch down a second bird before heading over to Piedmont NWR, where I'd drawn a tag during their winter lottery. This was a highly pressured area and I didn't much care for it, but at mid-day I found a tom everyone else had overlooked and then I called him in pretty as you please. I promptly screwed that up *bigtime*!

My persistent vision troubles were to blame for this one. I simply tried to make the final adjustment of aligning on the incoming tom while I *thought* that he was behind ample cover, when in fact, he wasn't. That old, familiar "take advantage of every opportunity given" adage began ringing in my ears.

At that point I could've simply moved on to another state and left Georgia behind, but I had a lot of time invested and I was determined to fill that third tag. Towards doing that, I decided to move my operations up into the mountains, which had finally begun to green up and look more "spring-like." Once there it didn't take long to start finding birds, but alas; just because I was hearing and seeing turkeys didn't mean that I could actually *kill* one! Another frustrating week passed by without a trigger pull, and due at least in part to my missed opportunity at Piedmont, I found that my attitude was spiraling downward. My last journal entry made before heading north was an epitaph-laced tirade that would make a sailor blush.

Having now hunted the Peach State a total of 24 days straight and thus been forced to cancel planned trips to Tennessee and North Carolina while my mind reeled in a psychological state of increasing agitation and vex, I was bound and determined to kill that final tom or go down in flames trying. However, there was no way that I would miss Indiana's Wednesday opener. I also had a permit slated to begin on Thursday in Illinois, but if things went well in those two places, I hoped to come right back and try to find that one Georgia mountain turkey which was willing to sacrifice his life for my mental well-being.

Gary Shepherd hunted with me on opening day back home. Mostly due to the self-imposed and manic-driven craziness with how I'd conducted my seasons during the last decade or so, Gary and I hadn't spent much time together since 2003. You will probably recall some stories that I've shared about Gary and my cousin Bob Torrance from those earlier times. Well, Bob was once again living out in the boondocks, and he had lots of turkeys around his house, so the three of us had a bit of a reunion there. After we failed to kill any turkeys, I took off for Pope County in southern Illinois with plans to meet up with Gary again the following week. He had a farmer friend with lots of ground in Lawrence County, and was anxious for me to come up and help him kill his first turkey. Gary and I both had tags for that county, as well, besides the two I'd drawn for Pope.

The first day in Pope County was a windy bust, but I found lots of scratchings and fresh sign on a wooded ridgeline. It then rained all night long, only to quit about 4 a.m., and at daylight a tom gobbled close to the scratched up area. The damp leaves allowed me to silently move in and get set up only 100 yards away, and although I seldom call to a roosted gobbler out of fear of keeping him in the tree too long, I gave this bird a single set of tree yelps. He practically tore the sky open in responding. A minute or so later I glimpsed the tom gliding towards me, and although I couldn't see him when he hit the ground, I heard the impact and subsequent drumming. Not long thereafter, I was standing on his neck.

A second bird 200 yards away gobbled at the shot, and then he gobbled three more times before I could carry my dead tom back to the setup tree. He then gobbled one more time to a yelp on a glass call before shutting up completely. I gave him about an hour to silently drift in, and then I hung my turkey up in a dogwood tree and commenced a long hike to another favorite spot. When that place didn't pan out I circled back to pick up my dead gobbler. It was 9 o'clock by then, and after tucking up into my original setup spot and calling a little bit, I kept thinking that I was hearing the "chump" at the beginning of a tom's drumming sequence. The wind was gusting heavily by then, so I couldn't be sure. However, promptly at 10:10 I yelped fairly loud into the wind and a turkey definitely gobbled east of me. My next yelp got no response, but it didn't matter…I *knew* that this bird was coming in! Within a minute I saw not one, but two toms approaching, and I shot the strutter. Both of these dead gobblers killed from the same setup tree were absolute brutes. In fact, they ranked #1 and #8 at the time in my own personal record list of turkeys as scored by the NWTF system which I'd modified so many years earlier. They still hold the #2 and #9 spots even today.

Returning to Indiana, I next took out Bob's adopted son Tyson. I had tried to get him a turkey back when he was only six years old, but he hadn't seen the tom that I'd called in to about a dozen yards. I didn't learn until later from his mom Tabby that he was supposed to be wearing his eye glasses. Tyson was now 12 years old and about six feet tall, but quite gangly and fairly uncoordinated. Too much growth in a young body, I suppose, with lots of "baby fat." His footwear were a pair of fur-lined "muck" boots too big for his feet, and they didn't afford him very good traction on the steep hills on which we were hunting down around Madison, Indiana. After our first day afield I decided that the best options for getting this kid a bird was to find a good spot and stay put in a blind. Tyson made way too much noise when following behind me, and he couldn't sit still for very long whenever we set up against a tree. Taking kids turkey hunting can often times be a challenge!

Lo and behold, the very next day things went far better than I could've ever imagined when a jake came charging in to my decoys. Tyson absolutely waylaid him from a range of 17 yards, but he'd never shot a turkey load before and the kick of my Benelli knocked him clean off of his stool. As I tried to control my laughter, he looked up with eyes and jaw wide open before exclaiming, "DANG!" But, his first turkey lay flopping in the leaves. On the way back to the house I fired up another gobbler and soon thereafter filled my own tag. It was a great morning of hunting with young Tyson, and we made some fun memories along the way.

Gary's buddy Louie Vinnard is a big-time farmer in Illinois, with a lot of his ground bordering the Indiana state line defined by the Wabash River. Louie had never killed a gobbler before, but his sweetheart of a wife Lynn despised turkeys of any shape or sex, and she encouraged us to "kill 'em all." We assured her that we would try our best to knock some off, but we only had three tags and they were for toms only.

The first day we came painfully close to getting one or two of those tags wrapped around scaly legs, but the fickle winds of fate only tortured us with close calls and "what if's." At noon we stopped in at a little roadside bar for lunch, and when we opened the door it was like living out an episode of the TV show "Cheers" where everyone at the bar always greets George Wendt's character entrance with a collective, "NORM!"

"LOUIE!"

They all wanted to know why he was wearing camo clothing, too. I suppose none of them had ever seen Louie in anything other than farming duds or a Sunday suit. During lunch a fellow came over to the table and told Louie that he'd been seeing five huge gobblers at 10 o'clock every day, parading up on the river levee at mile marker such-and-such. This guy was a commercial fisherman, so he cruised back and forth on the river all the time. The Wabash is bordered by these tall, grassy levees to control flooding, and they stretch along its banks for many, many miles. The spot this guy described was on Louie's land, so the following day, after striking out again due to nothing but pure, dumb, bad luck, the three of us arrived at the levee promptly at 9:15.

The quandary was in how to hunt there. A guy living a couple miles further up river was a long distance runner, and he'd mowed the levee top for a place to train. It looked like a manicured lawn up there. With no other options, I decided to gamble. Putting a jake and hen decoys in the mowed strip, I then erected my Double Bull popup blind 25 yards away. The blind itself barely fit on the flat top of the levee. Then, we climbed inside to await the arrival of those "huge" toms.

By 10:30 nothing had shown up except for the fisherman's boat slowing to look at us and wave, but not long after that I got a gobbled response to a loud call. That excited all of us, and it wasn't but a few minutes later when Louie said, "Is that a crow on the levee?" I looked out the blind window and said, "Oh, hell no... it's a gobbler!" There, 200 yards away from us, stood a big ole tom. No sooner had I spoke, than he craned his neck and head to full height, gazed hard at the decoys for a few seconds, and then began a steady march in our direction.

Louie's chair was already pointed at the approaching tom, but Gary's was faced in the opposite direction so that he could cover our flank. I wanted Gary to be sitting beside his friend to watch the show, so I told him to stand up and let me rearrange the chairs. I intended to kneel on my knees behind them. We were all so excited! This was really gonna work and Louie was just about to kill his first gobbler in a matter of a few more moments...

And then, like a tornado had descended from the heavens and lifted them both away, the blind and Gary were simply gone! It was only Louie and I, naked and exposed to the world like a boil on a baby's ass cheek, with an incredulous tom staring at us from a hundred yards away. He didn't stay there very long!

Gary's litany of curse words broke the spell of our confusion, and we looked down towards the river's edge to see a tangled mass of camo at the bottom of the long slope of the levee, with Gary wadded up inside of it! In trying to keep back while I was rearranging his chair, Gary had inadvertently stepped or been nudged over the edge of the levee top and lost his balance. Then, he'd tumbled against the blind wall and fallen, taking the blind with him. His gun had been safely shouldered at the time of the mishap, but now its muzzle was sticking out of the torn roof of my fairly-new and expensive Double Bull blind, and judging by the dialog emanating from within the crumpled cloth, Gary wasn't very happy about that, either!

Louie and I, on the other hand, had recovered from our initial shock and now we could barely control our laughter. No; I take that back. We could not control our laughter, but only after calling down to Gary and making sure that he was physically ok from his lengthy descent. He assured us that he was fine, other than a bruised and battered ego, and he felt ashamed and embarrassed for ruining Louie's chance of killing a turkey. As I slid down the levee to help extricate my friend from his tangled entrapment, I assured him that the value of mirth provided by the mishap far outweighed any excitement that a dead turkey would've generated, while Louie laughed his agreement from atop the levee. I don't know if I have ever laughed so hard during a turkey hunt, and at dinner that night with Lynn, Gary's wife Karen, and Gary's granddaughter and her husband, we must've told and retold that tale fifty times, laughing until tears rolled down our collective cheeks.

The next morning we failed yet again to pop Louie's proverbial turkey hunting cherry, so back to the levee we went. That day, however, Louie had to attend his grandson's first Little League game, so it was just Gary and I sitting in my patched up blind at 9:30. I had also replaced the jake with a strutter decoy and a new Dave Smith "Leading Hen." The wind was howling ferociously by the time of our arrival, and it threatened to blow us all the way to Vincennes. I had to actually sit on the bottom edge of the upwind side, and then hold my arms out to brace the blind and keep it from blowing away.

Shortly after our arrival I'd seen a bird fly across the river to our side. It was just a glimpse, and could've been an owl or a cormorant, but my initial impression had been, "turkey." Then, at 9:50 I heard a gobble in the same direction. Nothing answered when I called, and at 10:15 I was still trying to hold the blind to the ground in those 40 mph gusts when I suddenly heard drumming. Even over all that wind, I was sure of it! Glancing out of every window in the blind, I couldn't see a turkey anywhere, but when I heard the sound again I knew that a bird had to be *close*. I told Gary to be alert. There clearly wasn't anything in either direction on the levee, and I could see nothing down over its top to the landward side, but I had conscientiously set the blind a bit further inland this time out of fear for a repeat of the previous day's disaster, and now, the only place where I couldn't actually put eyes on ground was directly towards the river. Obviously, there had to be a tom down there intently staring up at my strutter, and I knew that it was only a matter of time before he came up for a confrontation.

And then, I looked out the front window to see two strutters where a moment earlier there had only been one! "Gary, kill that tom, but don't shoot my strutter," I hissed. When the real turkey separated from the fake just a little, Gary laid him out stone cold dead as a wedge. He was a brute, too...weighing 25- 1/2 pounds and sporting spurs of 1- 5/16." But, he wasn't the only one to suffer mightily from that shot, for my brand new hen decoy sounded like a baby's rattle when I shook it. Well, at least she did until I tipped her upside down, and then the pellets poured out of her shot-off beak! Gary was awfully hard on my equipment during that trip, but as I always tell my work-mates, you gotta be tough to be Doc's tools!

Gary and I flank Louie with his first turkey

The next day we finally put everything together and got Louie his first bird, and the following day I filled my own tag. I stayed one more day to try and help Louie kill another tom, but when that failed it was time to bid farewell to my new friends Louie and Lynn Vinnard. Louie had seed corn to get in the ground, and I had revenge on my mind as I traveled back down to Georgia.

When I reached the Peach State once again, I'd already spent 24 days of the season hunting there. During that time I'd killed two toms, but they had each come only after lots of work and hardship. In truth, I wasn't having much fun in Georgia because it seemed more like work than turkey hunting. Striking out time and time again, or hearing nothing all day long, had really worn down my generally positive attitude and I was feeling a bit fatalistic; like I was bound for failure and powerless to change the outcome. I knew that I needed to turn things around quickly, if I didn't want to be forced to come back the following year for a fifth lifetime kill in the state (a goal which I had recently embraced).

Unfortunately, the first couple of days following my return did not bode well. In a spot where 16 days earlier there had been at least two hot toms, I now heard zero. The silence forced me to assume that I was now hunting ghosts. That was a discouraging development, but not totally unexpected, so I began driving around in hopes of finding an actual live gobbler someplace else. However, in the back of my mind I was already actively contemplating and calculating the options in giving up and trying to salvage the season by heading to a new state. But, I have never been a quitter, and that drive to finish what I'd started kept me digging hard. The memory of my tenth day in Georgia, (which now seemed like an lifetime ago), when I'd boogered a tom that was coming in on a string, kept rearing its ugly head as I cruised along backroads and mountain byways.

And then, rounding a turn on a gravel road, I suddenly drove up on two gobblers and several hens. They were practically oblivious to my presence as I stopped in the middle of the road to stare, and I could've easily shot one out the window and been on my way down the road to Pennsylvania or anyplace else. A lesser man might've done that. Not me. I would leave this place with a well-earned victory, or I would go down swinging for the fences. Cheating would only serve to cheat myself. Of course, several hours later and after a failed attempt at killing one of these birds, there was just the slightest twinge of regret...but only in myself for not capitalizing on the brief window of opportunity which had presented itself after I'd parked my van and worked those birds into "questionable" range. Again, it wouldn't have served me to scratch down a tom with a long shot, or, even worse, to cripple one of them, so I'd passed on that chance with a clean conscience.

For another three days I pursued this flock of birds relentlessly, and while my time in the Twilight Zone of Georgia continued to flummox me with frustration, I was at the same time encouraged by the amount of knowledge about those birds being gained every day. They were much too regular in their habits, and I truly felt like it was only a matter of time. And then, on one gloriously fine morning, I *FINALLY* (the 29th day of hunting in the same state) found myself laser-focused on my sight beads aligned with the glowing orb of a gobbler's cotton-white pate at the nearly-certain range of 21 yards. When that trigger pull dropped him like a sack of potatoes I didn't know quite what I was feeling… was it joy, elation, excitement? It felt more like simply a sense of relief; as if the lid had finally been removed from a pressure cooker that was about to blow up. Whatever it was, it felt *good*!

My final Georgia tom from a difficult 2014 season

During that eternity spent in Georgia, I'd only heard gobbling on about 2/3 of the days. Even when I had been lucky enough to hear one, most of the gobbling had ceased completely after only about an hour. Furthermore, I hadn't actually set up and/or worked turkeys more than just a very small handful of times. Overall, it was one of the most painfully dull experiences of my hunting history, with the final tom being the only one of three killed which had been called in during the supposed "prime" morning hours. The other two were afternoon delights, and while those are certainly fun, it's not the same. Turkey hunters live for those mornings filled with raucous turkey talk, and I am no different. The brief hiatus when I'd ventured up into Indiana and Illinois and actually enjoyed a few days of what "real" turkey hunting is all about had only further accentuated how difficult the "Georgia experience" had been for me. I most certainly wasn't looking forward to coming back to do this anytime soon, and now with five toms under my belt, I could see no compelling reason to do so, at all. Goodbye, Georgia; good riddance!

Pennsylvania, as I've written previously, can be drastically different from one year to the next. In 2014 she was everything Georgia wasn't. Oh, I had a mini-dry spell in the middle of the trip when I heard no gobbling, but that was due to cold, windy, and rainy weather. All the other days supplied everything a turkey hunter could want...great climatic conditions and lots of gobbling toms who cooperated just enough to make a feller feel like he's earned the occasional victory gained. Bill George and Doug Pickle were there for comic relief and trips to Haller's General Store for daily ice cream treats, and we also ate like kings back at camp. Doug and I both avoided the numerous competing hunters present on the public lands well enough to shoot two toms each, and Bill added another to the camp tally with Doug's assistance. We had a grand old time with Bill's folks Bill, Sr. and Beryl, too. They are wonderful people and gracious hosts who put up with our shenanigans and are always such a profound joy to be around.

Another Pennsylvania tom that gave me a thrilling hunt in 2014

Maine is big fun, too. I've been enamored with the state since long before I ever turkey hunted there, as it's a place where I just like to hang out. The turkey hunting can be pretty special, as well.

Back in 2014 I was sort of looking for new areas to hunt, and in driving around one day I saw a gobbler strutting in a pasture with a fantastically beautiful overlook in the background. You could see forever into Canada from there, and I think that old tom must've loved the spot for that reason alone, because there wasn't a hen visible anywhere for which he might've been displaying. There were signs posted around the property that said, "Hunting by Permission Only," so I gave the phone number at the bottom a call and the landowner told me to make myself at home and hunt the place like I owned it. WOW! That was a welcome change from the way the rest of the country often responds to a hunting request!

To make a short story even shorter, I set up on that tom at 9:43 a.m. and I pulled the trigger on him at straight-up 10 o'clock. The following day was real foggy, and I only heard some far-off turkeys gobbling a time or two. I would've enjoyed hunting at that beautiful piece of property more, except that I'd previously arranged to meet up with Les Peters that afternoon and he was eager to show me some more gracious Maine hospitality.

Results of a "flash hunt" in Maine

Les was a good friend of Doug Pickle and a real interesting character. The kind of guy who becomes your best friend the minute you meet him. Earlier in life he'd played in a semi-famous rock-n-roll band that opened for nationally and world famous acts like Jimmy Hendrix, Cream, and others. Now he worked at L.L. Bean in their firearms department and did carriage rides in Acadia

National Park during the tourist season. His wife was a nationally renowned artist who specialized in horse paintings, and they owned a little farm where they raised and trained the specialized carriage pulling teams used in their summer business.

The first spot Les took me was a place I absolutely fell in love with the moment we drove in, even though we heard nothing while there. Nothing; not even a peep! Of course, I had a powerful feeling that it was gonna go down like that, since the weather forecast was for rain beginning sometime around noon. I've long held a strong belief that those conditions portend miserable gobbling results at dawn, and that has proven itself to be the case time and time again. But, this place just cried out as a perfect turkey farm. It was comprised of three fairly large grassy fields laid out along the moderately sloping spine of a tall ridge, the top of which offered a stunning panoramic view. A ten-yard-wide strip of hardwoods separated each field from the next, with ancient stacked-stone walls bordering the perimeter of the entire farm. It was not only a beautiful piece of ground, but Les had heard nearly a dozen toms gobbling from the uppermost field only a week prior.

Despite the property's potential, it was one of those deathly still mornings when no other birdlife was talking. We didn't even hear the first owl hoot, crow caw, songbird trill, or turkey gobble. In fun, I accused Les of bringing me to a "gar hole" devoid of turkeys, but I could tell that he was even more anxious than me to hear gobbling. I assured him that I did, indeed, recognize a honey-hole when I saw one, and then we built a great stick blind along the edge of a rocky little "island" in the top field and sat staring at decoys until noon. Both of Les' 71 year old knees were in bad shape, so a run-n-gun style of hunting to cover ground and find birds was out of the picture.

After a delicious lunch of fried whole-belly clams at a local diner, we came right back and slipped into our blind at around 1 o'clock. By 1:40 I was getting serious with some loud calling when a hen starting answering me back. We had a lovely little discussion for twenty minutes or so, but she wouldn't come out of the distant tree line 200 yards in front of us. Then, a barred owl in a tree beside us let go a "who-cooks-for-you; who-cooks-for-you-allllll" cry, and a tom over near the hen shouted out the first gobble of the day!

The next time I yelped with a glass call the tom bellowed right back, and I just had this feeling that nothing else I did would matter. This bird was on his way out into the field, he was going to see the decoys, and he would then come over and get shot. That is pretty much what happened, too, although there was a bit more drama involved when two mouthy hens led the way. Over the course of the next twenty minutes we exchanged pleasantries, gossip, recipes and such as only a bunch of gabby women will do, all while they closed the distance between us with their boyfriend tagging along. I kept hearing loud drumming that I felt sure wasn't coming from the fuzzed up tom in front of my gun barrel, but it wasn't until I'd pulled the trigger that a second gobbler revealed himself by flying away. He'd been hidden in a slight swale while approaching from a different direction in the field, and although he looked 747-normous in exiting the scene, I was perfectly thrilled to death with the magnificent tom flopping in the tall grass.

Les Peters showed me some beautiful country and this fine tom

With both of my Maine tags now filled and three new friends met in Les Peters, Roger Karadin (the landowner where I'd shot my first tom), and Henrik Green (one of Les' good friends and a great guy who lived in a totally awesome hand-built cabin where we'd spent the night), I turned my attention to one last state before heading home…New Hampshire.

On my first day there I met another wonderful pair of folks who would instantly become hard-and-fast friends. I'd failed to hear a bird at Pisgah State Forest during the morning, so I was cruising around in the non-huntable afternoon hours when I happened upon a beautiful old farmhouse near the town of Swanzey. Vince Hanscom and his wife Donna took a liking to me about as quickly as I did them, and they welcomed me to not only hunt the turkeys which gobbled around their property "all the time," but to camp wherever I could find a spot flat enough that I wouldn't roll out of bed. Vince was retired from the Merchant Marines, and he was this infinitely talented fella who could do just about anything. Donna was equally adept, and she also grew and continually cared for the most amazing garden of flowers and plants in the yard of their renovated 1780's-era house. They had recently built a new barn with a solid roof structure on the back to protect Vince's "portable" saw mill, and he (like myself) was a big fan of DeWalt tools. We yacked about all kinds of carpentry stuff for most of the afternoon, and like I said, the three of us bonded almost instantaneously. I found both of these folks to be the quintessential rugged individuals one would expect to find carving out a life in a place that was subject to long, severe winters, but more importantly, they seemed to be the perfect loving couple who had come together fairly late into middle age, and were obviously made for one another.

The next morning I got used and abused by one of their "pet" turkeys who ran me all over the county, and then a rather intense weather pattern the following day assured that I wouldn't even hear a single gobble. The third morning the original tom was right back to his old tricks though, and long before the noon quitting time I'd already decided that he was one of those "asshole" turkeys that needed to die, but which a feller would be far better off simply leaving behind. Still, I gave him one last try on Day 4; only to yet again have him make a fool out of me. By 10 o'clock I was outa there and driving around looking for a new bird, and I found one only a few minutes from the end of legal hunting hours. I didn't even have time to go after him.

At dawn I was right back up on his mountaintop, though. The results of that day's efforts were quite similar to the abuse I'd been receiving down at the Hanscom's, with one important difference…this new bird liked to gobble a lot. However, he had multiple hens continually surrounding him, and while they were just about as talkative as their boyfriend, they were also of the jealous kind. I originally made the fatal mistake of trying to challenge their dominance, so they did exactly what I most didn't want them to do by taking the tom over hill and yon and away from me.

With only two more days to go before the end of the season, I got in tight to the previous roost site long before dawn the next morning. Although the tom and his hens weren't "home," he did gobble within hearing distance, so I hot-footed it across a huge cut-over area to close the gap. My setup tree was a large maple that had somehow avoided the chainsaws, and I gained its vantage point long before any of the turkeys even thought about flying down. A particularly yackity hen was roosted off to the side of the tom, so I focused my attention on her…answering her calls immediately, but not in an overly-aggressive manner.

I didn't want to challenge her authority, but I was most definitely trying to get under her skin a little bit.

It worked. When the hen flew down, she pitched out in my direction and very nearly landed on my head before veering off at the last second and setting down 30 yards behind me. Once on the ground, she got real fired up and demanded that I answer her calls, but all I did was give her an occasional two-note yelp. What that accomplished was making her mad. Then, before she could come in to whoop my butt, the tom flew to ground and headed for us both in a trot. His morning went steadily downhill soon thereafter.

When I got back to Vince and Donna's place, they told me that their local tom had been gobbling his head off all morning long from the beautiful little pasture out back. Oh, well...he'd be even bigger the following year, and I was definitely planning a return trip to take vengeance on him, as well as spending more time and sharing more laughs with my new friends Vince and Donna.

In recapping that 2014 season, I could say that it had been one of lofty highs and dreadful lows, with many challenges and frustrations along the way. Most of the troubles were due simply to a recurrent theme of hearing very little gobbling after the first hour of daylight, and it didn't much matter in what part of the country I'd been hunting...toms were henned-up and hush-mouthed *everywhere*! There were also many days of total silence, when I would occasionally catch myself wondering why the heck I was even out there when I could've been home working on my house. I'd also split up with Jen (yet again) after eight years of sometimes fun times but more often tumultuousness, so my mind had been a troubled knot of negative thoughts and raw emotions at a time when it should've been soaring free and unfettered. Furthermore, I knew in my heart that I hadn't hunted particularly well all year long, and that bothered me a lot because I don't like to half-ass anything. However, even with the problems encountered I had managed to scratch and claw my way to a total of 72 days afield. True: 29 of those had been spent in only one state (Georgia), but I'd topped that lofty figure just once before, so in that regard alone, it had been a glorious year.

Something I found very interesting were the reports coming in from friends around the country relating the same kinds of odd turkey behavior as I had experienced all year long. Toms were gobbling very little after hitting the ground, and remaining quiet all day. Perhaps that was due to a winter which had hung on and refused to give up. In Indiana, we had set all-time marks for number of days when the temperature dropped below 0 degrees, and it had even dipped to -18 a half dozen times! Lots of snow also seemed to push the gobbling peaks back three or four weeks, as well as the leaf cover on our trees. Toms were gobbling well in June, though, and my friend Tracy Deckard had seen two hens with 16 poults on June 2nd.

A beautiful beaver pond in Maine

Chapter 9

2015

The year 2015 started out with a bang when I guided a Texas rancher's beautiful daughter to an Osceola; a tom which completed her world slam. Then, I followed that up with a successful hunt in the afternoon with one of three guys who were already at their motel awaiting a phone call informing them that they were now up to bat. A second guy from the party connected on Day #2, but it would take another two days before Charlie Southworth shot his bird from a popup blind located just a few yards to the side of where Kyla's victory had taken place on opening day.

At that point we were four for four in four days, but what I haven't mentioned is that I wasn't exactly in tip-top physical shape. In late January I'd fallen off a 2-step ladder at work and landed on my elbow, thereby tearing the rotator cuff of my dominant right arm to shreds. Surgery had followed on February 9th, and immediately thereafter I'd begun the painful and slow recovery process. When the season started I was still under strict doctor's orders to keep my wing immobilized with an elastic sling that held it tucked up tight against my body. Guiding turkey hunters one-handed was tough, so I was thrilled with the initial successes.

The season would end up being a wet one in Florida, but not even all of that water could grow spurs on the first bird I shot. I killed him during a brief window of opportunity available before my next clients were due to arrive, and the only way that I'd been able accomplish the feat was by mounting a monopod on my gun's barrel. The shoulder was still much too painful to raise my hand all the way up to the gun's fore end (I shoot left-handed). Though difficult, it was pretty cool to have scratched down an Osceola like that, but the tom's slick legs were, admittedly, a bit of a letdown. Spurless toms always make me feel a little hollow, even though I know better. The truth of the matter is that *any* tom taken from Green Swamp WMA is one of which to be especially proud!

My "one-handed" gobbler from Florida in 2015

After successfully guiding two more clients (Nick Dalasio and Steve Mullinex) I was free to hunt on my own once again, and that evening I got a tom to gobble at an owl hoot. Little did I know at the time that this bird would end up becoming one of those "named" gobblers that get under a fella's skin, and despite numerous opportunities to send him flopping during the course of the next two weeks, he always found a way to avoid death. Some of those instances were simply good luck on his part and bad luck on mine, but many of the others were unexplainable from a logical point of view. He just seemed to lead a charmed life, like royalty. This tom was also not afraid to gobble, and he spent most of his days in a long palmetto flat situated between two tall cypress strands. It had been burned so thoroughly a month earlier that the place looked like a courtyard, and with his penchant for carrying on almost defiantly in its far back end, as if proclaiming his greatness to the world, I eventually started calling him, "The King."

Of course, some of my difficulties in bringing that rascal to bag were simply physical in nature. My shoulder was indeed feeling better every day, but that was only by a matter of degrees, and its lack of mobility was a major factor in keeping The King alive on at least five different occasions. I was also being very conservative in my methodology, as I generally considered this turkey to be one of those evil birds that don't much cotton to hunting pressure. He'd shown me that tendency early-on, so I was playing him accordingly. Heck; I was in no big hurry to end our chess match, for despite failing every day, I was having fun with this tom and learning along the way.

For instance, there was one particular spot in the north end of his domain where wild hogs had rooted up a good portion of ground in amongst a bunch of what David Caudill always referred to as dwarf cypress scattered among pines. I have no idea if this is a particular subspecies of the tree, or if they were just young cypress, but most of the specimens in this area were only five or six inches in diameter. Many were even smaller; more like saplings. Green two-pronged shoots of pinkroot grew throughout the hog rootings, and knee-high ferns poked up through the pine stray wherever the underlying soil hadn't been turned over. It was a really pretty place, and there were many, many turkey tracks visible in the exposed sand and mud. The King liked hanging out there, and oftentimes could be heard gobbling in that vicinity.

On about our seventh day of messing with each other's melons, I found him roosted back in the middle of a rank swamp 400 yards east of his favorite spot. When I say rank, I mean *rank*, too: deep water, big, tall cypress trees, and absolutely no way to get in there with him. He must've flown in there the evening prior, and would thus need to fly out, because there simply wasn't any place for bird nor beast (let alone, man) to walk. Anticipating where he might land, I set up on dry ground outside of the swamp, hoping that he would pitch down into a nice open spot in front of my gun barrel and in the very place from where he'd gobbled for two solid hours the previous day.

Suddenly, a hen flew out of the swamp and over my head. She kept right on going, too. A few minutes later a second hen did the same thing, headed in a different direction. That was odd behavior, but I saw it as a good omen because now I knew for sure that I would have two fewer competitors. What happened next was simply bizarre, as the tom gobbled a few more times and then flew right at me, landing in a tree about 40 yards away. I hadn't uttered the first peep to make him come that way. After standing tall on a limb and staring in all directions for about a minute, the goofy bird then flew right back to his original roost 125 yards further into the middle of the swamp. All this happened at around 7:30 a.m., and then we both sat silently until 9:25, when a hawk scream forced a gobble out of him. Twenty five minutes later he once again flew out to the swamp edge and landed in a tree 80 yards from me, and after another ten minutes of staring out at his surroundings, he finally flew down into the middle of the burn 200 yards away. I never saw nor heard anything else from him the rest of the day, and at the 1 o'clock quitting time I walked away shaking my head. What a weird bird! I decided right then and there that he needed killin.'

After flying home that afternoon for a doctor's appointment and missing only one day of hunting by returning the same night, I came right back after The King with a vengeance. And yet, he continued to show me new ways of avoiding a face full of shotgun pellets. Some days he would gobble good on the roost, some days not so much, but he always had something to say sooner or later and would eventually find his way to the dwarf cypress/pine patch. I'd already built a nice blind in there, and should've simply hunted from that spot until it paid off, but I don't like to sit in one place day after day. That feels more like deer hunting to me, and I despise hunting hooved carp!

But, on the 13th day of hand to hand combat with The King, I slipped into my blind before daylight. I hadn't heard much from this bird for two days straight, and thought that he might've even moved on elsewhere in quest of new hens, so when he gobbled from only about 175 yards away I felt a sense of relief. I was also strangely confident, with a feeling that today might be the day. Still, I played him as usual...very conservatively. I only gave him one muted tree yelp at 6:55, and he gobbled to it. Then, I said nothing else and he pitched down at 7:20. Once on the ground he gobbled a few more times, but again, I was playing it coy and didn't answer right away.

Only after he'd been on the ground for ten minutes did I offer up a couple of clucks, and then I cut into the tail end of his next gobble with a short cutt of only a few notes. That was it. My intent was to say nothing else whatsoever, and 15 minutes later he gobbled from only 75 yards away. Not long after that I saw his white-topped head gliding above the ferns. It was a beautiful sight to behold as he came in fuzzin-n-buzzin with a hen following behind. Just by his demeanor and the way he carried himself, it was obvious that today, for whatever the reason, he was intent on looking for me with conviction. One last gobble at 40 yards was his last, and after he stood tall at about 30 yards to look things over, I ended our long-standing chess match with a permanent check-mate.

This magnificent tom had been a difficult bird to kill, and our final rendezvous had happened in a gloriously beautiful place that practically screamed "Osceola" to me. The hunt itself had also been everything I could ever hope for, and I felt really good about how each of us had performed our duties and obligations to play the game in an honorable manner. My respect for The King had warranted no less, and I was thrilled to carry him on back to camp.

Overall, my month spent in Florida could best be described as one long period of hot, humid, rainy weather, with lots of bugs. I'd never been there for that long before, so I was really ready to go when the time came, but as always, the "Florida Experience" had been a blast. Camp life with all of my close friends had been exemplary, and the good times and laughter nearly continuous. I left for Virginia the next day with a smile on my face and warm feelings in my heart.

The King

*Florida legends Craig Morton, Joe Ross, Bill George,
and Doug Pickle find respite from the rain under Bill's new "circus tent"*

Steve "Papaw" Mullinex in some beautiful Florida habitat

Wednesday's are "All-The-Quail-You-Care-To-Eat" nights at the Redwing Restaurant, in Groveland. This table full of dear friends in 2015 included David and Marie Caudill, Charlie and Cathy Parrish, and "The Princess" Robin McCormick

I reached Doug Pickle's house at 2 a.m., and he woke me up at 3 o'clock to go meet up with a friend and his son who were taking me to their private lease. Although bleary-eyed and exhausted from the long drive, I hopped up out of bed ready to roll. Not too much later, Kevin and Shawn Myer were pointing me down a path where they'd heard three toms gobbling the day before my arrival, and then they scampered off to hunt in their own blind situated along a powerline. At the least, I intended to slip back into the woods and curl up to take a well-deserved nap, but turkeys gobbling in a couple of different directions offered me no respite! You know what they say: no rest for the wicked, and before too long I was locked into battle with a tom and forgetting all about how tired I was. The hunt's culmination didn't come easily though, and it was almost 10 o'clock before I pulled the trigger. By then I was so tired that it wasn't until picture time back at the truck that Shawn looked my gobbler over and discovered that he had a total of four beards...my first bird with more than three.

Doug and I then guided on the very first Virginia One-Shot Governor's Hunt along with Ken Greene and Richard Shively. Despite our approximately 180 years' worth of cumulative turkey hunting experience, the four of us failed to call in any birds for our clients. That's one of the exquisite agonies of this sport...there are no guarantees.

After that illustrious event I hunted at Quantico Marine base and managed to scratch down a tom on the first morning. Then, I spent another week or so hunting with both Doug and Ken. We all had a large time of it that spring, and I enjoyed our moments in the woods even more than the last time we'd hunted together back in 2007. Maybe it was because I already had two great toms in the cooler, or perhaps I was just beginning to mellow, but for whatever the reason, I found myself content to simply go with the flow and let my hunt mates dictate the course of action. It doesn't really matter why; I thoroughly enjoyed my time spent with these two guys, whom I love dearly and consider as brothers of the woods.

Delaware. Yes, I had returned yet again! My experiences in that state had fluctuated from one extreme to the other over the course of my personal history

My first Quantico Marine Base bird in 2015

there, but now that turkeys abounded on their public lands, it had become sort of a "go to" destination for me. I never would've thought that even possible early-on, and I still despised certain aspects of the state, but I had nothing other than positive outcomes to point towards in how I felt about their turkey hunting.

So too in 2015, when I spotted a tom and several hens while driving around on the afternoon before my hunt period was to begin, and after a lengthy battle the next day, I took my fourth public land First State tom. It was almost with a feeling of regret that I had to leave my great camp site at Redden State Forest and head for home.

This Delaware gobbler roosted in the big tree over my left shoulder, but it was two hours after flydown before I killed him

My plan was to hunt in an area of Orange County where I'd chased turkeys twenty years earlier. I had no idea whether there were still birds to be found in that chunk of Hoosier National Forest, but I couldn't think of any good reason why they wouldn't be, and on the first morning I even heard one from my campsite. However, I really wanted to hike further back into the spots where Ron Ronk, Steve Seramur, and I had experienced so many memorable hunts, so I left him alone. I'm glad that I did, too, as I heard at least five others during the course of the morning. I didn't kill any of them, but it sure felt great to be back in my old familiar stomping grounds.

The next day I heard three more toms in a different direction, and after striking out once again, I decided on the third morning of my "coming home" party to cross the steep ravine beside my campsite and hunt the bird I'd heard initially. That morning's hunt ended up being epically good; full of intrigue and excitement. And, only after I was standing on the tom's neck did I realize exactly what I'd shot. There, projecting from the barrel-chest of a bird weighing almost 24 pounds protruded *five* beards. I'd now shot a 4-bearded tom in Virginia and a 5-bearded tom in Indiana only a week apart!

My 5-bearded Indiana tom from 2015

My old buddy Tracy Deckard came down that afternoon, and the next morning he killed a tom with me on the opposite side of camp. We must've heard 400 gobbles during that hunt; at one point becoming the focal hub in a battle between three different toms ripping it as hard as they could go, while coming in with ill intent directed at that sweet sounding hen (me) who kept telling them promises that she had no intentions of keeping. Great hunt, with a great friend. Yep; it sure felt good to be back "home" again in Indiana!

When I got to Pennsylvania it was raining, but you know the drill; a little rain (or, even a lot of it) isn't likely to stop a turkey hunter from making a fool of himself. I walked about as far out on some paper company lands as I could go before daylight, and then the rain *really* started coming down. By that time I was already drenched, and when the downpour stopped an hour later I was still far from the van and a change into dry camo's. Instead, I just continued to tough it out...miserable and bedraggled looking as an old wet hen.

The emerging sunshine soon got a nearby bird gobbling, so I merely slipped underneath a low hanging shrub of a tree and pointed my gun barrel right down the muddy logging road that I'd walked in on. My first yelp was stepped on by the tom's strident gobble, as was a second, and then it was just a matter of waiting him out...which didn't take long. Almost before I had a chance to get nervous, he came around a bend in the road 75 yards away with a jake trailing behind, and not long after that the older bird became an even soggier mess than when he'd first appeared, due to flipping and flopping and splashing his death throes in a big mud puddle. I didn't mind the extra water weight in my turkey vest, or the long hike out.

The next morning I went right back in there because of how much turkey sign I'd found along that muddy road. I heard a half-dozen gobbling toms over the course of the day, but it wasn't until a few minutes before noon that I finally called one of them in and shot him full in the face at 29 steps. When I got back to Bill's camp house I found out that Tracy Deckard (who had followed me up from Indiana) had also killed a tom. His bird was rather special because he wore not just one, but two metal legbands! I think Doug Pickle might've felt a twinge of regret afterwards, because he'd "given" that location to Tracy before dawn.

Tracy Deckard's bejeweled Pennsylvania gobbler

For the next two days I took Bill George's daughter Belinda back to my killing spot, and although we came close to getting her a bird several times, in the end all we gained were some experiences and memories. These weren't bad outcomes at all: just not exactly what we'd worked so hard to achieve. On the second of those days I'd had a pair of toms headed towards destiny as the noon quitting time loomed over top of us, but they progressed so slowly that we eventually had to stand up and walk away. That was the third time of her PA trip when Belinda had been whistle bit. Pennsylvania's latter portion of all-day hunting hours didn't start until the following week.

When a neighbor of Bill's heard a tom gobbling insanely only 200 yards off of the main gravel road leading to camp that afternoon, a decision was called for. Did Belinda want to hunt this bird, or did she want to hike in the two miles or so back to where we'd spent the last two days? The answer was almost a given, really, for what teenage gal would opt out of sleeping-in? Besides; it was supposed to rain heavily, and furthermore, Belinda had stepped on a hot coal at the fire pit the night before and her foot was hurting. Both of these circumstances further pointed towards a short hike as opposed to a long forced march. Bill, Doug, and I snuck in after dark and got everything set up.

Bill George and his daughter Belinda pose with her hot PA tom

The three of us served as Belinda's guides and cameramen the next morning, and if that tom gobbled once, he must've gobbled 300 times! Actually, Belinda counted more than 250 gobbles before flydown, and the tom certainly didn't slow very much once he was on the ground. I've seldom encountered a turkey so vocal, and we got gobs and scads of good audio recordings, as well as some great video footage. We even put out a couple of GoPro cameras right in amongst the decoys, and those angles provided some really interesting shots. It was a great hunt; it just didn't last very long!

Massachusetts was up next, and for the first four days I struggled in a section of Warwick State Forest near the town of Orange. I can't even remember why I chose that location, but there were a few turkeys around...I just couldn't seem to make things happen in my favor. The public ground was also a patchwork of small landholdings surrounded by private property, and while most of them weren't posted (hence; huntable), I've never been able to feel comfortable in stepping on someone else's property without first asking for permission. Furthermore, this area was people-dense, and traffic on all the roads was heavy. I even had a lady call the cops on me one morning because she didn't know why my van was parked along "her" road (I was, in fact, parked in a State Forest pull-off). After talking to the cop (who was a turkey hunter), I then had a discussion with the lady to ease her mind that I was legit, and she eventually told me that it was ok if I hunted her field, too.

Since the next day was Sunday and I couldn't hunt in Massachusetts, I opted to drive over to New Hampshire and visit with my new friends Vince and Donna Hanscom. Despite their assurances that the local toms had been ripping it from their back pasture quite regularly, I only heard one distant gobble at daylight. The rest of the day was hot as blazes, so any other turkey talk was neither expected, nor detected. By noon I was on my way back to Massachusetts, and the next morning I shot a great tom in the State Forest lands behind that woman's house.

Massachusetts was tough in 2015, but it finally came together

Three days later I filled my second tag. In looking back through my journal, I noted that upon leaving Massachusetts I hadn't ever felt like I was really "into" birds, nor learning much as the hunt progressed. I'd spent eight days there, and yet, it had generally been a struggle. Usually on a trip of that duration it ends up being accrued knowledge gained that tips the scales in my favor, but I left for New Hampshire feeling like I didn't know anything more on the final morning than I had upon arrival. I'd just persevered until eventually putting myself in a couple of good situations.

Vince and Donna insisted that I stay in their guest bedroom. I ordinarily (and actually prefer to) sleep in my van, but I graciously accepted their hospitality and then tried to sneak out in the morning without disturbing them or their wonderful St. Bernard dog, Miss Bayley. It was raining when I reached their pretty little back pasture, but the drizzle stopped soon thereafter. The Hanscoms and I had by now established an "inside joke" amongst us, whereby they would claim that turkeys frequently gobbled east of the house in my absence, and yet I would never hear any while there. This proved true once again, but I did hear a bird hammering it far to the south.

I didn't even wait for any other birds nearby to begin gobbling, and by keeping a steady pace, I eventually closed in and set up only about 125 yards from the roosted tom, who was belting out gobbles at a frenetic pace. We were basically seated on the same elevation and sharing a narrow "shelf" near the base of a mountain which climbed up and away to my right, and I anticipated (or, at the least, hoped for) an easy hunt after flydown time.

Ordinarily, I don't call to turkeys while they're in the tree, but I wasn't really sure if he'd flown down yet when I uttered my first yelp on a Cane Creek glass pot. His answering fusillade of gobbling didn't really settle the issue either, so in about two more minutes I decided to call again. Just as the peg in my hand had begun making the first circular motions for producing a yelp on the glass, I detected a flurry of activity close on my right hand side. That "something" was airborne and coming directly at me, and without knowing what, or why, or exactly the circumstances, my poor feeble brain had only the time to decipher that it was under attack! Although I know not from where it came, and am equally certain that I couldn't reproduce it again unless under similar circumstances, a sound then came involuntarily out of my throat that could only be construed as the shrill essence of pure fear!

Whatever the creature was then bounced against my leg, and in pushing off to go back the way it had come (leaving me with a 2" scratch on my calf), I realized that the beast was a bobcat! He ran up the mountain a dozen yards, and then turned to face me with a look on his face that said quite plainly, "what kind of critter screams like *that*?" Then, he turned and ran away, leaving me stunned and a bit shaken.

The turkey, however, continued to gobble hard, so I remained seated. An hour and a half later we were both still in our respective positions. I had long ago decided that this tom was indeed still treebound, and in making that determination I had yelped a couple of times to garner answering gobbles. Trust me when I say that anytime I touched peg to glass, my head swiveled around like an owl to look out for that danged bobcat!

Two hours into our standoff, the tom finally flew down and began moving away. I quickly arose and gained 40 yards in his direction, but when he gobbled once again it seemed like he might be coming back, so I picked a nearby setup tree which offered good cover. From there we dueled for another half an hour before he definitely started moving away. This time I hustled 50 yards closer and cutt hard at him as I was sitting back down at my third setup tree of the morning. I'm sure that it was this small, incremental series of movements which were the deciding factors in turning the hunt to my favor, and before long I got that old familiar feeling in my gut. When the tom first appeared at 40 yards, there was a hen tagging along beside him. I'd heard her answer me several times during the long duel with her boyfriend, but now she became only a bystander to his death once he'd steadily strutted in to a range of 21 steps from the end of my gun's muzzle.

With my New Hampshire tom now cooler-bound, and having survived the cat attack, I found myself with a week and a half of May remaining. That left plenty of time to hunt another state before Maine, so I headed to Vermont. The first six days there were a total bust, with not a single gobbler heard or seen. Then, I lucked into a great spot when I stopped by a dairy farm to inquire about turkeys, rather than cows. The owner's son said that I was more than welcome to camp and hunt there so long as I wished, and he also told me of a little hidden field where he'd been seeing a pair of toms quite regularly. It was only about 9:00 in the morning when he told me this, so I thanked him profusely and drove on down to the lower farm, where I parked along a dim tractor path and then walked back in to the honey-hole. What was there? Why; two fuzzed up gobblers displaying for a hen, of course!

Slipping into a brushy ravine that began along the roadway leading into the field, I hunkered behind some briars and yelped. The gobbles bellowed forth were the first ones I'd heard in nearly a week, and in pretty short order all three turkeys came towards me in a trot. But, due to my rather unorthodox setup, I didn't have any chance to shoot until they'd gotten close. In fact, when I pulled the trigger I was actually aiming *up* at a gobbler's head craning tall to look down into my ravine at a distance of seven yards away. The final three days of the season were hot and rainy, and I never even heard another gobble, but at least I'd succeeded in chalking up another Vermont tom.

Only Maine was now open, so I once again ventured up to hunt with Les Peters. In talking to him on the phone while at a laundromat en route, he'd suddenly blurted out, "Hey, there are three jakes and a tom right now under my bird feeder beside the house. I've got things to do for the next couple of days, but you're more than welcome to hunt my place." That was music to my ears, so by 5:30 in the afternoon I was pulling into his driveway, where I saw five jakes milling around in his horse pasture behind the house.

Les' farm was only about 20 acres or so, and most of it was in pasture for his pair of Morgan carriage-pulling horses, but there was also a bit of woods in the back. He told me that I was very likely to find a tom in the corner of the property where they regularly dumped out used straw and horse crap into a compost pile. Then, he offered to walk me around the wooded portion of his property and introduce me to "Patrick," a ruffed grouse that Les claimed would follow him around like a pet dog. This, I had to see!

Sure enough, we had no sooner entered the woods than Patrick suddenly appeared, and he did, indeed, follow us for the entire time. It was only when we headed back across the pasture that the goofy grouse halted, looking forlorn as we left him all alone. I'd never seen anything like it!

The next day's weather called for cold temperatures and prolonged rain. Planning for the worst but hoping for the best, I carried in a blind and a comfortable chair to the scratched-up hay pile long before daylight, along with a strutter and hen decoys. What did I hear at daylight? Nothing. What did I see? Patrick the ruffed grouse, standing just a few yards away from my blind and looking wet and miserable. I was hoping that he would come inside out of the weather and keep me company, but while not looking exactly content in the rain, he did seem to be resigned of enduring it, and he stayed right there as hours passed without any turkeys showing up.

By 10:30 I was getting cold, so I then walked to the house and heated up a can of soup. Les' wife Kathy had been hearing turkeys gobble from the compost area nearly every day at 11:30, so I gulped the hot lunch down quickly and got right back to my blind, where I found Patrick still maintaining his vigil. I brought with me two additions, though...a second hen decoy, and a length of fishing line. All morning long I'd been staring out at that statue-still strutter decoy, so now I decided to tie a jerk string on him to create a little bit of movement. It worked great, and Patrick seemed to approve.

A very wet "Patrick" the ruffed grouse/dog

At 1:41 p.m. Les sent me a text message that the tom and three jakes were back under his bird feeder. I called loudly on my diaphragm, and twelve minutes later I could see a number of turkeys in the horse pasture. When I called again, they began yelping and coming towards me...five jakes and a hen in total. The jakes all rushed up to my strutter and began ganging up on him, but whenever I would give the decoy string a yank and spin him to face them, they would back away. It was comical for Patrick and me to watch, until one of the jakes got tangled up in the string and yanked it from my hands. After that, my poor non-moving strutter got pummeled by the gang of hooligans.

I texted Les at 1:56 to tell him about the jakes, and at 2:01 he returned my message to say that the tom was still eating bird seed. At 2:19 I cutt really hard on my glass call, and I could hear an answering gobble from up beside the house. Texting Les to tell him of how I'd finally made the tom gobble, I soon received the following reply, "Last supper. Headed your way. Bang!" As I was reading that message the tom gobbled from half his original distance, and I called one last time before setting the pot call aside.

I could've let him come all the way in to the strutter, but with those aggressive jakes still present it was questionable what would happen. Rather than risking them running off my tom, I shot him just twenty yards short of the object of his angry stare. Then, Patrick and I eased out to inspect our fallen adversary. I was thrilled with the entire way this hunt had progressed, and Patrick seemed pleased, too. In fact, he almost let me pet him before stepping back warily. This otherwise "wild creature" definitely maintained a "look, but don't touch" relationship with his humans. Not quite a pet dog, but pretty darned cool none-the-less.

Henrik Green, Marivi Mejico, and their wonderdog Alex

For the final few days of the Maine season I stayed at the log cabin built by Les' buddy Henrik Greene. He worked at L.L. Bean with Les, and is an accomplished fishing guide, as well. Henrik is a great dude, and we had tons of fun. Although he'd only killed one turkey to date, Henrik is a dedicated deer hunter and had decided to hunt turkeys only with a bow. That made things a little problematic, but I finally called in a whole passel of jakes which came over a grassy hill and charged our position like warriors from the movie, "Brave Heart." Henrik promptly shot two of them a minute apart, from less than fifteen yards, and still to this day I have no idea where they were hit due to the speed of the arrows and the lack of dead turkeys. We blood trailed both of them a good ways, and never found either one. Henrik and I were both terribly disappointed and saddened by that development, but as I've come to discover in my own forays into bow hunting turkeys, that outcome is bound to happen…and, often. A lot of things can go wrong between the release of an arrow from string and its killing end striking vital organs. That's why I no longer do it. The birds themselves deserve so much more. When I pull the trigger, I expect to send a bird floppin' in the leaves every time, unless something crazy occurs or I screw up. Obviously, that happens with gun hunting too, but not nearly as often as with a bow.

Before leaving Maine, Henrik introduced me to his buddy Matt, who is a lobsterman. I bought twenty lobsters from him at $4.70 per pound, and we packed them carefully in a cooler with ice on the bottom, a layer of seaweed, a layer of lobsters, a layer of seaweed, a layer of lobsters, etc. Driving straight through, I arrived home having only lost two, and then we had one tremendous Indiana lobster fest at my buddy Tom Skirvin's house.

My tallies for the year amounted to 70 days of hunting or guiding in nine states, with 32 toms called into camp. Sixteen of them stayed. Considering how badly my shoulder had been wrecked in January, it ended up being a glorious season overall. Furthermore, by the time it ended I was feeling quite good physically, even though I wouldn't be allowed to go back to work until August. I'd even received a regular paycheck for the entire duration of turkey season for the first time ever, because Workman's Comp was paying me just slightly less than a 40-hour rate every week!

I ended the 2015 season needing only a single bird from eight states to complete my third U.S. Super Slam. Additionally, there were just 28 states where I had killed less than five birds in total…a new goal that had developed during the course of the year, for no other reason than the number five had always been one of my "lucky" numbers. Ultimately attaining that figure in every state gave me a new way in which to focus and keep striving ever-onward, and it helped knowing that this was something I could hope to finish up in the relative near future. And, if I never achieved it, I could certainly rest easy throughout eternity in knowing that I'd had one helluva good run! For the present time, I was really looking forward to looking forward.

Views afforded the turkey hunter inspire and invigorate

Chapter 10

2016

I began the 2016 season with an absolutely crazy plan of guiding a group of five hunters at the same time. Insanity: pure insanity!

But, we got one bird killed on opening day, and two more on the second day. The other two members of their party must've decided that too little action on a heavy-thunderstorm laced opening day didn't fit their expectations, and they just left their partners behind and went home without so much as a sorry, thanks, or a screw you! In some regards I was mad about that, but in other ways I was perfectly fine with their premature departure…I hadn't cared much for either one of them from the beginning, and now I had two spots open for a father and son who seemed like real fine fellers.

John and Chad Flick were friends of Craig Morton. They just happened to be in Florida during the first few days of turkey season, and had inquired about a hunt, but I'd had to tell them that all my spots were full. Now, all it took was a phone call and they jumped at the chance. I also wanted to prove that the quitters had made a stupid decision by abandoning their commitment to me and their friends, so the Flick crew and I hunted the very same spot where I'd place them on opening day. Despite cold and very windy conditions that chilled all three of us to the bone, Chad got his first Osceola at around 9:30. It was another twenty minutes before we could take any pictures though, because we were all shaking and shivering too much to hold the cameras steady! A return trip to that very same "log cabin" blind the following morning provided much better climatic conditions, and a much shorter hunt, after a bird roosted

Heath Adkins, his dad Gary, and Brian McGlothlin show off Gary's tom with a boogered-up tail. His long spurs more than made up for it

Brian's Osceola was as pretty as they get

Chad and John show off Chad's tom while standing in our blind

directly behind us flew down and walked by my side of the blind at less than ten yards on his way to a confrontation with my DSD Strutter and John's Heavy Shot blend of 4's, 5's, and 7's.

I took my next client to a new property that I'd acquired up around Brooksville: wooded acreage surrounding a golf course where turkeys were regularly visible strutting on the fairways and greens! Gregory York was the kid's name, and he was 13 years old. His dad Greg filmed the hunt for their YouTube channel, and he got some great footage when I called in a pair of toms that were initially reluctant to commit the final few yards, but which eventually succumbed to a hen scratching so enthusiastically beside my decoys that she was kicking leaves and debris ten feet.

Greg and Gregory with a fine Osceola

Four days of humbling hunts at Green Swamp kept my head from swelling too much from all of our early successes, and then I brought my final client back to the golf course property. Bradley Graham and I had a great hunt there; just not an easy one. Despite lots of gobbling from numerous toms, it took us three days to get things done. This property had never been legally hunted before and I strongly suspected that poachers from an adjoining WMA had been messing with its turkeys. Why else would every bird I worked during those three days act so "hanky?" But, we persevered, and the troubles encountered proved to be worth the hardships endured when Bradley smote down a dandy of a gobbler with spurs of about 1- 3/8 inches. The timing was perfect, too, as we barely made it back to the van before torrential rain with heavy lightning, thunder, and wind threatened to kill us.

Bradley Graham's first Florida tom

It would take an additional five days to find my own first success at Green Swamp, and that came about in a rather unexpected way. The previous afternoon I'd found a lot of fresh sign on a woods road running down along the edge a very large palmetto flat of probably 100 acres or more, so I was confident while standing there the next morning when a tom started gobbling about 300 yards away. However, he was basically on the opposite side of the palmettos from me. Now; there ain't no way in hell's creation that I'm gonna willingly wade through a palmetto field like that (I always envision unseen 7-foot rattlesnakes coiled up underneath those thick palmettos and subsequently striking me about thigh-high as I fight my way through the tangled mess), even if there wasn't a turkey roosted where he could've seen me coming from a mile away, so I began circling around its edge, instead.

Three separate small "fingers" of pines projected perhaps 40 yards out into the ocean of palmettos along my path, and I figured the tom to be roosted in the last of these. As I cut across the first point, I found that the ground underneath the pines had been rooted up by hogs and there was a lot of turkey sign visible on the exposed soil...tracks and droppings in quantity. By the time I reached the second finger the tom had quit gobbling altogether, and I worried that I might've bumped him since it was getting to be so light out. That ground, too, was rooted up and showed sign of heavy use by turkeys, so I sat down against a tree to await developments. It looked like a great place for turkeys to gather and hang out anyway, so if perchance I hadn't spooked him, the tom might already be working along the palmetto edge in my direction, hoping to rendezvous with hens right where I was at.

An hour later I was still sitting there when the tom suddenly gobbled at a hawk's scream. He hadn't moved an inch from the third finger of pines, and when I yelped, he gobbled back at me. Then, not two minutes later, I saw a turkey fly up and out of that finger, heading north across the sea of palmettos. There was a loose cluster of pines about 150 yards out into the palmetto flat, and the bird headed straight for them and landed in the very top of one. A minute or so later a second turkey joined the first, and with the aid of my ever-present Swarovski mini binoculars hanging around my neck, I was able to ascertain that they were both hens.

I received three or four more answering gobbles over the course of the next ten minutes, and my hopes soared in thinking that the tom was, indeed, moving in my direction. It really looked like I was in the proverbial catbird's seat until the tom suddenly picked up and flew out to land in a tree about 30 yards from the pair of hens. Despite answering my next yelp with another gobble, he continued to just stand there craning his neck downward and staring at the ground below him. The hens were doing the same thing. From where I was at, I could see nothing but thick palmettos and scattered galberry bushes in this field so far as the eye could see, but *something* down below those turkeys sure held their attention.

Nothing changed until 10 o'clock, when each bird in turn pitched to the ground going almost straight down. After twenty more minutes I decided that they weren't likely to be coming towards me through all those palmettos, so I needed to go to them. A rather dim and narrow hog trail seemed to be pointed in that direction, so I began working my way out into the palmetto flat; not at all sure of what I was getting into, but confident that there were turkeys somewhere out ahead of me.

When I reached the pines and eased through a line of galberry bushes on the opposite side of them, I entered a whole new world; it was almost like opening a door and slipping into another dimension that I never even knew existed! From a drone's view up in the sky, this place would probably look like a winding glade of interconnected openings in the groundcover, while from the down-low perspective of where I'd come from, the whole area was just a continuous sea of palmettos. Generations of wild hogs had rooted-out and kept open what was now a beautiful carpet of green pinkroot shoots, and everywhere I turned to look, there were turkey tracks and droppings. That made sense, as it was a veritable smorgasbord of food sources for the birds, but how they ever found this place was a mystery that I didn't even contemplate...not after I heard the unmistakable "pfft...dddMMMM" of a drumming turkey! With no better option available, I merely sat down in the palmettos, raised my gun up on a knee, and yelped one time with a mouth call. The tom didn't gobble in answer, but rather, he quite simply and suddenly materialized from around a ledge of palmettos directly in line with my shotgun and only 19 yards away. I then spent another hour just sitting there in wonder and amazement at the beauty of that spot.

What a cool place to kill my 50th Osceola

Two days later I filled my season quota from another place that had often been good to me in the past. Then, I was honored to spend a couple more days hunting with my hero, David Caudill. He really wanted to call in and kill one more turkey "on his own," so I would do the scouting, drop him off and get him set up, and then come back and get him when he was ready to call it quits. Mostly, I just sat back behind him a couple hundred yards listening to the show without his ever knowing that I was there. David's health had deteriorated greatly in the last year, and he was now terribly frail and on oxygen. I was hoping against hope for one final bird to cooperate and give this man the parting gift that he so rightly deserved, but turkeys being turkeys, they refused to cooperate. After two days he'd had enough. I think when we left the woods on that last day, each of us knew that it would be his final outing in a place where his heart so very much longed to remain.

Florida had been a season of contradictions and extremes in 2016. Come to think of it, she often is! When I arrived it hadn't rained in over a month, but then it stormed nearly every day for two weeks. My clients had killed out in a bare minimum of time, and yet, I had struggled to get my birds on the public lands of Green Swamp East. Yellow flies (deer flies) and biting insets had been horrendous, but the good times with all of my "family" had been exemplary, even though we were watching David's life ebbing away before our very eyes. His dear wife Marie was also becoming very fragile and had fallen three different times at camp. One of those tumbles broke some ribs and necessitated an ambulance ride at 3 a.m., but the tough old gal was back in camp where she wanted to be the very next day. Trauma had also befallen Charlie's wife Cathy, who had accidentally run over their German shepherd Hemmie and then received a terrible bite when trying to rescue him from under the Jeep's tire. That wound required many stitches. Then, to top off the list of bad tidings, I had ventured up to Green Cove Springs on my way out of state and stopped in to see my Grandparents old house on the St. Johns River. It was very depressing to discover what a terrible state of disrepair and neglect had befallen that beloved place. So many wonderful memories had come rushing up from my heart as I'd driven in on the long and familiar driveway, but those were remembrances from a lifetime earlier: now it was a wreck. I took some pictures, but still to this day I hate looking at them.

Florida's live oaks are an intriguing sight to behold

Just like I'd done the previous year, my next three stops were Virginia, Delaware, and Indiana. And, once again, I would be spending the vast amount of my Virginia days with Doug Pickle and Ken Greene. We always have a great time together, no matter where we hunt. These two fellas are turkey hunters to the center of their souls, so we're of like minds and motivations.

The three of us would again be guiding at the Virginia One-Shot Governor's Turkey Hunt, with my client this time being a 9 year-old kid who couldn't for the life of his mother quit squirming. But, the fact that he ran off turkeys all morning long was nobody's fault other than mine, because I hadn't brought along a blind to hide his movements. I felt bad about letting him down like that, even though he was tickled to death by all the stuff we saw and heard during the course of our morning's outing. Then, he won a bunch of prizes at the after-hunt banquet. Doug's guy killed a brute of a tom, winning both hunter and guide brand new guns for the biggest turkey taken during the event.

After that we got down to some serious turkey hunting for ourselves, and the first tom I killed was a bird called in from just about as far away as Ken and I could hear him gobble. We hadn't moved closer because of three others surrounding us, but the distant bird was simply ready and willing to die on that particular day. Ken's intent to film the hunt had been aborted due to a

Doug Pickle and I with birds killed on the same day, but from different farms

Ken Greene and our "flash hunt" tom in Virginia during 2016

camera malfunction, so the vision of that tom strutting all the way across a huge expanse of pastureland is etched only in our memories.

The other tag I filled with Ken came after a mid-morning gobble nearly blew our hats off as we were easing down a new and unexplored road cut into the property. We hadn't had a clue that there was a turkey within miles of us at the time, and all we could do was hurriedly set up against a couple of six-inch pines, call once, and hope for the best. This flash hunt worked out great for us; not so much for the tom. Then, with a Delaware tag slated to start the next day, I made a two-hour drive over to Georgetown.

For the second year in a row I'd drawn a Redden State Forest permit and I was eager to kill one final bird in that state before hanging it up for good. There's a great, free campsite behind the headquarters, and all of my toms taken on that property have been big, robust gobblers with impressive physical attributes, but there are just too many negatives involved in Delaware turkey hunting for it to warrant much more than casual excitement. Too many people, too much congestion, too much household garbage everywhere that you walk on their public lands, and much too much stinking chicken crap spread over every inch of dirt and everywhere you go. Yes; a lifetime tally of five toms would be plenty!

True to form though, I once again had a fantastic time in Delaware, even if it did take me three days to pull the trigger. I'd passed up a bird on the first day

My fifth and final Delaware turkey

because he just looked scrawny (a risky maneuver when you're only allotted six days on a permit), and although it did seem kinda foolish to "shop around" for a bigger, better bird, my gamble paid off in the end with a tom that weighed over 20 pounds and had a beard stretching to 11- 1/8." His wicked-sharp spurs measured 1- 5/16 inches, too.

Returning to hopefully fill my third tag in Virginia, it rained for three days in a row. All that moisture affected the birds' attitude negatively, because I heard only one gobble at daylight during that entire timeframe. I did booger up an opportunity during a late morning hunt when I failed to act and make a move to a different setup spot despite my brain telling me that a quick twenty-yard sprint would put me where I needed to be before the gobbler arrived. I didn't, he did, and that was that.

The next morning also proved a bust, but after Ken joined me in the afternoon, we had an absolutely splendid time and called in two separate toms an hour apart. Each of them gobbled good, came in like they'd read the script, and died well. He shot the first one, and then I killed the second.

There's a place near my Indiana home that is just about the most beautiful hardwood ridgeline I've ever seen. In fact, you can walk there from my house and be standing on its highest crest in about twenty minutes. This is public land, but over the years I've invited a few select friends to stay at my place and hunt there while I was elsewhere jumping from state to state. Jim Spencer and his wife Jil Easton are outdoor writers from Arkansas who have done that very thing on three different occasions, and after they'd killed a turkey up there for the first time, Jil gave the place an appropriate, if not overly imaginative name: "Pretty Ridge." Back in 2016 it hadn't yet been so-named, but I knew and loved that ground intimately. The magnificent views and huge timber evoke a feeling of "home" to me. Dave Owens had even put boots on that ridgeline earlier in the season before I arrived, and then he sang its praises to me when recanting the tale of his gobbler taken.

When I arrived from Virginia the weather was (what else?) raining and dreary and I didn't hear any gobbling at all, but on my next trip up there I heard four. The one I eventually killed was a dandy, too, although it wasn't just the tom's physical accoutrements that made the hunt so special. It was the whole package of being able to walk there from my very own house, battle with a difficult gobbler for a long period of time on just about the most beautiful place on earth, and then leisurely stroll back home with his glorious magnificence

A fine gobbler from Pretty Ridge, Indiana in 2016

draped over my shoulder. I sat there on Pretty Ridge for a long time after the shot, listening to other turkeys continuing to gobble and feeling very blessed, lucky, and satisfied with my lot in life.

My first week in Rhode Island was a gobble-less affair. Well, I actually did call in a group of five jakes that gobbled once, but that was it. Then, on the seventh day I heard a tom gobbling insanely, but he ended up being nearly inaccessible by conducting his shenanigans from the middle of the State Fairgrounds. The next day he flew down and began gobbling while walking steadily away from me, and I think that he must've kept right on going clear out of the county because he never did return. By the eleventh day of my trip I was practically morose. Never before had I worked so hard for so long and been rewarded with less opportunity in the turkey woods. The soles of my boots were practically worn to nubbins from hiking far on that granite-laced ground just looking for sign, but even that had been a dismal failure. I was disappointed, demoralized, frustrated, and confused. Also, mad as hell. It was terrible.

Then, I found a tom willing to gobble like a real turkey. He was on public land, too, although Rhode Island law does allow hunting on any property which isn't conspicuously posted. After setting up on this bird several times throughout the morning and feeling as if I might actually kill him on two or three separate occasions, he was finally run off by another "hunter" who bumbled in on us and began incessantly blowing a peacock call. Still, the hunt itself had been everything I needed to buoy up my floundering attitude, and I spent the afternoon hours sneaking around and learning as much as I could about the area and how this turkey was using it. I found lots of his visual sign like scratchings and droppings in the laurel and rhododendron filled valley where he'd spent so much time gobbling all morning, and I also discovered where he hung out in a spot up higher on the ridgeline, closer to where he'd been roosted at dawn on a broad shelf.

The following day started out tough and then it got tougher as a combination of high winds and heavy machinery from the neighbor's property combined to rob me of any chance at hearing the tom's early gobbles. However, several times I was pretty sure that he'd sounded off from across the paved road, in the same direction he'd fled from the other hunter. I felt certain that the old boy would eventually come back, and precisely at 11 a.m. he did exactly that. I'd been patiently waiting all morning, so I was ready.

At my first call the tom immediately ran towards me and raced by at less than fifteen yard's distance without ever slowing down long enough to get shot. Then, we began a frustrating game of tag in a maze of tangled laurel greenery. He won the early rounds of our running battle before moving off towards the neighbor, who was presently running a track hoe and loading boulders into piles. Due to all of the noise stemming from that endeavor, I lost contact with the turkey. I couldn't hear myself think, let alone the gobbling of any tom! I strongly suspected that the bird had circled around the machinery and climbed uphill onto that shelf where he liked to hang out, but I didn't want to bumble my way up there and bump him unless I had current Intel of where he might be standing. A recently bulldozed trail ascended that ridge and dumped out at a simple log blind which I'd built the previous day, but again, I needed confirmation of the tom's whereabouts before making any sort of a move to get there. The woods were too open to risk boogering the only bird that I'd worked in nearly two weeks.

The guy driving the track hoe and his helper had stopped work for lunch the previous day promptly at noon, and now I was really hoping that they'd do the same thing. Time was of the essence, since hunting hours ended at 1 p.m. But, the noon-hour came and went with them still toiling on. Then, at 12:22 the heavy machinery finally shut down. Almost immediately thereafter I heard truck doors slamming as the guys drove off to go get something to eat, and no sooner had they exited the scene than I heard a gobble. The tom was, indeed, right up there on his favored shelf, so I climbed towards him. Another gobble as

I neared the top confirmed that the bird was far enough away that I could make it to my blind, and when I called from there, he hammered back a response.

The tom ripped into another yelp thirty seconds later. There wasn't much time on the clock to play things coy, so I then offered up a few more perts, clucks, and soft yelps. His next gobble sounded like he was closer, but he'd circled down directly below me, and when I yelped hard he obviously turned back uphill and gobbled with an urgency in his voice. After cutting into the tail end of that last gobble, I shut down...the cards had all been laid on the table, and now it was time to play the hand.

An eternity ticked slowly by as my stopwatch counted down to the zero hour, but I wasn't worried. I had a feeling deep in my guts that this thing was about to happen, and then I heard the most welcomed music that I could hope for...the "chump" of a tom going into strut. It was almost magical the way his white pate suddenly appeared rising up above the lip of contour between us, followed directly thereafter by the bird's total magnificence morphing as a vision before my very eyes. Climbing atop a little mound of earth in full strut, he then stepped behind two large pines which afforded me the perfect opportunity to align my gun barrel ahead of his path, and when he stepped out to the left of those trees at 24 yards, I let 'er rip. Time of trigger pull was 12:45 p.m.; a mere fifteen minutes before legal shooting hours expired.

A quick trip to Vermont brought me right back to the farm that I'd found in 2015, and it treated me well once again. I took my time, enjoying every minute of having permission to hunt on a great piece of ground, and then when I called

A Rhode Island reprieve after 12 days of tough hunting

in a tom with two hens and two jakes, I almost blew it.

I shoot a Benelli M2. It's a great gun, but that brand has an inherent flaw which is widely known as the "Benelli Click." If you bump the receiver handle ever-so-slightly backwards, it will disengage. Then, when you attempt to fire, all you'll get is a sickening click sound. In order to correct things, you've got to open the receiver and reclose it securely, but sometimes in the heat of battle, panic can take over. That's what happened to me when I pulled the trigger on a strutter standing 27 yards away. Several frantic moments later I successfully jacked in a fresh round, re-aimed, and killed the tom. He'd miraculously failed to alert at any of my movements getting rearmed. Sometimes it's lucky to be good, and sometimes it's good to be lucky.

Vermont can be rough, but once you find turkeys it can be great

Later in the afternoon Dave Owens stopped by my camp. He'd just finished up his own U.S. Super Slam that very same morning in New Hampshire, so we drank a cold beer in celebration and then drove around all afternoon yacking it up and looking for turkeys. Dave is a good guy and a great friend. I always thoroughly enjoy spending time with him, and I think the world of his turkey calling and hunting skills.

The next morning I killed a tom within eyesight of the barn where I was camped. In fact, I stepped it off at 225 yards. He was a gorgeous gobbler, with feathers absolutely ablaze in color, and I'm pretty sure that it was the same tom which had flown away from me across the Connecticut River the previous day. It felt good to put the hammer down on this old boy.

A great hunt produced my first Maine gobbler of the year

Followed up the next day with another

Seeing as how it was only May 24 when I shot my second Vermont gobbler, I decided to head on up to Maine for the season finale. Two days and two dead gobblers later, it was time to turn into a guide for hunts with Les Peters and Henrik Green's girlfriend Marivi Mejico. The day with Les was another one of those that I dread, weather-wise. The forecast was for rain sometime around noon, which is a sure bet for hearing zero gobbling at daylight. We got exactly that, and no more, too. Marivi's hunt was everything Les' was not, with the only basic similarity being that we went home empty handed. Otherwise, we'd worked numerous birds all day long and been oh-so-close to success on several occasions. In short, we did everything *but* kill a tom! I really wanted to help Marivi take her first gobbler. She'd grown up poor in the Philippines as the middle child of seven, picking bananas and coconuts to help the family eke by, and had come over to the states at age 19 so she could send money back to her family. Marivi might just be the best natural cook that I've ever been around. She also has a heart of gold, is funny, irreverent, and saucy in all the best ways, and not at all hard to look at. Unfortunately, we only had that one day to hunt before I needed to head for home and a scheduled birthday party for my girlfriend Jen on June first. All we could do was make plans for next year...

The previous spring I'd brought twenty live lobsters back to Indiana, but this year we needed more. Carefully packing thirty of those beautiful crustaceans into two coolers, I immediately cut out of Maine for the 20-hour trip home, and just like the year before, I arrived at Tommy Skirvin's house having lost only two to the rigors of travel. The feast that afternoon was truly epic...again!

So ended my 2016 spring season...a year dominated by rain and many days of hearing no gobbles. Thus, I was forced into longer stays in nearly every place I went, so my states hunted tallied only seven. I did manage to get in 68 days afield, which wasn't too bad all things considered, and the 62 toms called in to less than 40 yards would rank as the third highest total ever at that point, so there were certainly some good numbers put on the board. However, it felt a little bit like an "off" year for me...but only until I realized that most folks would rank such a season as a lifetime dream come true. Three months free from work obligations while out traipsing around the country and spending nearly every day in the turkey woods should never be considered as anything less than glorious, and it's truly the only way that I ever want to conduct my life!

This stream has cut through the limestone bedrock and dumps into a beautiful little "swimmin' hole" back home in Indiana

Chapter 11

2017

The very first year I hunted in Florida (1988), I had encountered a great deal of hardship in killing a bird, and in fact, I'd ultimately gotten skunked over the course of those 18 days. During that horrendous experience I'd met a fella who wasn't too much older than me, and in talking with him around the campfire one evening, he confided to have already killed 15 toms on public land. I remember being awed by that figure, as in my limited experience I wasn't so sure that there were such a number of live turkeys on public lands in the entire state of Florida!

Fast forward 29 years to a memorable day in 2016, when it dawned on me that the bird at my feet was number 50 for me personally. While proud of that figure, I also realized that if I never shot another Osceola it would be alright. Oh; I most certainly still enjoyed hunting them as much as ever, and undeniably, bringing one to bag felt nearly as good as the very first time I ever did so back in 1989. Things were just different. Maybe I wasn't as mad at 'em as I used to be, but I didn't feel such a strong need to be the one pulling the trigger. Thus, it was with malice aforethought that I decided going into 2017 that I would book more clients and spend less time hunting with a gun in my hands. That way I could still satisfy the turkey killin' itch and also make enough money to help pay for my state-hopping addiction.

The highest number of clients I'd ever taken out in a single year was seven. For the coming season I'd booked eleven (and actually ended up doing 13). The hectic pace needed to accomplish all of that started on opening day when three fellas from Tennessee scored their victories with a countdown-triple, and then Steve Boardman took our fourth tom of the weekend at the golf course property near Brooksville. Bill Glasgow would be my second Canadian hunter from Ontario, and he upped that tom tally to five a couple days later. Then, Mike Desjarlais killed another golf course gobbler; as did Andrew Magee. That made seven toms in only eight days of hunting!

"Canada Bill" Glasgow and his burnt-sod tom

Mike Desjarlais and his tom on a massive old live oak that fell a long time ago but didn't die. That limb growing upwards is bigger than most trees in the hammock

That tally should've been one higher the very next day, but Jonathan Haga missed. I did not expect that, at all. Jonathan is a great friend of Bradley Graham, who had killed a bird with me the previous year. Both of these Virginians are seasoned turkey hunters, but Haga subsequently told me the vision of that big Osceola tom strutting across 200 yards of burnt-black sod had shaken him up like nothing else before and he must've lifted his head up off the stock to watch in awe. Thus, he shot high. I really took a likin' to this guy and hated like hell that he'd missed, so I decided to give him a second chance. My next clients weren't due to arrive for nearly a week, so I figured there was time to get him a bird in the next day or two.

Well, for the life of me I couldn't find a longbeard willing to cooperate. We heard a little bit of gobbling and even called in a bunch of jakes one day, but success plumb evaded us. Fruitless days piled up like rotten apples, and no tom was brought back to camp. Then, I acquired a permit for Green Swamp West, where the turkeys had been gobbling their heads off. Charlie Parrish had heard seven only one day earlier! For some stupid reason I assumed that it would be an easy thing to kill a bird there and send Jonathan home victorious, but once again I was wrong. The only gobbling we heard was so far away that it might've just been a dream. However, with nothing else making a peep in any other direction, I took a compass bearing on the suspected tom and began a forced march into territory totally unfamiliar to me.

Walking a compass line is something you should *never* do in Florida! The further we went, the wetter the ground got. Eventually, we ended up wading waist-deep through weed-choked, tepid swamp water, all while crawling over rotten logs and fighting through thick willows. It was bad-bad, and I knew that I had really screwed up. But, there was a turkey gobbling somewhere out ahead of us and I was confident that he was smart enough to be standing on terra firma and not swimming like a duck.

Now, Haga is generally a positive sort and real funny by nature. Back then he was also kinda large, and the deeper into that hellhole we waded, the hotter, the sweatier, and the more worried he got. In short, he wanted out of there in the worst way! I truly think that he thought I was leading him to certain death by snakebite, drowning, or being eaten by an alligator. Maybe all three. I considered any of those things a distinct possibility, too!

Finally, the water level began to shallow and we eventually managed to stagger up onto dry sand. By then Jonathan was huffing and puffing badly, and the look on his face could've been the visual image for a dictionary definition of the word, "anguish." Once clear of the water, he sprawled out on his back and raised both arms to the sky, proclaiming loudly, "Thank you Lord for letting me live to see my son one more time!" I think he meant it, too, but I nearly split a rib laughing so hard.

We never did hear that danged turkey again, and Jonathan left for home vowing to return the following year if I promised to never *ever* again take him anywhere near a swamp of any kind, shape, or form.

Sometimes you just can't buy good luck

My next three clients were from back home in Indiana, but we'd never met before. Two of the guys were great and we bonded immediately and strongly. I consider them tight friends still to this day. However, their buddy was a real piece of work; basically a know-it-all and an asshole. In all my years of guiding I've only encountered a couple of guys that rubbed me the wrong way, but he was certainly one of those. Still, it was my obligation to provide him a chance to kill an Osceola, and he did just that on the second day. Mike and Jon had gotten their trophy birds the previous morning, so at that point I was 10 for 11 guiding and feeling pretty darned good about myself.

That's when I screwed the pooch by missing a tom. Man, was I ever mad about it, too! I'd been playing this difficult bird like a violin for three as-yet unsuccessful days in a row, while learning more about him with every encounter. It was just a matter of time. And then, on what should've been a victorious play in my favor on our ever-changing chess board, the tom altered the game a bit by not flying down from his roost for more than an hour after first gobble. He hadn't gobbled much all morning anyway, and once on the ground the obstinate old cuss never uttered a peep. I didn't know if he was coming in or going away.

However, I'd watched the tom land only 75 yards from me and I knew fully

My good friends Jon Bronnenberg and Mike Piqune in 2017

well that I was sitting in the perfect "killin' spot" if he came sneaking down the cypress strand edge like he'd done for two days in a row. I was keyed up and anxious to see this duel come to its conclusion, but perhaps too much so, because I was sweating and hyperventilating. Coupled with the weather being so very hot and humid, my hated eyeglasses were fogging up something fierce. The only calls I'd uttered were barely audible flock-talk stuff, and the tom's failure to respond must've lulled me into a state of complacency because I somehow missed seeing him cross an opening between us. Suddenly, he was just right there in my lap, and although not terribly spooked, the tom did catch a glimpse of something not right in his world and he turned to leave. I couldn't really see my sights clearly, but I took the shot anyway...and missed. That was pure stupidity on my part!

The next day was one featuring total silence so far as gobbling was concerned, so I took off on a mileage-eating walkabout as a way to exercise my frustrations at being such an idiot and blowing a golden opportunity. Then, while walking out at 1 p.m. I bumped into a guy named Brian who was real nice and personable. We conversed amiably as he told of having hunted Florida's public lands for over a week without even coming close to killing a bird. Basically, he and his girlfriend Laurie had been getting beat up pretty bad by the bad birds of Green Swamp. They were thinking about calling it quits and going home to Tennessee, so I told him about my guiding successes on private property and offered to put them on birds if they were interested. Brian thanked me and said they'd think about it, and an hour later my phone rang. They wanted in.

The three of us had a great hunt the next morning, but when Laurie couldn't

Brian and Laurie pose for a "Christmas Card Worthy" picture of her tom in Florida during the 2017 season

get on the tom that raced in to our decoy setup, she told Brian to take the shot. The following day we hunted the golf course, and once again it produced; this time, for her. Both of these birds were absolute studs bound for the taxidermist, allowing this great Tennessee couple to head for home victorious and happy.

As for me, I had failed to fill a tag in Florida for the first time since 1988. But, I'd watched Osceolas dying at a stunning clip. If you took out the six days spent guiding for Jonathan Haga, we had knocked down 12 toms in only 12 days... an amazing success rate! Green Swamp, however, had been a whole different matter. She had thumped my butt pretty good. That wasn't something totally unexpected, as it's a foreboding place and yields up her turkeys only reluctantly, but I'd wasted five prime days with Jonathan when I could've been hunting

I wanted to take a picture of my Osceola gobbler atop this old relic, but then I missed him

there solo. And now, even though there were nearly three weeks of the season remaining, a prior obligation in Texas meant that I had to leave Florida earlier than I really wanted to go.

Jen and I were on the outs again (the last time?), but her brother-in-law Bob Plentl had a lease near Brady, Texas and had proffered an invitation to come and hunt there with he and his son Eric. We only had three days to get things done, though. Furthermore, both of these guys were *not* turkey hunters in the least, and that always makes guiding infinitely harder. Getting them to sit in one spot for longer than half an hour was impossible, and I'm quite sure Eric would've rather been home playing video games, anyway. Overall, it was a very tough guiding task, but everything worked out well in the end and each of us walked away with a bird. I even got to mess with a genuine Texas rattlesnake while I was there, and the wet spring had all the cacti blooming magnificently, so it was a positive, fun experience.

My first West Texas tom

Back then, there was a decent population of turkeys in East Texas. I'd been there once before and killed a bird. However, when I rolled up to the same spot in the Angelina National Forest, I found signs posting that it had been closed to turkey hunting. That forced me to do a little scrambling and research on the fly, but I soon enough found out that nearby Sabine County was one of only 16 counties where you could shoot an Eastern gobbler. There were some Sabine National Forest lands within its borders, so that's where I headed. The last time I'd visited East Texas there had been 34 counties open to turkey hunting, so things had definitely taken a downward plunge.

In driving around prior to committing to a particular spot, I saw a couple of hens cross the road. I also ran into a very helpful fellow hunter who didn't mind sharing his knowledge of the area, and although he told me that the local turkey population wasn't great, there weren't very many other hunters to contend with, either. Hey; I'll take hunting in a place with moderate turkey numbers and negligible competition any time!

The next morning I only heard one bird gobbling at dawn, but he shut down early. I found another in mid-morning after walking several miles "trolling" for gobbles, but that didn't pan out, either. Then, when I was less than 400 yards from my van while headed back for lunch, I was able to fire up the original tom and subsequently kill him.

And a Texas Eastern taken during that same 2017 season

The trip from Texas to Maryland was long, but when I pulled into an isolated chunk of Pokomoke State Forest ground in late morning, I found that the leaf-covered parking lot itself had been ripped to shreds by scratching turkeys. That was certainly a welcomed and unexpected development! However, I hadn't even had a chance to exit the van before two trucks pulled down the lane towards me. Each vehicle carried two camo-clad hunters, and as they drove on past we waved acknowledgement. Then, they stopped at the other end of the parking area side by side and with their engines still running. A few minutes later they both turned around to came back my way, with the first truck pulling up alongside me with its passenger side window open. We exchanged pleasantries and talked a little bit about the weather and how many turkeys all of us *hadn't* heard at dawn, and then they left…only to be replaced by the second truck, with nearly an exact conversation replication before it, too, drove away.

I was flabbergasted! Did these guys not see how our vehicles had quite literally been parked right on top of the most thoroughly scratched over 1/2-acre that I'd ever seen? Or, had they for some reason thought that I possessed "claim" to this area because of being there first? If so, they had to be just about the most respectful turkey hunters that I'd ever encountered. Then again, perhaps they simply knew something which I didn't…that this place had already been worn out by hordes of other hunters, and there were now present only the ghosts of gobblers done dead. Whatever the reason for their inexplicable departure, my own path was clear and I began gathering together my hunting stuff. Then, before I could even complete that task, a loud gobble blasted out from only 125 yards away!

I didn't kill that tom due to a bevy of hens who carried their boyfriend off in a jealous fit, but I did discover that the ridge where I lost them was even more scratched up than the parking lot! Building one of my famous "log cabin" blinds in amongst sign so fresh that it practically still had turkey shadows in it, I then hung out there for the rest of the day, and at 6 p.m. a tom gobbled from private land three hundred yards due north of me. When I slipped in close to the property line I could see him out in a pasture whirling and spinning for a group of hens, and I continued spying on them until the sun dipped low and they eased off into the woods.

Sleep that night came hard, and by 2 a.m. I couldn't stand the suspense any longer and began reading the autobiography of the Red Barron. By 4:30 I was already dressed in camo and ready to go, and soon thereafter (since the distance to it was only about 125 yards) I was comfortably seated in my blind on a Cabelas Gobbler Lounger, where I catnapped until daylight. The sense of nervous anticipation which had kept me awake all night was for naught, though, because I heard zero turkey sounds to greet the dawn. By 6:30 it was obvious that this tom wasn't going to gobble on his own, so I sent forth a loud lost yelp from my trusted Cane Creek glass call before settling back to finish reading my book. My confidence was running high no matter what I wasn't hearing. There was too much sign of past turkey shenanigans all around me to think that the tom wouldn't eventually show back up.

At 8 o'clock I heard "something" that could've been a gobble. Several additional and similar sounds over the next 20 minutes convinced me that they were indeed distant gobbles, and eventually I could tell that they were coming closer. Had the tom from last night traveled much further to roost than I'd anticipated? Or, had he been hush-mouthed at dawn and led silently away by his hens? Either way, it now looked like he was headed back to his little hotspot beside the parking lot, and I was anxious to give him a proper greeting when he arrived. I kept my calling rather tame; mostly just cutting into the tail end of a few of his gobbles with two and three-note yelps, or gentle, almost whispered perts and clucks. I didn't care if he answered any of them...my only concern was that he *heard* me!

When the tom finally arrived on the scene, my first glimpse of him was a splash of bright red color poking up behind the fanned tail of my strutter decoy. He stood out there at about 75 yards for the longest time, simply staring, until finally turning to leave. At that point I gave him a sharp two-note yelp from a diaphragm, and if turkeys really do have heals, he turned on his before beginning a determined march to knock some sense into the interloper (my strutter deke) who would dare to hang out with three of his ladies (again; my fakes) in their favorite courtship spot. The only problem with that plan was my Benelli pointed at his head.

The whole ridgeline and parking lot had been ripped to shreds

Officially, I only needed one more tom from Massachusetts to reach the tally of five that I was striving to achieve in every state except Alaska, so that's where I headed next. Unofficially, I hoped to hunt there many more times, simply because I like it so much. But, for this trip I wanted to make a return to the beautiful farm where I'd met an older gentleman who also shared permission to hunt there. Fred Solari and I had formed an immediate friendship and maintained contact throughout the years, and despite the steepness of those mountains, he was still willing and able at 86 years young to climb up and hunt a place where turkeys could almost always be counted on to hang out along the

*A Maryland railroad track-walking
tom that died just as he's pictured*

high side of a big pasture that offered breathtaking views of the surrounding mountains and valleys.

I really wanted Fred to experience a hunt using a DSD strutter decoy, so I climbed up there early and got my blind and decoys all set up on an ideal little flat shelf that projected 30 yards out into the steep field. Then, I headed off towards the opposite side of the valley in order to give him some space, while Fred slowly made his way to the blind. When gobbling time arrived I could hear birds on both sides of the blind, and shortly thereafter, at 5:44 a.m., a shot. I assumed that meant Fred had killed a tom, although I would find out later that he missed. I, on the other hand, succeeded only in calling up jakes all morning long.

The next day Fred and I returned to that little honey-hole up on the mountainside, but this time he insisted that I stay with him and shoot first. The tom I killed just after flydown weighed over 23 pounds. I'm not sure what Fred's weighed, because he missed him. And then, he missed another. Finally, at about 9 o'clock I managed to call in a pair of toms to 25 yards, but Fred had his gun barrel shoved way out the blind's window and was waving it around so fervently that the turkeys alerted and left. Fred didn't mind even a little bit that he'd boogered so many turkeys. At his age, it was all about having fun, and the day's adventure had certainly supplied *plenty* of that.

The next day, in the same spot and with perfect weather conditions, we heard exactly zero gobbles. We saw zero turkeys. We had zero turkey encounters of any kind. If a person hadn't known what I knew and seen what I'd seen the previous day, he would've thought that there had never been a turkey on that property in time eternal. That's the way this sport can go, sometimes, and with Rhode Island beckoning, I headed off in that direction with no idea how long it might take to kill a bird on their difficult public lands. I wanted to be there on opening day though, and if things went well, I hoped to return later in the season to help Fred find success.

Me and my good friend Fred Solari in 2017

My 2017 hunt in Rhode Island was perhaps the best time I ever spent there, so far as turkey encounters are concerned. Whereas the previous year it had taken me 13 days to kill a bird and I'd only heard gobbling on perhaps four mornings in total, this time I got on a tom the very first morning and killed him on Day 3. I had that rascal in gun range all three mornings, and basically spent just about every available woods-hour in the vicinity of him and his flock. I'd also had big fun with Jeeper and Mark Plante, who are like brothers to me. Good times, good food, and good hunting just can't be beat!

A very satisfying hunt for a wily old Rhode Island tom

Connecticut is a cool place, except for one fact rather common in some of the northeastern states: there is no free camping. Not even on their state forest lands or WMA's. That's rather annoying to a traveling turkey hunter working on the cheap, so I did what I always do in situations like that and stayed at a Walmart parking lot. I didn't sleep very well though, because I'd found something during the afternoon scouting session that had me tossing and turning all night long in anticipation of the morning's hunt.

In cruising around looking things over, I had driven down a seldom-used road labeled with a "no winter maintenance" sign at each end. Stopping midway through this mile-long lane to take a pee, I absentmindedly gazed out through the State Forest lands which ran along one side of the road and saw what appeared to be an entire ridgeline scratched to pieces. It was nearly identical to the place I'd found in Maryland, except that there were probably five acres of ground scratched, re-scratched, and scratched some more. I'd never in my life seen such a glorious thing!

It was raining when I got there the next morning, and the forecast was for the same thing all day long, so I carried in a blind with a chair and my strutter decoy, plus three hens. Then, I set up right smack dab in the middle of all that magnificent turkey sign. At daylight I could hear multiple toms gobbling from the private land across the road, but I didn't care that there were none on my ridge, for I have seldom been so content to sit in one spot and simply await a tom's arrival. I knew that they would be coming, and sure enough, within the first hour of daylight birds began filtering in all around me. At one point I had a minimum of three toms, five jakes, and four hens within gun range, so I decided to bide my time and wait for the chance to fill both of my public land tags with one shot. Not long after making that decision the opportunity presented itself, and after sitting in that turkey wonderland for another couple of hours enjoying birds that continued to gobble and scratch around on that hillside with me, I headed back over to Massachusetts.

A Connecticut "true" double

The unique tribute I left for my Connecticut toms

I was determined to help Fred Solari get another chance at a tom, but like I said earlier, he was 86 in 2017. Tough as nails, this man, but still getting up there in years. My hero David Caudill, at the very same age, was on oxygen and barely able to travel 100 yards in the flatwoods of Florida. Those "hills" of Massachusetts most certainly weren't flat by any stretch of the imagination, so we arrived at our farm extra-early to allow the old man plenty of time to reach our favorite spot. Leaving him behind to make his way to the top of the field alone, I carried so much gear that our presence on that flat shelf took on the appearance of a goose hunt...a Double Bull blind, two chairs, both guns, a jake and three hen decoys, as well as all the regular calls and stuff in our vests. It would've been a hump up there carrying nothing, so by the time I arrived loaded down like a pack mule I was breathing pretty hard and ready for a rest. However, there wasn't time for any such luxury.

After the blind was put up and all the decoys arranged, I began to get a little worried because Fred hadn't showed up. The sky was turning pink by then, and I expected gobbling to begin soon. I flashed my penlight downhill repeatedly to signal him of my location, since Fred could get lost in a closet, but still there was no sign of him. Obviously, something had gone wrong, and I immediately feared that he'd died in trying to ascend that dad-blamed mountain. What was I thinking, taking Fred on such a lung-busting hike?

Leaving our setup in place, I headed back down to look for his body, but about halfway to the road I saw a flashlight twinkling off to my right. He'd inadvertently taken a wrong turn and wasn't dead, after all! My heart was relieved tremendously at that, so I went over to get him straightened out, and then we completed the remainder of his journey up to the blind together. The last 50 feet of elevation was the steepest, and it took Fred a long time to ascend it. By then I was really chewing at the bit because I figured turkeys should've already been gobbling and on the ground.

Finally, Fred made it to the blind and had no sooner gotten settled into his chair than a tom about a hundred yards away let loose with a tremendous gobble. I couldn't believe that we hadn't been spotted already, but as hens began yelping too, I added my own calls in order to keep up with their diatribe. Turkeys immediately began flying down inside the wood line, and then one bird glided out and landed right with our decoys...it was a jake. Another followed, and this one landed about five yards from us! By the time those two young birds had begun posturing up against my own fake jake, a whole string of turkeys was emerging from the woods and headed towards us...two more jakes, a couple of hens, and two big longbeards.

Fred was very insistent that I shoot first and fill my second tag, and since I knew fully well that there was no arguing with the old codger, I did just that. Then, after the rest of the turkeys simply stood around watching their dead buddy flopping, Fred promptly missed the other adult gobbler: his *fourth* miss in four days! That final gunshot broke the spell for the surviving members of the flock, and they all left. By 9:30 Fred was getting cold, so we packed up and headed down off the mountain. Man, I sure enjoyed hunting with my friend Fred Solari, as he had as strong a love and admiration for the wild turkey as anyone I've ever met. But boy, he couldn't shoot for shit!

The Massachusetts farm where Fred Solari and I hunted. This picture does not convey how steep the land is in hiking up from the house at the right, to our field edge in the center of the photo, above the shadow line

When I pulled up to Vince and Donna's place in New Hampshire, Donna and their big St. Bernard Miss Bayley were standing in the driveway, having just returned from a morning walk. Donna had a strange look on her face when I jauntily hopped out of the van to greet them, and then she told me that Vince had died in January. A melanoma had invaded his brain, and in only a few short weeks it had killed him. To say that I was shocked would be a tremendous understatement.

I felt so terrible for Donna. She and Vince hadn't been married for too awfully long, having only met in mid-life as they had, but they always impressed me as the perfect couple who accentuated and brought out the best in each other. Their lovingly restored 1780's-era house was a fine example of what two people devoted to one goal could accomplish in working together, and since I am an historical restoration carpenter anyway, their home was what had originally prompted me to stop and ask for permission to hunt the farm. The three of us had become friends immediately, and I looked forward to seeing them every time I came back to New Hampshire.

Vince was a jack of all trades with a strong skillset in everything he did, and his attention to detail in whatever task he'd chosen to accomplish was yet another trait which I admired, and which I thought we shared. In fact, I could see myself in him whenever we talked, and I had generally stood in awe of his attitude, demeanor, and outlook on life. Donna is, likewise, a highly capable woman in a variety of fields, but now she had been thrust into the whole new reality of trying as best she could to carry on as the two of them had worked previously as a team...no small task, there! When I offered my help, she told me that Vince hadn't been able to finish some repairs started on the old barn, so I gladly jumped at the chance. She also told me that I was more than welcome to stay and hunt the farm to my heart's content, but at that very moment I just wanted to be there for my friend in her time of grief. I parked my van in the new barn and camped up there for a few days, hunting most mornings until the noon cutoff and then working on the farm.

Just as always, Donna told me that turkeys had been gobbling around the house a lot. It was our running joke line...they would tell me about all the turkeys waking them up in the morning, and then I would hear none. Not this year! I heard no less than seven on the first day. But, numbers don't tell the full tale, and I generally mucked it up. The weather also turned cold and rainy, further adding to my difficulties. Then, after taking Donna to town for some ice-cream one afternoon (both to take her mind off of things for a little while, and to bring me luck), I watched two toms fly up to roost in the distant corner of their pasture. One of them was limping badly.

The next morning I called in six male turkeys, but the only longbeard in the group was that wounded tom. He was really messed up and could barely walk, although he did strut quite a bit. I felt very good about putting this poor creature out of his misery, and those feelings were validated back at the barn when the scales only registered his weight at 12.75 pounds. With the extensive injuries to his leg, this bird wasn't long for the living world.

After finishing up some chores around the farm for Donna, I gave her a warm and loving hug before heading down the road toward Maine. Although I knew that she would welcome me back, I wasn't sure if I wanted to ever hunt there again. Vince had been a huge part of the story for me, and his death seemed somehow like the end of the New Hampshire chapter in my life. I had also finally succeeded in killing a turkey in the beautiful little pasture back behind the house, so maybe it was time to move on. Donna and I are still Facebook friends, and although it's true that I haven't returned since that time, I hope she knows that I value those memories spent on the farm with her and Vince more than I could ever convey in words.

The Hanscom barn, with my gimp gobbler resting atop the cooler

"Gimpy" on an old New Hampshire stone wall

In 2016 I had wanted badly to help Henrik Green's girlfriend kill a gobbler in Maine, but we were limited on time and didn't get it done during our only chance to hunt together. Accomplishing that task thus became a priority for 2017, so after shooting my own two toms during the first four days of the trip, it was Marivi's turn. Poor Henrik simply didn't care much about turkeys and was content to stay at home, while Marivi was a different case, altogether. This girl truly "got it." She was an eager student, too…fascinated by everything that makes turkey hunting so special, and wanting to learn all about the sport. We had a great time for two days in a row, and she shot a jake on each outing.

This tom came from my favorite Maine property

Another cold-weather victory from the 2017 Maine season

Marivi Mejico and her first turkey

Marivi the Filipina Princes was now a Turkey Huntress!

I usually don't hunt Maine until very late in the season, but a shakeup of the schedule in 2017 had moved it forward quite a bit and now I still had a couple of weeks to hit a few more states. Vermont was first up on that list, and she provided an eventful few days, to say the least. For starters, I missed a tom. I'd been striving hard for the last few years to cut down on such "unfortunate instances," but this faux pas made three for the season. That was really disheartening, as it was a totally boneheaded move on my part, too. I'd been lying prone in an apple tree-studded pasture and simply misjudged the distance to a gobbler standing at 46 paces; only knocking a few feathers off of him. Luckily, I saw this tom several times later on, so that helped to assuage any worries of perhaps crippling or causing him a slow, painful death. I somewhat made up for that mental error later in the same morning with a real nice tom taken 22 minutes before the noon cutoff.

Two days later, while hunting another remote section of this extensive dairy farm, I heard at least five birds gobbling at dawn. They were all across a paved road and on ground owned by someone else, but I'd learned the previous afternoon that at least three of them had no issues whatsoever in crossing that road and hanging out on the hilltop where I could hunt. I'd built a nice, comfortable rock and stick blind up there, which was tucked under a tangle of brush growing in the middle of a copse of cedar trees. Running away to the east of my hide lay a disked field littered with big dustbowls and gobbler turds, and with temperatures predicted to top out over 90 for the third day in a row, I planned to just hang out in my shady blind and wait.

I'd very consciously placed a few decoys so that they weren't visible to anyone driving on the road running down below the field, since the farm wasn't posted and anyone could legally stop to hunt it. But, the landowners told me that nobody else had asked for or received permission, and they hadn't seen anyone hunting up there all season long.

All five toms ripped it hard early, but then they hushed up soon after flydown. I couldn't blame them; it was too danged hot for sex! But, when I cutt hard on a glass call 30 minutes later, one of the birds gobbled in answer. For the next hour he would only pipe up when I called, and then a second bird also began chiming in. This latter one seemed much more enthusiastic and actually moved towards me, but I could only hope that he'd arrive before I boiled to death in my own sweat!

Starting about forty yards to my left and running downhill towards the road was a "hedgerow" of sorts, and after this heat-tolerant bird had come across the blacktop, he climbed uphill along the opposite side of that brush-line and popped out into my side through a tractor path. One look at the dekes was all it took to bring him marching in with a purpose. The only problem was that his tiny little beard and longer central tail feathers revealed jake status. Thus, he was perfectly safe from my ill intentions.

After a brief skirmish with my own fake jake, this fine young bird of the year was content to saunter around in the decoy spread like he was among friends. Once in a while he would gobble, and several times he walked by my blind within spitting distance, but mostly that silly bird just hung around "in camp" doing nothing in particular for over an hour. For the final 15 minutes, he contentedly preened his feathers from about 40 yards away, until suddenly, I heard a *close* yelp from a boxcall. It had come from the hedgerow, and when the jake suddenly stood tall and alert, I knew what was about to happen. Quickly diving down below the rocks in front of my blind to keep from getting sprayed in the face with pellets, a shotgun's explosive detonation soon followed, and when I cautiously arose to look around, I saw the flailing wings of a dying turkey beating the earth where the jake had just been standing. Then, a fellow emerged from the tractor path and strode quickly towards him.

It was easy to tell the exact moment when the interloper spotted my decoy spread, because he jacked another round into the chamber of his pump gun. Luckily for us both, he didn't raise the firearm to his shoulder, because if he'd so much as begun that motion I was ready to yell and/or fire off a warning shot of my own. Instead, after gazing at my dekes for several very long and tense moments, he figured out that they weren't real and then he simply walked out, grabbed the jake by its neck, turned on his heels, and left the same way he'd come. There was no "sorry" offered, or anything else. I never said a word, either, as there was nothing to be gained by it. The deed had done been done. In all fairness, I am quite certain that the guy didn't see my decoys until after he'd shot my "pet" jake, and I'm equally sure that he never knew that I was anywhere nearby, since my van was parked up at the barn. He must've heard a gobble, snuck up along the hedgerow, yelped one time, and filled his tag.

After he'd gone, I merely went back to doing what I'd been doing prior...sitting in wait and calling periodically. The wind kicked up, the heat reached nearly 95, and the turkeys continued to do whatever it is that they grudgingly do in such miserable conditions. And then, over the howling wind I thought that I heard a turkey answer one of my yelps. Less than 30 seconds later I definitely heard a gobble, and a minute after that, a third. Each one was closer than the last and nearer to the road, before the fourth gobble sounded like it was on my side. Not ten minutes later a big old badass Vermont longbeard waltzed his way into my life, and I pulled the trigger on him exactly one hour after the jake had lost his. It was a strange way to end a strange day, but I'd killed a dandy gobbler and had kept from getting shot in the process, so I was one happy feller while driving towards New York.

This Vermont day ended with a great tom after not *getting shot*

It had been four seasons since I'd been back to one of my favorite places in the world. Trevor was now 23 and guiding in Kansas for waterfowl, deer, and turkey, but he was "back home" to hunt with ole Doc. We had an absolute blast of it, too. Trevor had permission on farms scattered over several different counties, and *all* of them were good. On the second morning we shot our first True Double together, and then two days later I filled my second tag. Then, I had an interesting hunt with Trev's girlfriend Mackenzie.

This gal was really into turkey hunting, and had been trying all season long to call in her first tom alone, without Trevor's help. But, she agreed to let me tag along as a witness to her history. The turkey of choice was one that had evaded her for the last week or so, and he was a bird which was always visible in a corn stubble field along the highway. He and his nine or ten hens would roost in some big maple and hemlock trees on a steep bank which was across a roaring brook from the long edge of the field, and every morning they would fly down into the stubble and stay there all day. A secondary creek branched off of the main one near the roost and ran along the short side of the field, and between it and the farmed land ran a barbed wire fence choked with big old autumn olives. Thick willows bordering the creek combined with that invasive shrubbery to make up the only vegetation on any side of the field, so our best setup option was to simply crawl under the olives and sit up against the fence posts. We put out no decoys. Mac had hunted and patterned this flock so thoroughly that it was going to be strictly an ambush situation.

Sure enough, the tom gobbled right where he was supposed to be, and four minutes later a half-dozen hens flew down into the field and began feeding towards us, paralleling our fencerow and thirty yards out from McKenzie's gun barrel. I could barely hear the tom gobbling because of the rushing water in the creek right behind us, but it seemed like a no-brainer that the tom would soon follow his lovely ladies to an untimely demise.

An hour later I'd counted 41 gobbles, and yet, the tom was still tree-bound. It was very foggy that morning, so perhaps that was why he refused to come down, even though it hadn't affected his hens similarly. They continued to peck around right in front of us. Mackenzie was seated at the next fencepost to my right, and I'd just whispered to her how many gobbles I'd counted. The very next part of that sentence was going to be, "He should be here any second," but I never got the words out of my mouth because right then, coming down through those tangled willows and landing like a helicopter right in the flowing creek only six feet behind us, was the gobbler! There is absolutely no way in the world that the tom should've or would've done that, but he did! The only circumstance I might envision of a turkey landing where he did was if he'd been flying overhead and you folded him up like a goose. It was (and still is) the most illogical and inexplicable thing that I'd ever seen a turkey do, and it saved his life. Oh, he did circle up through the willows and nervously step out into the field without ever knowing exactly what we were, but by then McKenzie was so flustered and discombobulated that it's a wonder she was even able to pull the trigger. I'm not so sure I could've. Who knows where that round of shot ended up, but it didn't hit any turkey flesh.

Poor Mac...she was beside herself in anger, bewilderment, and frustration. She'd worked really hard, all season long, and it seemed like nothing was going right for her. I did my best to assure her that I'd been in that same head-space a thousand times before, and that all she could do was to keep plugging along. Sooner or later the turkey gods would smile down favorably and she would find herself on an ever-upward trend. I coaxed her to stay positive, because good things were bound to happen...eventually! After all, it's the hopes of tomorrow which keep turkey hunters going ever onward!

After Mackenzie went to work I got together with Trev and we guided one of his Florida friends to a first New York turkey, so the day wasn't a total bust. Then, I headed down the road to my final destination of 2017.

Trevor Bays and I with our first True Double

On the first afternoon in Pennsylvania it was drizzling rain. Earlier in the day I'd worked a tom with a tremendously long and thick beard in a favorite section of public lands, so that's where my attention was directed. Sitting along a dim woods road with a lone hen decoy stuck into one track, I had just about given up hope of luring in the gobbler before dusk when I stood up and saw a bobcat coming towards us. He was only 30 yards away, and I could plainly see that he only had one ear. In fact, his whole appearance projected that of a haggard old housecat. When he spotted my deke, he froze and stared at it for a long time. Then, he stepped off the road, turned back to his original direction of travel, and paralleled the roadway without ever even glancing in the direction of the fake hen. Then, when he'd drawn even with the decoy, he suddenly flashed like a bolt of lightning and hit the fake hen *hard*, skittering it down the road. That scared him, and the cat ran...directly at me! Stopping only about five feet from where I was leaning up against a tree, he stared back at what he'd intended to be his wild turkey dinner.

I leaned over so my mouth was probably only four feet from his ear and whispered, "How'd that one taste?"

That old mangy cat sunk down to the ground like he'd been shamed, and then his head turned slowly upwards until we were looking at one another eye to eye. I could read the terror in his feline brain even before he turned back and began slinking away, with each step getting longer and faster until he was sprinting through the woods. I couldn't help but laugh out loud.

Rain, rain, and more rain followed over the next month. Well, that's perhaps a bit of an exaggeration. It only felt like an eternally long wet spell. The actual rain had only lasted while I was wasting four days trying to kill that big old gobbler at the bobcat spot, leaving both the woods *and* my attitude a little soggy. Not until I'd abandoned the foolishness of hanging up on one particular tom and forsaking all others did the hunt, and the weather, turn around, and the final two days were both beautiful and fun. In fact, on May 31 I called in four toms, a jake, and two hens. The one I shot was a true limbhanger, putting a satisfying exclamation point on both Pennsylvania, and the season in its entirety.

This 2017 Pennsylvania gobbler was a brute all the way around

2017 had been quite a ride! For one thing, I'd called in 95 toms to less than 40 yards...by far my highest total in a single season up to that point. I'd also called in 18 birds shot by other people...yet another all-time best to date. Unfortunately, there had also been ten misses in total (three by myself), and that ranked as the second most ever: it trailed only the year 2000, when there had been a confounding 13. The misses were a totally unacceptable outcome, but weirdly, that was a phenomenon experienced and commented on by friends all across the country. Everybody I knew had been missing turkeys all year long. The weather had also been rather funky. Florida was suffering through the driest year I'd ever experienced, and yet once I headed to Texas, rain had followed me for the rest of the season. The good part is that it had almost universally been light rain and mist, which makes for (in my opinion) optimal hunting conditions. I'm not a huge fan of sunny days, and almost all of April and May had been perfectly cloudy and overcast.

I also ended the year only four states short of achieving my third U.S. Super Slam, and just 14 shy of a fourth. Additionally, I was 24 away from a fifth, and the eleven states hunted were the most I'd hit in a single year since 2010. In doing all of this, I'd spent 69 glorious days of spring traipsing around the turkey woods.

But, there had been some terrible things that happened in 2017: most notably, the deaths of three great friends in Zane Caudill, his dad David, and Vince Hanscom. My dear old friend Zane had succumbed to a stroke back in the summer. That had been a real shocker, as had been the news about Vince. David's death was more expected at age 88, and in fact, when he was confined on what would end up being his death bed, I had flown down to Florida in order to spend a little more time with this man, whom I've made no qualms about describing as my hero. Bill George and I were able to set up a video camera in the room with us, and then we spent three wonderful days sitting there for hours while listening to him recant stories of his life. On the final afternoon I was able to tell David how much I valued his friendship and that I loved him. Saying goodbye in that way meant the world to both of us.

I'd also finally come to terms with the fact that Jen and I were done. I wasn't what she needed in order to find happiness and peace in her life, and she wasn't right for me, either. The only tragedy was that it had taken us ten years to figure it all out. It was hard to let go after spending so much time together, but now I was confident that it had been the right thing to do...for both of us. Any loving relationship should be a shining example of the whole being better than the sum of its parts (take, for example, Vince and Donna), but we quite simply were not that. I wish her the best, always and forever.

And then, as if to cap off the year of mixed blessings, on May 29 I felt a sore spot on my head. After killing my final tom the next day, I headed for home, but I didn't feel well; it was as if I was coming down with something. By the time I reached Indiana seven hours later I was sick-sick, and for the next three days I lay around wrapped up in blankets, trying to sweat out what I thought was a bad case of the flu. The sore spot on my head was increasing in size and extremely painful to the touch, and I felt worse every day. It made me wonder if perhaps I'd been bitten by a venomous spider. A trip to the doctor diagnosed the head wound as Shingles, but then I developed a terrible, non-stop headache on the opposite side of my brain. Three days later I practically crawled into the doctor's office again, feeling like death was at my door. After extensive bloodwork the final diagnosis was a combination of Rocky Mountain spotted fever and Lyme's disease, in conjunction with the Shingles. After treatment began I started feeling better, but it wasn't until a month and a half later before I felt good again.

I hate ticks!

The odd thing is that I'd only seen one of the little bastards on my skin during the entire season, and I'd been spraying my clothes with a home-mixed solution of permethrin spray for the past four years. The one I'd pulled off of me in Pennsylvania must've been an especially potent specimen, because I sure was sick for a while! Once recovered, it was time to begin planning for 2018...

I refuse to waste ink to picture a despised tick, so here's a cool scorpion from Florida

Chapter 12

2018

Jonathan Haga came back to Florida once I'd sworn not to get his boots wet. I had certainly put him through a lot of punishment after his miss in 2017, so I figured that he was due for a nice, easy hunt. He got it. Meanwhile, his buddy Bradley Graham shot a bird in Green Swamp WMA. Those Virginia boys are good people, and will always be welcome in our camp!

Bradley Graham, Charlie Parrish, and Jonathan Haga are much happier with their opening day gobblers than it looks in this picture

Next up were Mike Piqune and Jon Bronnenberg; two fine fellow Hoosiers and good friends who had hunted with me the previous year. They brought along their buddy Doug Johnson, and rounding out a five-some were the fellow whom

I hadn't much cared for the previous year and his young son. By the second day they had all killed birds, but once again, the "odd" man of the group didn't think my herculean efforts to produce five toms in two days were deserving of a tip. Somehow, that didn't surprise me at all.

My next client was another fun guy to hunt with. Jeff Winningham had learned the game from none other than Harold Knight and David Hale a long time ago, so he knew how it was played. And yet, Jeff never tried to "guide the guide." We just had a great time together, meshed real well as friends, and got it done... twice. After he headed for home it dawned on me that my clients had killed eight toms in only five days of hunting!

Jeff Winningham with his second tom in two days

I had drawn a quota permit for a real interesting property which I hunt every once in a while, and since they allow you to bring a guest, Bill George accompanied me there. After roosting a bird in the evening of "scout day," we snuck in closer than I realized the next morning. The tom's first gobble was so close that it scared me, and in looking upwards, I could actually see him laying down on a limb. He gobbled like that for a while, then stood tall and belted out a few more before pitching out and landing less than 25 yards away. Soon thereafter, Bill put him down for the count.

Dropping off some gear and Bill's tom at the van, we hustled towards another bird that was still gobbling hard. About 300 yards short of his location we came across strut marks gouged deeply into the road, which was made of crushed shell packed almost as hard as concrete. The bird was gobbling from just around a bend in the road ahead of us, where it entered into a jungle-like swamp, so we followed his smokin' hot furrowed sign a little closer and set up where I could shoot to the corner. My first yelp from there was ripped into like the tom thought that I was the only hen left alive in Florida, and it wasn't but a few minutes later when he retraced his strutted path to a meeting with destiny. Two toms, tagged out, and it wasn't even 9 o'clock.

Bill George and I with our early morning delayed double

This is sign turkey hunters love to see

We were now ten days into the season and Trevor Bays hadn't as yet killed an Osceola in his quest to take a single season Grand Slam. I wouldn't have even dreamed about charging Trev for a hunt on private ground, but since the agreement with my landowners is based on their receiving a fee for every bird killed, I could take him there for that lesser amount. Trev's buddy Matt Laymon came along and did most of the calling. Matty is an absolute wunderkind on a diaphragm, and Trevor quickly killed a dandy of a tom in one of my favorite spots. Those boys are like sons to me, and both of them are pure death on turkeys, as well. That gobbler never stood a chance.

Matt Laymon and Trevor Bays in a Florida honey-hole

The following day I inadvertently ran off two gobblers that were sneaking silently to me in Green Swamp WMA. I've long espoused the need to focus hard and take advantage of any opportunity presented in the turkey woods, for the simple fact that you never know when, or if, you might get another. Spooking those birds by not being alert and writing in my journal when I should've been tightened up and honed-in seemed to anger the turkey gods, because from that point until the day I left Florida, I and anyone else hunting with me were doomed. That included my last two clients, and while it was true that their hunts were constrained by self-imposed time limits of two days apiece, I still felt bad for having failed them.

During the final 18 days of the 30 total spent in Florida, I only called in turkeys twice. Even worse, my calling wasn't even answered by a tom for the last 20 days straight! After the way in which the season had started, those dismal figures didn't even seem possible, and it bruised my ego badly. By then I was ready to get gone and go someplace where turkeys actually existed, and gobbled, and occasionally died. I was ready for Arkansas.

The Turley's (Danny and Patty) used to live in Florida, where I'd met them originally, but they had moved to a place way out in the sticks of the Natural State. Both of them love their turkey hunting almost as much as they love to talk, and that's saying a lot (pun intended). They're mighty good people and big fun to hang out with. I managed to kill a real difficult bird on the second day while accompanied by Danny, and it was one of those hunts that just felt good and satisfying all the way around. Then, I called in another wily old tom for Patty. At that point I headed up to the Ozark National Forest solo, and two days later I filled my second tag. Arkansas had been one of the four states needed to complete my third Super Slam, so now I was down to three.

Arkansas often produced scenes like this "back in the day"

Patty Turley with a big old Arkansas gobbler

I hadn't planned to hunt at home in 2018, but at the last minute I decided to do something really crazy. One of my all-time favorite foods is Boudin, and it hardly seemed right to be so close to Louisiana without stopping in to sate my appetite. And then, once I got a taste of that delicacy, I figured that I might as well make it worth my time by purchasing 150 more pounds of the stuff, driving 16 hours home to get it put into the freezer, and then heading out for the next destination on my schedule, which was North Dakota. And, since turkey season was currently underway in Indiana, I could take advantage of that opportunity by hunting on the State Forest ground surrounding my house. This "Plan B" worked to perfection, as it supplied me with a dandy of a bonus turkey, taken on perhaps the most beautiful ridgeline in the world. I'd heard no less than seven gobbling toms up there.

Another home-bird from "Pretty Ridge" in 2018

North Dakota was another state on my "short list," but it's a long drive to get there from home. My first trip to the Standing Rock Indian Reservation had been in 2006, meaning that I hadn't been back in twelve years. When I pulled up to the same ranch where I'd hunted previously to ask for permission, an incredibly beautiful young woman came to the door. She told me that the previous owner had retired and moved away, and the ranch was now being run by his stepson, who was also her husband. But, she told me that I was welcome to hunt it once again.

Their ranch is very picturesque, in a stark, barren, North Dakota kind of way, and its northern border is formed by the Cannonball River, which is an estuary practically teeming with waterfowl, pelicans, and a variety of wildlife...including turkeys. Those birds aren't afraid to cover ground in their daily wanderings, and they most definitely aren't the least bit hesitant to fly the river. In fact, three out of the four birds I killed that spring did just that very thing in order to come to my calling. One of them landed right beside me and was strutting six yards from my gun's muzzle when I pulled the trigger. Now, only two states remained for Slam #3!

I've made no efforts to hide my enchantment with Iowa. It has great turkey hunting, and the place where I go is very unique and beautiful. Rumor has it that the mushroom picking can be awesome there too, but I've never hit it at the right time. I'm always either too early, or too late. The only real negative has been the price they charge for a hunting license. If it was cheaper, or if you could kill two toms for the same fee, I would visit more often. While I didn't

I couldn't shoot this tom until a deer between us got out of the way

This picture along the Cannonball River can't show the 40-mph winds that seem to blow there non-stop

My final North Dakota tom from 2018

need another Iowa gobbler for my third Slam, I most certainly did if I wanted to eventually complete five of them, and the great bird I killed in 2018 upped my tally to four. That assured me of a return trip in 2019 for another crack at finding some of those tasty morels!

My Iowa hunt in 2018 was nothing less than phenomenal

Ohio also has some good turkey hunting, but there are a lot of turkey *hunters*. For the first few days in the Wayne National Forest it seemed like every time I got on a bird, someone else messed me up. Then, I found a pair of hot toms so far back into the boonies that I had 'em all to myself. I shot the leader of the two as he strutted down a ridiculously steep slope towards me, and when the flopping was over and he'd quit rolling, my third Ohio tom was quite literally lying right at my feet. Taking this tom meant that I only needed one more state for my Super Slam, but with another tag in my pocket, that trip to Minnesota would have to wait for a little bit.

Most folks who know me are aware of my stance on ice-cream. In short, I think of it as the world's most perfect food. Additionally, I claim that it brings good luck in the turkey woods, so my friends and I often make "ice-cream runs" throughout the season. Hey: I don't have any real superstitions which guide my course through life, but ice cream comes mighty close to qualifying as such! Maybe it works, and maybe it doesn't, but at least we get to regularly enjoy a delicious treat, and when I found the top of an old ice-cream stand far back in the woods on the hike out with my tom in tow, I just had to stop for a picture or two.

This Ohio tom rolled down the steep hill to stop at my feet

The perfect backdrop for a Doc Weddle victory photo

So far, my trip to Ohio had been a mixed bag of good gobbling early, coupled with long hours of nothing. The temperature had also been consistently hot as blazes, and the vegetation was so far advanced that it felt more like summer. Spiders were already spinning aggravating webs across the trails, morel mushrooms were completely done, and there was just this general feel that I should be moving on northward. Still, the gobbling every morning had been good enough to keep me anxiously looking forward.

However, after the fifth day of the trip it felt like a change of scenery was needed, so I headed to an area recommended earlier by a wildlife biologist. When I pulled up into the Zaleski State Forest headquarters in late afternoon, the only person there was a guy welding on some sort of apparatus designed to thwart beavers from plugging up a culvert, and when I asked him about turkeys, he claimed that the crew heard gobbling every day from right where we were standing. He also divulged that they often saw birds along a winding gravel road that looped back behind the shop on land open for hunting. I could hardly contain the grin on my face as I jumped back in the van to take a little "property tour."

I didn't have to go very far though, because almost immediately, a hen ran across the road in front of me. Since there was still time left to hunt, I grabbed my gear and began exploring on foot, following a well-worn deer trail that eventually crossed the same gravel road which the wildlife tech had told me about. They had recently bulldozed a new parking area right where I exited the woods, and scattered about in the dust were a number of turkey turds; some of which were exactly what I was looking for...J-shaped, and fresh!

Dropping back down the trail about 75 yards, I set up and began calling. Not ten minutes later I heard turkey feet walking in the leaves, and then I saw three toms pop out into view fifty yards away. After turning uphill on the trail, they ventured out of sight towards the bulldozed area with me silently and cautiously following behind. As I neared the road I heard a gobble up ahead, and for the next 45 minutes before sunset I tried my best to kill either that bird, or one of his buddies. I failed, but I did succeed in watching all three fly to roost about 40 yards off the gravel and very close to the same flat, scratched up area where I'd earlier been seated.

I could barely sleep that night in anticipation, and long before necessary, I was already sitting at the very tree that I'd used the evening before. It offered a great vantage point and commanding view of the oak flat around me, as well as the deer trail, and I figured that the birds would pitch down close to me, whether I ever called, or not. Getting in "super-tight" to roosted toms was a tactic that I'd employed to a high degree of success all throughout my early turkey hunting career, but it wasn't something that I did very often these days. There were several reasons why I had gotten away from the practice. For one thing, it entailed getting into the woods *very* early, and when you hunt frenetically from dawn to dark for three months straight, you just can't afford getting up in the middle of the night to go sit in the dark for hours and hours before daylight. Something has to give in those circumstances, and you end up napping away too much of the actual daylight hunting hours.

I also wasn't as mad at turkeys as I'd been in the early years. Killing the bird wasn't nearly as important as the hunt itself, and I gradually became more and more content to simply put myself in the vicinity of toms before they ever began gobbling, and then conducting the hunt accordingly once they'd had a chance to hit the ground. "Sleeping with the enemy" was undoubtedly a highly lethal hunting method, but in some regards it was almost *too* lethal. True; I'd never shot one out of the roost and always waited until they'd gathered dirt under their toenails before administering the coup de grace, but hunts like that didn't always make me feel warm and fuzzy. To be perfectly frank, they sometimes felt more like an execution, or cheating.

That day in Ohio, however, I was there to kill a turkey. If one happened to land in gun range, then shame on him. As it got lighter I detected some shuffling about in the treetops nearby, and then several times I was pretty sure that I heard turkey poop falling down through the limbs. In short, I was *close* to the birds, and the unanticipated loudness of an initial gobbling flurry nearly caused me to jump out of my skin!

For some reason known only to those goofy three amigos, they decided to then pitch down into the gravel road itself instead of right there in front of me. The first gobble I heard on the ground was fifteen minutes later and 200 yards away. I had to move, and I needed to do it quickly!

Scurrying stealthily up the deer trail, I eased into the bulldozed parking area only after I could tell that the toms had gone around a bend in the road. A lot of the brush and limbs scraped up by machinery in clearing the new parking lot had been piled against an oak tree, so I wormed my way into this ideal "natural" blind and hit my glass call. Immediately, one of the toms hammered a reply, and when all three then hit it again, I stepped into the tail end of their gobbles with a demanding cutt/yelp series of calls.

Not long afterwards they gobbled from just around the corner, and then one of them strutted into view...coming right up the gravel lane like a fashion model on a Paris runway; only prettier! He had a long, pencil-thin beard that was quite unlike the next tom sporting one much shorter, but thicker, or the third tom, which looked like a twin to Number 2. Each of them were separated from the next by about 20 yards as they approached, and when the first gobbler reached good killin' range, I waited until he stood tall before touching off a round. Instead of piling up in the gravel stone dead, the tom merely ran back the way he'd come and then slowed to a nervous walk as he approached his next buddy in line. Then, they all three kept right on walking away, looking much more confused than scared.

How had I blown such a perfect opportunity to kill that bird? I hung my head in shame, and then, when I lifted it back up, the answer was clearly staring me in the face. There, about three feet in front of my gun's muzzle, was a horizontal oak limb of perhaps two inches in diameter with a neat half-circle shot out of its top. If I'd only seen the danged thing beforehand, I could've simply sat taller, but I hadn't. I was bummed. But, at least my mistake had resulted in a clean miss and not a crippled tom to worry, fret, and lose sleep over.

Not two minutes later, as I sat there contemplating my "what now" options, the trio gobbled in unison at a pileated woodpecker. I distinctly remember thinking, "There ain't no way in Hell's name that I can call them back here." However, the fact of the matter was that I was sitting in a really awesome hidey-hole, they obviously hadn't been overly traumatized by my shotgun's blast, and judging by the gobbler turds all up and down the gravel road, they really liked this spot. What did I have to lose by trying?

The next time one of them gobbled, I stepped all over it with a demanding yelp and all three toms answered. Game on! I said nothing more, and sure enough, the next set of gobbles was closer. Then, another set came from even closer, still. As the first two toms materialized from around the bend in the road I could clearly see that they were the ones I hadn't shot at. The next gobble was off to their side, and when I cut my eyes in that direction, I could see their pencil-thin bearded brother easing down along the wood's edge. I guess the road incident had him a little leery of gravel under his feet, but he still wanted a piece of the action and couldn't resist slipping in on an alternate path towards doom. When the range to his head dipped under 25 yards I was already making sure that there were no obstructions between us, and at 22 yards I put him down for the count.

Unbelievable! I had just called up three Eastern toms to the very same spot where I'd missed them only ten minutes earlier. Never in my wildest dreams would I have thought that even possible. Soon thereafter, I was headed towards Minnesota still feeling shocked, and yet, elated.

My Ohio Double-Shock-Power tom

My first day in the last state needed for completion of a third U.S. Super Slam provided such a cool hunt that I was left practically tingling in excitement after it ended. The hunt took place in an isolated chunk of public land necessitating a hike of approximately one mile to circle around a private farm, and at dawn I was greeted by the glorious sound of no less than eight fired up longbeards scattered in all directions. The previous afternoon I'd spent hours watching a tom strut for a whole passel of ladies in the plowed farm field, and he looked like a good'un.

It was super foggy for most of the morning. I'm not even sure from which direction the field boss eventually came from, but suddenly he was just out there in the soup, gobbling amongst numerous hens which were being quite vocal, too. It was one of those magical times in the spring when it seems like every turkey for miles has something to say, and several of them came to the field, as well. I even called one to within killing range of where I sat in a corner of public land, but after glassing him and "grading out" his short spurs, I decided to wait and see how the day progressed. I really wanted this capstone bird to be something special, and since I was obviously hunting in a "target rich" environment, I wasn't in any hurry to pull the trigger.

After the fog had finally burned away I could see at least ten hens and a couple of jakes out there with the tom. This old boy exhibited behavior very similar to a bull elk in constantly herding his harem around the field, and he even went off a couple hundred yards a time or two to pick up stragglers and return them to the main flock. I'd never before seen a turkey make such a concerted effort of keeping his hens knitted together. Perhaps he might be susceptible to another lost hen, yelping over here in the bushes...

When he actually began fervently strutting his way in my direction it sort of caught me by surprise. After all, I hadn't really expected the forlorn yelps that I was offering up on a diaphragm to work quite that well, especially while he was in the company of so many other hens, but they did. He took his own sweet time reaching me though, and wore deep furrows in the turned topsoil as he spun and gobbled to try and make me exit the woods. When that failed, he gingerly stepped out of the field and climbed up to his demise, with a long-echoing shotgun blast signaling that I'd taken the final tom needed for my third Super Slam. In doing so, I'd called a great tom away from ten girlfriends, and those sharp spurs measuring 1- 1/4 inches left no doubts that this was the boss gobbler targeted the day before. I couldn't have been any happier as I stopped by the Town and Country Restaurant for some delicious homemade Rhubarb/Custard pie in celebration of my victory.

This Minnesota tom completed my third U.S. Super Slam

While "in the neighborhood," I then ventured over into Wisconsin. This state had been good to me a couple of times previously, but the first three days were a frustrating mess of boggy ground, hordes of mosquitos, and only a few long-distance gobbles. Seeking a change of scenery (or, at the least, relief from the skeeters), I then ventured up to a totally new area for me. It was a place recommended by my old friends Ron and De Ronk, and once there, I was thrilled to find out that it was topographically-speaking like night and day from where I'd been hunting. This new place actually had real soil and dirt, instead of being a region of seemingly endless boggy peat. And, more importantly, it held turkeys aplenty!

The logging road I started out on eventually took me back to a big selective cut of old timber, and once there I began finding turkey tracks. Some of them had been made by male turkeys, and while I was bent down looking at the imprints, a tom ripped out a gobble from only 400 yards away. I halved that distance before setting up, and he responded to my first call. From that point onward I only called perhaps four or five times in answer to his gobbles over the next

He only had half of a tail fan, but his 1- 3/8" spurs were wicked

A full fan for this Wisconsin bird, and spurs nearly as long

twenty minutes before the woods became deathly silent. Ten minutes later I heard drumming, and two minutes after that a tom and a hen came right up to me. At 19 yards I made the shot count. Then, while taking glory pictures, another bird gobbled. I came back the next day and killed him, too.

Good times in New York with the Bays family were next in store for me. On the first morning Trevor and I hunted a bird close to his Dad's Chenango County home, but on a different farm. I killed him. Then, we went to another spot and called one in for Zach Wyss. Zach is an old friend of Trev's and a hoot of a feller to hang with. He also gets just about as excited when he kills a turkey as anyone I've ever been around. This was only his second turkey ever, and the first longbeard, so he was *pumped*!

Trevor and Zach Wyss celebrate victory

For the next five days Trevor and I found ourselves mired in a rare bad luck streak while trying to fill my second tag. No matter what we did or where we hunted, we just couldn't seem to make anything good happen. We even traveled west a couple hours to hunt on a farm where the owner had heard 9-12 toms sounding off the previous day, but the following morning those same woods were silent as a grave yard. It was eerie. And then, on the very next day we found all of those gobblers traveling together in one big group. I'd never seen that many longbeards in a spring flock before; especially with no accompanying hens. The bird I shot ended up having two beards.

Y'all know that I've visited New York many, many times, but overall, I would have to rate my six-day trip in 2018 as one of the most uneventful and unrewarding hunts of them all. Yes, we killed three toms, but it had taken lots of work to get it done, and we'd covered many miles in scouting and hunting on a number of different farms. The highlight, of course, was just in being able to spend so much time hunting with Trevor Bays, who had grown into an incredible talent in his 24 years on this planet. At that tender young age he was already a serious and acclaimed waterfowl, deer, and turkey guide with insane skills in all three endeavors, but of even more import, he was loved and respected by a vast array of contemporaries. Trevor showed a maturity and awareness far beyond his years, and I had a feeling that someday his accomplishments in the turkey woods would far surpass those of my own. I also felt like it was just a matter of time before the student was able to snatch the pebble from the master's hand. I wasn't ready to roll over and die and let the young dog eat my flesh, but the time was coming...

Me and Trevor with my second New York bird of 2018

My turkey killing for the year was now done, but there were still three days left until the end of May. Trevor really wanted to knock out a bird in Pennsylvania, so he followed me over to Bill George's camp near Tionesta. Joining us there were Doug Pickle, Craig Morton, and Dickie Clark, along with Bill and his nephew Holton. With ten states in total under his belt, Trev was hoping to add one more before season's end, while I was content to just watch the show and serve as guide, gun bearer, or cameraman: whatever it took. Trev certainly didn't need me as a caller, since he was already one of the best I'd ever heard on a diaphragm.

All three days were filled with lots of gobbling activity, but the local turkey population refused to fully cooperate. Then, panic mode hit my young protégé after we failed to quickly score on the initial setup of the last legal day to hunt. What followed would illustrate perfectly-well an important difference between his generation and mine.

Whereas I would've been content to stay the course and hunt that bird we'd started the day with until we either killed him or failed trying, Trevor was ready to hit the road and make something happen. He is, after all, a member of the "immediate gratification" generation and had been raised in New York, where they just drive around until a turkey is spotted, and then figure out how to gain access to the ground where he's standing. Both of our respective methods work, but being as how this was Trev's last hunt and time was of the essence, away we went. The turkey gods had obviously decided to smile down upon us that morning, for not a mile down the road we drove up on two toms crossing the blacktop into a recently planted corn field. Right across the street was the Township Road Department building, and there, driving a skid steer, was a guy loading gravel into a dump truck. He told us that the land in question was owned by his sister, but it would be just fine if we hunted it.

We first made visual contact with those birds at 7:15 a.m. By 7:25 we'd already gained permission and left our vehicle in the Township parking lot. Trevor pulled the trigger at exactly 7:29. Talk about your flash hunt! That tom was Trevor's 19th of the season, and the 46th he'd watched die in 2018. Perhaps his "find 'em and kill 'em" strategy had some merit; most certainly, the method and its results warranted respect!

Trevor's flash-hunt Pennsylvania tom

Another great spring season had come to an end. While I'd "only" hunted in nine states, I had gained another 65 days' worth of turkey hunting experience. Furthermore, I'd polished off the last remaining states needed for completion of a third U.S. Super Slam, and now I was only looking at nine more for my fourth and another 22 to complete a heretofore unmentionable and totally insane fifth. Things couldn't have gone much smoother for the year overall, with May having been especially productive. I'd directly participated in the demise of 18 longbeards during that one month alone, and while this wasn't quite up to Trevor Bays' standards, I wasn't running too far behind him, either. It's not like there was any competition going on between us, though. He was doing his thing, and I was doing mine. Only at the end of the season would we find it interesting to compare notes, tallies, and stories. That's just what turkey hunters do.

Newborn fawns...a common sight in New York during late May

2018

Epilogue

Volume 4 of this continuing series takes us up through the final hunts of 2018...the year in which I completed my third U.S. Super Slam. Right now it feels like I've been doing this turkey hunting thing for all of my life, and yet, in many ways I'm no better at it than any other raw, wet-behind-the-ears newbie. Yes; I do have an extensive resume of experiences which make me feel confident and lethal whenever I'm setting up on a gobbling tom these days, but I still make bone-headed and silly mistakes quite regularly. In fact, I do so any number of times during every single day when I'm out there "playing the game." That's just the nature of the sport, and in pursuing a bird as wildly idiosyncratic as the wild turkey.

A tom turkey is a study in contrasts, if nothing more. One day he might run to a call that sounds no better than a sick goose on its deathbed, and the next morning he will not even bother to honor a real hen at your feet yelping for all that she's worth. He can be so totally vane as to viciously attack his own reflection in the shiny bumper of a car, or he can just as easily put the screws to the best and brightest of hunters who walk amongst us. His ability to apparently vanish silently into thin air is legendary, but he can (and often does) appear almost magically; as if he were an apparition popping up where moments before there was nothing.

What I'm saying here is that the wild turkey is an adversary worthy of the many hardships encountered in hunting him, and he deserves the respect and honor bestowed upon his feathered brilliance by every single one of us who thrills to his pursuit. My life would be a hollow shell of an existence without this magnificent bird to plot, plan, dream, and scheme about all year 'round, and I am grateful beyond measure for every moment of my life when he has pervaded my thoughts and steered my course.

Once I had conquered a U.S. Super Slam for the first time in 2006, I'd embarked upon the journey of doing it again. That dream reached fruition in 2011, and only then did I even acknowledge in my conscious thoughts that a third one was possible. Like I said earlier in the book, my Minnesota bird in 2018 was the capstone to Number 3, and along the way towards achieving that rather ridiculous goal I had begun thinking about where I wanted this Slam insanity to end. The only reason I've picked the number five is because it has always been one of my "lucky" numbers, and I'm quite confident that I will stop this silliness forevermore upon reaching that figure. Right now, as I write this last chapter following a 2023 season in which I conquered Number 4, I find myself needing only two states next spring to reach that hopping off point. I will be utterly delighted and satisfied beyond belief if I can kill birds in Arizona and Wyoming next spring. I will also be thrilled to never again allow the self-imposed "need" for killing a bird in a certain state to dictate my travels. From that point onward I will only be hunting when I want, and where I want. Of course, I don't plan to hunt any less during the seasons ahead, but I do anticipate feeling a sense of freedom unlike anything that I've known since beginning these quests.

Another thing that has altered my viewpoint and outlook on life is something which I brought up in the beginning chapter of this book, but haven't expounded upon any further. In January of 2023 I was diagnosed with a tumor on my left kidney. It was about two inches in diameter, and the doctor told me that it needed to come out as soon as possible. In researching options and outlooks on kidney cancers, I ran into some rather sobering statistics about survivability and such. Those numbers filled me with trepidation. Would I even live to see another turkey season? Might my world soon come crashing in on itself? Were my 63 years of life nearing an abrupt end, at the same age as when my own Dad had died? I felt fit as a fiddle and healthy as a horse, but could the dreaded "c" word be fixin' to take me out? How could that even be possible? Cancer was something that other people got...not *me*! It was a troublesome and worrisome time for a guy who hadn't ever much considered his own mortality, and who still considered himself to be fairly invincible. Heck; my plans all along have been to live well into my 130's, and I wasn't even close to being ready to check out. There was too much living left to do: still turkeys to kill, and books to write, and a house to finish remodeling, and love to find, and all that jazz. I didn't want to die. It was too soon. And yet, at the same time I realized that if everything were to end tomorrow, I would go out with a smile on my face. I've had a good run. No real regrets.

I explained all of this to my doctor, and I also told him that if this heinous disease was indeed going to kill me, then there were a few goals which I very much wanted to accomplish during the upcoming season. For one thing, I had a lot of people counting on me in Florida. My guiding endeavors down there had grown bigger every year, and now were limited only by the available land where I had permission to hunt. I also had just one single state left on the list before finishing the fourth Slam, and merely a half-dozen for #5. Dr. Kitley told me that there was no way he would agree to do the surgery before the season began and then allow me to hunt afterwards, simply because of the high risk of an internal hemorrhage developing while I was sitting under a tree waiting for hours on end while a gobbler took his own sweet time coming in. Did you know that about a quarter of your blood flows through the kidneys every minute? A leak could easily prove fatal, and I needed to remain close to a hospital for several weeks after the Da Vinci robot took out the hated parasitic tumor and part of my kidney.

Could I postpone the partial nephrectomy until June, after the season had ended? Although empathetic of my plight and wishes, the good doctor didn't want to wait that long. Of course, I let him know in no uncertain terms that if it was going to increase my odds of the cancer spreading to other organs, then I would agree to him performing the surgery at his earliest convenience and I would cancel my entire turkey season altogether. However, if it didn't up the risks substantially, then I would like to wait as long as possible and get in some hunting beforehand. He agreed that I would probably be fine to wait and conquer a few of my goals, and then we set the surgery date for May 15.

I didn't tell very many people about this whole ordeal. I didn't want to be treated differently, or for anyone to feel sorry for me, and I most certainly didn't want my Mom to find out. She is a natural born worry-wart, and at 87 years old, I was afraid that her fretting over my plight might kill her. I did, however, inform some of my closest friends, including Trevor Bays. Then, I made out my will and final arrangements, put all of my priorities in as much order as possible, and went on with living. What else can you do? Life goes on, whether you're here, or not.

Trev wanted to spend as much time hunting with me this spring as possible. I guess he thought that it might be our last chance if 'ole Doc was getting ready to kick the bucket. In case there's any question, I want it known right here and now that I am eternally grateful for his presence throughout this past season! We were able to hunt in a half-dozen states and wrack up many new memories. He also helped me with my guiding operation down in Florida. Someday I'll hand those reins over to him, but hopefully, that won't be for a long while because the surgery was a tremendous success and the doctors feel very positive about the outcome. Pathology reports couldn't be any better, too. The type of cancer I had was extremely treatable with surgery alone, and it hadn't spread to any other organs. No chemo and no radiation needed. That was a huge, huge, *huge* relief to my poor, feeble brain!

In many ways I feel like I've been given a second chance, and I intend to embrace it wholeheartedly. I've always been keenly aware and consciously acknowledging of what I view as the important things in life, but those have now been brought even further into focus. Believe me; it isn't the quest for money, or fame, or how much stuff you acquire before they plant your butt six feet under. What matters is the time spent with loved ones, doing those things that bring you joy, and helping to make the world a better place at every opportunity. The legacy we leave behind is the only thing that remains after we're gone. And while none of us has the power to fix everything that's wrong in the world all at once, my motto is: "One step at a time; one day at a time." We could all benefit from realizing that this ain't no trial run, and you're far better off enjoying yourself while there's still time. This life goes by so quickly...in the blink of an eye, really. I know that I've wasted too much of my own air-breathing allotment, but one area where I don't feel like it was frittered away are those days when I was out in the turkey woods. The countless hours chasing gobblers and gobbles around the country have been the moments of my essence when I was truly free and my mind was at ease. I regret not a single second of that time, and I plan to keep on keeping on out there until I turn to dust. I hope you do, too.

Ok; that's it. If perhaps you wish to purchase this or any of my other books, please order them directly from me. They are also available on Amazon and elsewhere, but the ones I sell from home allow me to personalize and sign them to the buyer, or to whoever is receiving them as a gift. The books in my own library most personally valued are the ones signed by their authors, and I would be more than happy to accommodate.

Unfortunately, with this volume I find myself in the dreaded position of having to raise my prices a little bit. Paperbacks are now $29 and hardcovers $39. Not only is this book bigger and chocked-full of pictures (both of which add to production costs), but my publisher has raised their printing fees and begun charging me an extra $3.50 per book sold through distribution channels like Amazon. Then, add in the U.S. Postal Service jacking up their shipping rates multiple times over the last few years. Of course, I didn't begin writing these books to make any money, but breaking even would be a worthy goal. Even still, I apologize. If this new price structure hasn't run you off, my mailing address is still the same:

Tom Weddle
PO Box 7281
Bloomington, IN 47407

I can accept funds via Paypall, sent to my email address of tdocweddle@comcast.net. This is the fastest way to get the books ordered, and most folks utilize PayPal these days. If you do order by this method, please utilize their "send money to friends and family" option, so they don't deduct fees on my end. Or, if you'd rather, send me a check or money order.

I hope you've enjoyed this volume. I told you in its beginning to expect less quality writing and more pictures, so I'm quite positive that I hit those lowered goals. With any sort of good luck, I intend to write at least one more book in order to bring my turkey hunting life on paper up to current time. And once again, in this rather informal manner, I would like to thank each and every person who has expressed kindnesses towards me during this rather difficult year. I acknowledge and embrace the love shown me, and I send back my own in return. "Thank you" doesn't sound like enough, and yet, it means the world to me and comes from the very center of my heart.

EPILOGUE

www.ingramcontent.com/pod-product-compliance
Lightning Source LLC
Chambersburg PA
BHW031145020426
2333CB00013B/510